CHARLES FREER ANDREWS

*Appendix IV contains a list of books
by C. F. Andrews*

CHARLES FREER ANDREWS IN 1937

CHARLES FREER
ANDREWS

A NARRATIVE

by
BENARSIDAS CHATURVEDI
and
MARJORIE SYKES

With a Foreword by
M. K. GANDHI

HARPER & BROTHERS
Publishers   New York

PRINTED IN GREAT BRITAIN

in 12-point Bembo type

BY THE BLACKFRIARS PRESS LTD
LEICESTER

Dedicated to

C. F. Andrews' fellow-teachers in all lands
who strive to make their teaching
a ministry of friendship

FOREWORD
by M. K. Gandhi

Charlie Andrews was
simple like a child, up-
right as a die and shy
to a degree. For the bio-
graphers the work
has been a labour
of love. A life such
as Andrews' needs
no introduction. It
is its own introduc-
tion.

New Delhi MKGandhi
8-12-'47

ACKNOWLEDGMENTS

During the eighteen months which have been given to the preparation of the book, Marjorie Sykes held an "Andrews Memorial Chair" at Santiniketan, on terms which enabled her to devote a large part of her time to this work. Without the leisure thus afforded, the excellent opportunities for library work which Santiniketan offers, and easy access to the files of Andrews' correspondence preserved there, it would have been quite impossible to complete the task within the time, and we are under a great debt of gratitude to the Governing Body of Santiniketan for thus making the work possible.

The list of those to whom we owe thanks is a very long one. The generosity with which they have responded to our requests for information has been one of the joys of writing this book. Without their help some of its earlier chapters could hardly have been written at all, and all of it would be the poorer. A part of what we owe to them is acknowledged in the footnotes to the text ; more appears only indirectly, as scattered phrases in letters and conversations have contributed to our understanding of our subject.

C. F. Andrews' own family, his brothers, Mr. J. B. Andrews and Mr. W. H. Andrews ; his sisters, the Misses Edith, Isabel and Lilian Andrews ; and his cousin, Mr. R. C. Lucas, have been unstinting in their helpfulness, as also a number of the men, still living, who were Andrews' contemporaries at school and college. Besides those whose names appear in the body of the book, to all of whom we are much indebted, Dr. Bethune Baker, the Rev. H. R. Baugh, the Rev. H. C. O. Lanchester, the Rev. C. T. Wood, the Rev. J. F. Williams, and Mr. Joseph Manton, have helped us in various ways with details of Andrews' life in Birmingham, at Cambridge, and in the Pembroke College Mission.

For the account of his work in Delhi from 1904 to 1914, we owe very much to the kindness of the Cambridge Mission to Delhi and the members, past and present, of the Cambridge Brotherhood and the staff of St. Stephen's College. Some of Andrews' students of that period, in particular Mr. Sudhir Rudra, Mr. G. Yazdani, Mr. Saharia, and Fr. G. Y. Martyn, have made valuable contributions, as have the many friends, Indian and British, who had no direct connection with St. Stephen's College itself, but who knew Andrews during the same years—Lala Raghubir Singh, Mr. G. S. Ingram, the Rev. T. H. Dixon, the Rev. W. E. S. Holland, Bishop Ferguson-Davie, Sir T. B. Sapru, Mrs. G. C. Chatterjee, the late Mr. S. E. Stokes, and the young men who were attracted by the missionary ideals set forth by Stokes and Andrews—Mr. K. K. Kuruvila, Mr. Shoran Singha, the Rev. Norman Tubbs, the Rev. Arthur Davies, Mr. J. S. Hoyland.

Many of those mentioned above have also given us information relating

vii

to the latter part of Andrews' life. We are very grateful for the readiness with which Mahatma Gandhi and the authorities at Santiniketan placed their files at our disposal, and with which others whom we approached have allowed quotations from private letters and memoranda to be made. The late Mr. J. B. Petit, who wrote to offer this kind of co-operation shortly before his death, was a recipient of letters of the greatest value for the understanding of Andrews' work in South Africa, and Miss S. Schlesin and Dean Palmer of Johannesburg helped in the same connection. Pandit Totiram Sanadhya, Mr. A. W. Macmillan and Miss F. E. Garnham gave us great assistance with regard to Fiji and Australia, and the copy of Andrews' journal which throws such light on his work in British Guiana was made available to us by the kindness of Mr. S. A. Waiz of the Imperial Indian Citizenship Association. Lady Denham kindly allowed us to quote from a letter of the late Sir Edward Denham, and Mr. H. G. Alexander sent valuable comments on the opium control campaign and other matters.

Of Andrews' life at Santiniketan, Pandit Khiti Mohan Sen, Dr. Kalidas Nag, and Mr. Sudhakanta Roy Chowdhury have told us much. The sections on the Punjab owe a great debt to Mr. Gurdial Mallik, Mr. Ruchi Ram Sahani, Mr. Bhai Parmanand, and to the courtesy of the editorial staff of *The Tribune* of Lahore. Those on Indian labour owe a similar debt to Mr. B. P. Wadia, Dewan Chaman Lal, Mr. N. M. Joshi, and Bishop and Mrs. Pakenham Walsh.

Very many men and women have contributed anecdotes and impressions which when quoted verbatim, are acknowledged with thanks in the footnotes to the text. In addition to these we have received similar help from Pandit Jawaharlal Nehru, Mr. D. P. Khaitan, Mr. T. D. Santwan, Dr. S. Jesudason, Mr. L. A. Hogg, Fr. J. C. Winslow, the Rev. P. O. Philip, Sir Maharaj Singh, Mr. G. Sitarama Sastry, St. Nihal Singh, Dr. Amiya Chakravarty, Mr. E. W. Aryanayakam, Mrs. Hutchinson, Dr. Garfield Williams, the Bishop of Ely (Dr. H. E. Wynn), and the Bishop of Lahore (Dr. Barnes).

Even such a list as the above is far from exhaustive. Other friends of Andrews have contributed to this book indirectly, by the reminiscences they have written for "Andrews Memorial Numbers" of Indian magazines, which have been of the greatest value. We owe much in this way to the contributors to *The Stephanian* and *Vishal Bharat*, and to Mr. Sri Ram Sarma, the editor of the special Andrews number of the latter. Many others, who might gladly have contributed, we have for various reasons failed to reach, and can only offer them our apologies.

Mr. Hemant Kumar Nilkanth of the Sabarmati Ashram, Ahmedabad, gave many hours to helping us in the selection of material from Mahatma Gandhi's files. Students of the Woodbrooke Settlement, Birmingham, where large parts of the book were drafted, were able and enthusiastic typists ; and most valuable assistance in this respect has also been given by Miss Ethel Faram of Friends House, London, and Mrs. Marcella Hardy of Madras. To all of them our thanks, and our deepest gratitude also to those who have given time and thought to read and comment on the manuscript, Mr. H. G. Alexander, Mr. H. S. L. Polak, the Rev. C. G. Robinson, and above all, Miss Agatha Harrison, whose informed co-operation at every stage of the work has been literally invaluable.

BENARSIDAS CHATURVEDI
MARJORIE SYKES

PREFACE

THE NEED for an authentic factual narrative of the life of Charles Freer Andrews was discussed by a number of his friends, including his literary executors, his Santiniketan colleagues, and the present authors, not long after his death. The material available was however scattered through a number of different countries, and none of us were willing to expose irreplaceable documents and letters to the risks of wartime travel by sea or air. For the first part of the story, moreover, personal investigation in England was essential, a thing well-nigh impossible under war conditions. It was therefore only towards the end of 1945 that definite plans for the preparation of the book were made.

Andrews was in the literal sense of the word a world figure; apart from the U.S.S.R. and the mainland of South America there was no major region of human habitation which he did not visit. To make any complete record of his life and work one would have to examine the files of hundreds, perhaps thousands, of forgotten newspapers and magazines in a score of languages, and seek out the men and women, some well-known but many quite obscure, in whose memories reposes a wealth of revealing anecdote which no one but themselves can supply. This we have been able to attempt personally only in England and India; correspondence with other parts of the world has brought us a certain amount of very valuable evidence, but no one could be more keenly aware than ourselves of the incompleteness of the record. Nevertheless, our material probably represents a true cross-section of Andrews' life and influence, and we believe it is in the public interest that the publication of a full-length biography should not be longer delayed.

In addition to the files of newspaper cuttings, letters and memoranda which Agatha Harrison in England and Benarsidas Chaturvedi in India collected during Andrews' life-time, we have had access to material of the highest authenticity in the shape of Andrews' own surviving letters. Two series of these, addressed to Rabindranath Tagore and to Swami Sraddhananda, provide an almost day-to-day record of Andrews' interests and activities for the periods which they cover. In the files of Mahatma Gandhi's correspondence, and in those of the Imperial Indian Citizenship Association of Bombay, which we were very courteously allowed to examine, are similar valuable letters contemporary with the events they describe. A third mine of information is Andrews' own published work. Nearly all his books, and many of his articles, are illustrated by incidents drawn from his own experience; for some events, such as his work during the Madras lockout of 1918 and the Orissa floods of 1925, articles written at the time by himself are our main and almost our only source of information.

When Andrews' description of events are not strictly contemporary, however, they must be used with caution. An amusing illustration of this occurred not long after his death. Many Indian newspapers had published biographical sketches, which began, on the authority of *What I Owe to Christ*, with the statement that Andrews was born in Carlisle. The sequel was that one of us, who was then in charge of Andrews' affairs at Santiniketan, received a reproachful letter quoting the relevant entry from the birth register of Newcastle-on-Tyne, and asking why we should conspire "to deprive Newcastle of its only saint"?*

Of that particular event Andrews could not be expected to have any personal recollection, but there are other instances in which the power of strong emotion to colour a man's memory has to be taken into account. Those who know the story of *What I Owe to Christ* will notice a number of discrepancies between our account of certain events and that given in Andrews' own narrative. Our version of such incidents is based in every case on incontrovertible contemporary evidence, which has been carefully weighed and collated. For Andrews' own book factual accuracy was comparatively unimportant, provided that the record of inner development was true. He wrote entirely from memory, after a lapse of twenty years or more, and memory is "a complicated flux in which events roll one over the other like pebbles in the bed of a stream. Every

* The confusion was due to the fact that shortly after Andrews' birth the family did move to Carlisle, but returned within a few months to Newcastle.

subsequent impression overshadows the earlier ones ; every new memory modifies the old ones."*

In this book we have made no statement without authority which we believe to be trustworthy ; and we are satisfied that our narrative is substantially accurate. But accuracy is only a part of truth : truthfulness of portraiture requires the selection, from the mass of material available, of those words and deeds which will best reveal the whole man, "in his habit as he lived." It is impossible to talk to anyone who knew Andrews in any degree without hearing anecdotes, humorous and very human, which possess this revealing power. Some of them have been included in the story, and he himself would have approved of their inclusion. "Nothing is so insipid in the historical records of saintly men," he once wrote†, "than to read about their superlative and superhuman excellencies, without any counterbalance of their human weaknesses." Any account of Andrews which omitted all mention of his own lovable human foibles would be insipid indeed.

"The biographer," says Lord David Cecil, "is there to explain rather than to judge. To get a clear view of a man we do not need to be told if his actions were good, but how and why he came to do them." That has been our aim. We knew and loved Charlie Andrews, and love does not find it easy to speak with detachment ; therefore we desire that the record of his life, set forth as truthfully and objectively as possible, should speak for itself. Yet the judgments of those who knew him are part of the record, and many of them have been included as such.

It was Dr. Sten Konow, a Norwegian scholar who knew Andrews at Santiniketan, who dubbed him "the Wandering Christian," and the title pleased him.

"A wandering Christian I,
A thing of shreds and patches,"

he commented, in apt misquotation of *The Mikado*. The wanderlust in him was the subject of many jokes. "Can you forecast C.F.A's latitude and longitude next July ?" wrote someone who

* Stefan Zweig, *Adepts in Self-Portraiture*. Introduction. For an example of the kind of analysis of evidence which has been necessary, see Appendix I.

† *Swami Sraddhananada : A Reminiscence* (1928).

was trying to secure him for a conference ; and the reply might well have been : "Ask me something easier !"

The jokes were a token of much affection, and very many of Andrews' friends in every nation would echo the words of a letter which reached him in 1934 from a Hindu fellow-worker in Orissa : "Within your beautiful works I see Him, the All-beautiful . . . He who can remind us of God, he alone is the true friend."* The secret of a life that could call out such a tribute was perhaps expressed most succinctly in the words quoted by his friend the Metropolitan Bishop of Calcutta on the day of his death : "It is not enough to give men *things*. You must give them yourself."

* Sarojini Chowdhury to C.F.A., 5th February, 1934.

CONTENTS

PART ONE

THE ENGLISHMAN

LIST OF ILLUSTRATIONS

CHAPTER I

EARLY YEARS

1871-1885

I

O N a cold morning of early spring a sturdy well-built man of thirty-five, black-haired, black-bearded, walked through the grey streets of Newcastle-on-Tyne to a dingy office in Westgate district and reported the birth of his second son :

        Twelfth February, 1871
        14 Brunel Terrace
        Charles Freer
FATHER   John Edwin Andrews, Gentleman
MOTHER Mary Charlotte Andrews, formerly Cartwright.

The father returned home to the cramped little corner house in the steep side-street above the Scotswood Road. He greeted his wife and looked from her to her child. Charlie had inherited his mother's lovely deep-set eyes ; he had also inherited from her his second name, Freer. It came from her maternal grandfather, William Leacroft Freer of Stourbridge, a West-country yeoman whose name his descendants were proud to bear. Long years afterwards the mother was to remember that her second son had been born "in a caul," and to speak of the old belief that this unusual feature foreshadowed some unusual distinction. *

Meantime there was little leisure for dreams. The family increased rapidly, and Mary Andrews was devoted to her children. There were two little step-daughters, six and four years old, besides Bertie, who was a baby of thirteen months when his brother was born ; before the family moved to Birmingham in 1877 there were three more younger ones to be cared for. The

---

* The "caul" is a kind of hood, formed by the membrane surrounding the foetus, which in rare cases covers the head of a child at birth. Folk-lore considers it a good omen and a charm against drowning.

I

mother was busy all day long, but she was never flurried; evening by evening, as they knelt beside her for their simple prayers, the children rested and delighted in the peace and serenity of her spirit. She was the centre of their universe. Her birthday in May, when they sang in the early morning outside her door, was their great festival. To the end of his life, Charlie's thoughts of Christmas were interpenetrated by memories of her telling of the Christmas story. Her singing of Highland songs (for there was a family connection with Clan McCallum) was the gateway to high romance. Her illness, when four-year-old Charlie, forbidden entrance to her room, was found by the doctor weeping silently on the stairs outside her door, was his earliest remembered experience of fear and grief.

In the winter of 1876-7, in his sixth year, Charlie was taken suddenly and seriously ill with rheumatic fever, and only his mother's devoted nursing through many critical weeks saved his life. The long months of pain marked the delicate child with more than ordinary seriousness, and made the bond between him and his mother one of unusually close intimacy. The deep understanding between them left an abiding impress upon Charlie's whole character and outlook. Long years afterwards, when the news of her death had reached him, he strove to put into words what her influence upon him had meant. It was, he felt sure, the source of the extreme and somewhat demonstrative sensitiveness which in later years would make his friends remark, in admiration or irritation according to the circumstances, that Charlie was half a woman. "It is because of this unchanging motherly influence," he wrote, "that the mother in me has grown so strong. My life seems only able to blossom into flower when I can pour out my affection upon others as my mother did upon me."*

II

Soon after this illness the family moved from Newcastle to Birmingham, a crowded and grimy city, but prosperous and powerful nevertheless—the Birmingham of Joseph Chamberlain in the golden age of Free Trade, manufacturing "trade goods"

* Letter to Rabindranath Tagore, 27th January, 1914.

for the ends of the earth, and supporting at the same time a distinguished intellectual life of its own.

The Andrews family lived at first at 6 Key Hill Drive, a quiet cul-de-sac off the steep thoroughfare of Key Hill. The little street runs along the brow of the hill, and the houses overlook the trees and green grass of the "old cemetery" on the slope below. Along the foot of the hill, parallel with the Drive, runs the ancient Roman highway of Icknield Street, forming the lower boundary of the old cemetery. Even now, seventy years later, there lingers a faint aroma of the distant days when the Drive was really a drive, leading through parkland to some country house on the edge of a little pre-industrial town. In Charlie's childhood the Lodge Gates at the end of it still remained, and could be closed to shut out the heavy horse-drawn drays which toiled up and down the hill.

Here in Birmingham the outside world began to make its impact upon the Andrews children. Bertie and Charlie went off each day down Key Hill and round into Icknield Street, past the window of the sweetshop on the corner, and up the high steep steps to the door of Miss Hipkins' dame school. Edith, aged five, accompanied her brothers, and Charlie was soon offering to fight a girl of his own size who had remarked disparagingly, though possibly truthfully, that his little sister couldn't sew!

The new experiences of school were accompanied by others whose centre was the Church. The "Catholic Apostolic Church" to which the family belonged had arisen in the distress and dark uncertainty of the years following the Napoleonic wars. Earnest souls had seen in those days of "the breaking of nations," a fulfilment of Biblical prophecies of the Last Days. The orthodox shunned the enthusiasts, but they met together in prayer and fasting, and looked forward eagerly to a miraculous coming of Christ in the clouds of Heaven which they believed to be close at hand. John Andrews, Charlie's grandfather, was one of their number. With the sober, God-fearing courage and rugged independence of spirit which had marked his East Anglian Puritan ancestors, he had thrown up the teaching post to which his conscience could no longer be reconciled, and with his young

3

wife had started life afresh. His son, John Edwin, was born in 1835, in the midst of this spiritual adventure. The passionate personal devotion and faithfulness of the father was reflected in the son ; he in his turn devoted himself to the ministry as an "evangelist," and "spent himself, during the whole of a long life-time, in incessant spiritual toil."*

Charlie's boyhood was thus spent in an atmosphere of close prayerful fellowship and mystical aspiration. The inner organisation of the faithful, and the appointments of their beautiful Birmingham church, were based on a detailed symbolical interpretation of the description of Temple and Tabernacle in the Old Testament, and of the meaning of numbers such as four, seven and twelve, which recurred in the Bible. The boy's beauty-loving spirit responded to the majesty of the services. The twin lights on the altar, the Seven Lamps that hung before it, the mighty nave and high dim roof, fed his sense of awe. Even when he was still quite small, sitting close by his mother's side, the great "farewell" chapters of St. John's Gospel which were read each year on Maundy Thursday, made a deep and lasting impression on his mind. But their rare beauty of language was felt rather than understood, and he was not abnormally "good" or precociously pious. "God," he expostulated during one seemingly endless service, "when I'm grown up I won't ever go to Church again !"

Sunday by Sunday a solemn hush fell over the great crowded church as the worshippers went up in turn to the altar to receive the sacrament. Then the quiet might be broken by words of prophetic utterance—the voice of one raised in warning, or the ecstatic cry of a woman, "speaking with tongues," followed by another and another, then dying away into silence. Preachers sometimes dwelt on the wonders at hand, when the Last Trump should in the twinkling of an eye summon the dead from their graves, and those who had been "sealed unto salvation" should meet the Lord in the air. The faces of preacher and people alike shone with expectant joy. Charlie shivered ; he had the faculty, not uncommon in children, of externalising the vivid imagery of the mind till it became objectively real for him—a faculty which

* *What I Owe to Christ.*

4

in his case persisted into after-life. These imaginative sermons had a powerful effect. His mother's hand and smile would re-assure him at the time, but on dark winter evenings, as he hurried home from choir practice at the church, turned into Icknield Street and came alongside the cemetery, the preacher's imagery was terrifying to remember. The headstones glimmered grey on his right—suppose the dead beneath them should rise *now* ! He panted up Key Hill—the ghostly stones still on his right—through the Lodge gates and into the comforting firelight and com-panionship of home. But he confided in no one—not even his mother. He was tongue-tied, like so many children, by the sacred associations of his fears.

III

The family grew in stature and in numbers ; the quiet home in Key Hill Drive no longer sufficed for their housing, nor Miss Hipkins' little school for their education. In 1879 they moved to No. 1 South Road, on the borders of Handsworth, which was then close to fields and open country. The boys attended Mr. Deakin's preparatory school, but it was the father himself who was his sons' greatest teacher. Vigorous in mind and body, his deep religious convictions were allied with an impulsive buoyancy of soul, a power of wonder and delight in the world, which kept him a boy at heart, and made him the ideal companion of his children. At Newcastle when they were still tiny he would take them to spend the day by the sea ; now he took the growing boys away from smoky Birmingham for long days in Sutton Park, taught them to walk and to swim and to play cricket, and kindled Charlie's passionate love of beauty. Hidden within him was the sensitive spirit of a poet—one who could write like this :

> There is a ceaseless music of the earth,
> Tender and deep, for those who have ears to hear,
> In mountains lone, and woods, and murmuring trees,
> And in the sky at midnight, when the stars
> Chant, without sound, the song of all the spheres.

For several years after his illness Charlie was too delicate for strenuous physical exercise, and his vivid imagination found wholesome food in books. At the back of an upper shelf in his father's bookcase he discovered a complete set of Sir Walter Scott's novels and poems, badly printed on bad paper, but, for him, "a golden store of wealth that could neither be diminished nor exhausted."* Days in the Sutton Woods became days of glorious fantasy, spent with Ivanhoe in the glades of Sherwood, or with Rob Roy and Marmion in the magic Scotland of his mother's songs. There were other great days—a day at Llandudno when the music of the sea held him spellbound, stirring dim memories of the waves on the Northumbrian coast, and holidays with his mother's sister, Mrs. Lucas, and the family of cousins on their Sussex farm. But Sutton and its wild and solitary woods came first in his heart.

As Charlie grew stronger, his father and he would go out together, over the fields or through the town, while the father talked as to an equal about everything under the sun, but especially about history, politics, and religion. He would picture the pageant of English life that the centuries had unrolled along the Icknield Way—that same Icknield Street along which they walked so often, and where the Roman legions had walked before them. Then he would turn to tales of British heroism in the more immediate past. Mr. Andrews believed implicitly that the British Empire was the noblest thing on earth. He gave Charlie an illustrated story book, *Deeds that Won the Empire*, which glorified even the Opium Wars with China. He told him thrilling stories of the Indian "Mutiny" and of Havelock, Outram and Lawrence. They set the boy's imagination on fire.

"Mother," he once said to her eagerly on his return home, "I want a bit of rice to eat with my dinner every day—please ! You see, I'm going to India when I grow up, and father says everyone eats rice there. I must get used to it before I go."

"You absurd boy !" laughed his mother ; but there was pain in her voice too, and he heard it.

The Catholic Apostolic Church was strongly conservative in political thought. "All power is from above, from God," Mr. Andrews would explain earnestly, "and to say that it comes from

* Unpublished Reminiscences.

the multitude is sheer blasphemy." He was a well-known figure in city politics, and was one of the founders of the Birmingham Parliamentary Debating Society, which chose him for its first "Speaker."

As "Mr. Speaker" he was something of an *enfant terrible*, and persisted in applauding Conservative speeches even from the "Chair" ; but as "Member for Salisbury," he could marshal his arguments with a first-hand mastery of the facts which bore witness to his ability and thoroughness, and present them with the zest of a born fighter. "This man is something positive," wrote a contemporary in the lively weekly leaflet published by the Society, "a man who can give and take hard blows with good humour, and come up smiling."* There was a memorable day when Charlie was about twelve years old. John Bright and Joseph Chamberlain addressed a vast and enthusiastic Liberal Party meeting on a field close by his home. His father attended, and recorded his dissent—an aggressive minority of one !

IV

Towards the end of 1880, in Charlie's tenth year, the two brothers had taken the entrance examination for the ancient and famous King Edward VI High School. Being instructed to try for every possible mark, both boys embarked boldly on the Greek paper. Their father had inspired them already with something of his love for the classics, but their linguistic equipment was still very meagre. Whether by virtue of the five marks which Charlie scored in Greek, or by virtue of the "handicap" for which his tender age qualified him, he succeeded in winning a scholarship, and he and Bertie started on their High School career. The change was at first far from pleasant for Charlie, who was still not robust, and the youngest and smallest boy in his class. The school bullies victimised him, and his true life was still lived at home.

A year or two later a great change took place in the Andrews' fortunes. Mary Andrews had inherited from her parents a certain modest wealth, and the investment of her money had up to this

* *The Speaker*, 1879.

time brought a welcome addition to the family income. It had made it possible to keep two servants, and with fourteen children, of whom thirteen survived infancy and grew up, their help was needed. One day, when Charlie was twelve or thirteen years old, news came that the trusted friend to whom his father had confided the care of his wife's money had lost the whole of it in speculation and absconded. Before the day was over the worst fears had been confirmed. The family gathered, according to their custom, for evening prayers, and Charlie listened half afraid as his father began to read the psalm appointed for the day :

"For it is not an open enemy that hath done me this dishonour : for then I could have borne it ; but it was even thou, my companion, my guide, and my own familiar friend . . ."

There was a pause. The curse which the psalmist had uttered upon the treacherous friend was never read. John Andrews closed the book and began to pray with his whole heart for the man who had wronged him. His prayer made an unforgettable impression. It was linked in Charlie's memory with another day, when his father had quoted to him the words of Jesus in St. John's Gospel, "Greater love hath no man than this, that a man lay down his life for his friends. Ye are my friends, if ye do whatsoever I command you." "That, Charlie," he had said, "is the ideal of a Christian gentleman."

Material comfort gave place to struggle ; only one little serving-maid could be retained. Pence had to be hoarded, and only for the most urgent reasons could they be used for the steam-tram that would save the long daily tramp to King Edward's. Bertie had to leave school and begin to earn his living ; only Charlie's scholarship enabled him to go on with his education. Mary Andrews, always a skilful and thrifty housewife, exercised endless ingenuity to make the benefice of a minister of religion cover their household needs. With a wistful smile she would cut down her husband's "pocket-money," knowing how impulsively generous he was towards anyone who asked him for help. Her older children watched and understood, loved her more dearly than ever, and learned unselfishness in little things.

CHAPTER II

SCHOOL AND COLLEGE

1885-1895

I

A T Christmas 1885 Charlie, not yet fifteen, stood first in "Classical III." In "Classical II" he came directly under the care of the Rev. A. R. Vardy, the Headmaster of King Edward VI School and a brilliant teacher. The parents' hopes ran high. Charlie might perhaps be able to win a scholarship to Cambridge. And later, please God, he would follow his father in the sacred ministry of the Church.

They spoke seldom of these dreams, but Charlie knew of their hopes. The first he fully shared. King Edward VI School was no longer an uncongenial place. The physical weakness of childhood had been overcome, and he could now hold his own there. Always serious-minded, he set himself to justify his parents' confidence, and to make the most of his opportunities. He was a shy, awkward, thoughtful, studious schoolboy, rapidly making his mark in the classroom ; the first of the other school circles where he distinguished himself was the Debating Society. In October 1886 he made his maiden speech, and after that took part regularly in the debates. He brought to them the political opinions he had learned at home. In October 1887 he opposed the motion that *This House condemns the Government use of coercion and suppression in Ireland* ; the following year, "with a very powerful speech," he argued that *Home Rule is NOT compatible with the integrity of the Empire.* His speeches exhibited the same sound preparation as those of the "Member for Salisbury" in the Birmingham Parliamentary debates. His wide knowledge often astonished his schoolfellows, but what most impressed them was that Andrews, summing-up a debate on the motion *That*

9

Shakespeare was greater in his delineation of female than of male character, should dare to demolish with telling quotations the arguments of no less august an opponent than the Head himself!

In one debate Andrews supported cricket against tennis. Cricket had become an enthusiasm. Charlie and Bert, with a gang of other Handsworth lads, ran a club of their own, with cricket in summer and "hare-and-hounds" in winter. In his last two years at King Edward's Charlie was selected for the school cricket team. This was a triumph of perseverance rather than natural aptitude, and fellow-cricketers long remembered the serious look on his face as he walked to the wicket to open the innings for his side. Nature had not made him an athlete, but by painstaking, steady determination he made thirty runs in his first match against Stratford College, and saved the day for King Edward's.

On the other hand, he had considerable artistic talents and longed at one time to be a painter. Alone in Sutton Woods with his water-colours on holidays he would strive to seize the impression of light and colour, and some of his sketches are still preserved. He amused himself and his classmates with his cartoons of classics and cricket. He attended evening classes at the Municipal School of Art, and his gifts so impressed his teacher that he offered the boy a scholarship for the full professional training there. The suggestion fascinated him, but Mr. Vardy strongly advised him to complete his classical course, and the advice was accepted.

His intellectual ability was outstanding even in a set of brilliant contemporaries.* School prizes fell easily into his hands. At the Speech Day of 1889 a younger brother looked on proudly as Charlie welcomed the Governors of the school in Greek verse, and then went up to the dais amid laughter and applause for six prizes in succession, three for classics and three for English. His tremendous power of concentrated work, his quick and sure hold on essentials, the memory which could retain with ease long passages of English, Greek and Latin verse, are remembered by

---

* Several became Headmasters of well-known schools ; two were brilliant mathematicians ; one a distinguished surgeon.

all who then knew him. Nor was it only a superficial nimbleness of mind. His powers, in fact, ripened later than is the case with many brilliant boys and his comprehension of the great human themes of the classics was deeper ; for he had the soul of a poet, and a knowledge of pain beyond his years.

This deeper quality of mind is revealed in the last reference to him in the school magazine. The chief item of entertainment on Speech Days was a scene from some great Greek play. In 1890, in his last term at school, Andrews took the part of Sophocles' Philoctetes.

> "He made a really great impersonation . . . brought home to us with fresh power the majestic desolation and the infinitely tragic pathos of this great creation of Sophocles. He had evidently deeply entered into the spirit of the hero, and he was eminently successful in portraying his feelings alike by gesture, expression and tone."*

During the last two years of his school career Andrews was Assistant Editor of the School *Chronicle*. Contributions to the *Chronicle* were anonymous, but it is known that he was the author of a School Song. His imagination had been fired by the great traditions of King Edward's. In March 1890, died one of the School's most distinguished *alumni*, Bishop Lightfoot of Durham. He was succeeded in the bishopric by another great "Edwardian," Dr. Brooke Foss Westcott, and the *Chronicle* contains proud appreciations of the work of both men. They are probably written by a maturer hand than Andrews', but it is certain that he read them with a responsive thrill, though he could hardly then have foreseen what a profound influence Westcott was soon to exercise upon him. His own school career was crowned in the same month by his election to the Open Classical Scholarship at Pembroke College, Cambridge. Half of his father's ambition was on the point of fulfilment.

II

Charlie Andrews was now nineteen years of age. One day during the summer vacation his father spoke to him openly of his hopes that he would find his vocation in the ministry of their

* *King Edward VI School Chronicle*, 1890.

Church. They were out walking when he did so, and the half-anticipated, long-dreaded words roused in Charlie's breast a tumult which stamped on his mind with unnatural clearness the very stones of the commonplace street through which they were passing as he spoke. The boy's mind rushed back over the years —the tiny estrangements of conscious, unacknowledged wrong-doing which had imperceptibly clouded the perfect frankness of childhood ; the slow change by which the formerly awe-inspiring Church Services had become through weekly familiarity a matter of indifference. He observed the forms of piety, but they were little more than forms ; the current of life had passed them by.

The father paused for an answer. Charlie was silent.

Day after day the conversation haunted him, the guilt of his silence burdened him. Time after time he tried to speak, but the words would not come. What followed must be told in his own words :

> "An evening came, when as I knelt to pray before retiring to rest, the strong conviction of sin and impurity came upon me without warning, with such overpowering strength that every shred of false convention was torn aside and I knew myself as I really was. The sudden agony that followed . . . broke in upon me like a lightning flash, leaving at first nothing but black darkness behind it. I buried my head in my hands and knelt there with God in an anguish of spirit that blotted out everything else and left me groping for the light. . . . At last a new wonderful sense of peace and forgiveness came stealing into my life at its very centre, and the tears rushed out, bringing infinite relief."

He slept, rose refreshed at half-past five, and went to Church to return thanks at the six o'clock service. He had never thought of attending the early morning service before.

> "As the blessing in Church next morning was pronounced, the flood of God's abounding love was poured upon me like the great ocean, wave upon wave, while I knelt with bowed head to receive it."*

In that spring-tide of the spirit all things and all men were made new. Close behind the church were the wretched slums of Camden Street. He had never before given them much thought, although other young men from the church used to visit there. But now in the faces of the needy he saw the Christ, and all the lovable kindliness of his boyish nature was transformed into a

* *What I Owe to Christ*, p. 91 ff.

passion of love and pity. Soon he knew the name of every child, the sorrows of every home. He looked with new eyes upon the degradation in which a prosperous city was content to leave its poor. His cousin, R. C. Lucas, who was staying with the family, visited the slums with him. In the squalid street Charlie turned to him with sober determination written on his face. "We have got to end all this," he said.

His conversion awakened other sides of his nature also to new life. Once more he responded to natural beauty with a gladness as keen as in his boyhood. When the harvest moon shone in splendour, his heart was too full for sleep. He went out and walked until dawn, and as he walked he sang joyfully to himself. Soon afterwards he was spending a holiday in the country, not far from Lichfield. On a golden afternoon of September sun he had come to a hilltop overlooking the little city, and seen the three great spires of its Cathedral rising through the trees. Down he went, and entered the quiet spaciousness of the long nave, filled with the soft radiance of summer sunlight. In a serene exaltation of spirit he seated himself there. Evensong began, the clear voices rising into the vaulted roof . . .

When Charlie became once more conscious of his surroundings he had known the mystic ecstasy, seen the unimaginable Light. He went slowly out into the evening. A tramp begged an alms, and the boy emptied his pockets into the man's astonished hands. Hours later, weary and hungry, he returned to the house where he was staying. His mother, hearing how it was that he had no money for the railway fare, smiled in amused tenderness. "So like his father !" she said.

III

The next month Charlie Andrews went up to Cambridge. Trees dreamed along the river in the blue hush of St. Martin's Summer ; red creepers burned on the grey walls of Pembroke courts ; King's College Chapel lifted its delicate majesty to the pale October sunlight, and within, the music rose and lingered among the springing arches overhead. In this companionship of beauty old friendships were renewed and deepened. J. H.

Srawley,* with whom Andrews had once walked every day through Birmingham to school, was two years his senior. Now they met each Sunday in Srawley's room at Caius, to read poetry and to discuss religion ; Andrews counted among the great experiences of life Srawley's reading of Browning's *Saul* in the firelight. He found new friends also. Charles Hermann Prior, Senior Tutor of Pembroke, a man of great gifts and warm affections, at once recognized the depth and truth of the young freshman's religious experience, and quickly won his confidence. Many years later Andrews edited a small memorial volume of his friend's sermons†; he included the one to which he had listened as a freshman on the first Sunday of that memorable term : "Come thou with us and we will do thee good."

Religion was now the centre of life for Andrews ; every morning at 7-30 he was at the College Chapel service ; every Sunday at the Holy Communion. But the circumference of his interests was drawn with generous and inclusive enthusiasm. He entered into everything—"all teeth and keenness," to quote a good-humoured sally. He rowed, with no special aptitude, but with his whole energy in every stroke ; in his second year his enthusiasm contributed to the triumph of one of the more mediocre Pembroke eights ; each man carried his oar, which adorned thenceforward the walls of his rooms. He was popular among the College athletes ; and on the long fireside evenings, when undergraduates sat in each other's rooms and argued about everything under the sun, he was remarkable for the extraordinary variety of the subjects on which he could talk with knowledge. Men gathered in his rooms to smoke a friendly pipe ; he attracted the scholarly and the insignificant alike. At midnight perhaps, when the guests were gone, the host would lie down and sleep for twenty minutes and awake refreshed to study.

The members of the Cambridge Inter-Collegiate Christian Union, with their passionate personal devotion to Christ and the fearlessness of their faith, attracted him greatly, and he joined in their meetings for prayer and for evangelism. Then he found

* Now Chancellor of the Diocese of Lincoln.
† *The Presence of God*, C.U.P., 1904.

that the men of the C.I.C.C.U. held a doctrine of eternal torment
for the damned which shocked him deeply ; it seemed so utterly
at variance with the character of the Christ whom his mother had
taught him to love and whose forgiveness had renewed his life.
His moral revolt against this teaching led him to question the
soundness of the premise, which was that every part of the Bible,
every sentence, had been directly inspired by God and was therefore equally valid and binding on the Christian.

It is remarkable that in what Andrews himself called the "keen
and biting air of Cambridge in an age of intellectual inquiry,"*
he never surrendered the "fundamental certainty" that the nature
of God is Love. God and Christ and Immortality, he testified
again and again, were for him things that could not be shaken.
He could not be unaware that questions were being asked which
struck at the roots of all such faith, but these questions did not
come home to him, either then or later, with the torturing
insistence with which they have pressed upon so many honest
minds. "Scientific doubts" seem to have been silenced for him
by the sight of Sir George Gabriel Stokes, the most distinguished
physical scientist of his day, worshipping Sunday by Sunday in
the College Chapel—a man whose personal faith so shone forth
that the undergraduates called him, and not in mockery, "the
Angel Gabriel."

But the fact that the particular religious difficulties with which
Andrews wrestled at Cambridge may seem to be comparatively
superficial must not blind one to their desperate urgency for himself. Many of the peculiar tenets and observances of the Catholic
Apostolic Church depended upon that very conception of the
literal verbal inspiration of the Bible whose validity he was driven
to call in question. The practical personal consequences of re-
nouncing them would be distressing in the extreme. Every tie
of home affection bound him to his parents' church, and in the
religious exaltation of his conversion he had been "sealed" to
its membership and service. Yet within a year of entering
Cambridge he had to tell his father that he could not enter its
ministry. The sense of estrangement was hard for both of them.

* *What I Owe to Christ*, p. 120.

15

Andrews found a satisfying intellectual foundation for faith in the teachings of Bishop Westcott of Durham and the younger Oxford thinker, Charles Gore, who had himself been Westcott's pupil at Harrow. Late in 1889 Gore's group of Oxford scholars had published a collection of essays called *Lux Mundi*, "an attempt to put the Catholic faith in its right relation to modern intellectual and social problems."* Such was the interest aroused that by the time Andrews went up to Pembroke, less than a year later, the tenth edition had been sold out. The book contained a striking essay by Gore himself on *The Holy Spirit and the Inspiration of Holy Scripture* in which (as against all "magical" doctrines of inspiration) he urged that "the supernatural fertilises, but does not annihilate, the natural. The Divine Spirit intensifies, but does not supersede, the human faculties. The inspiration of the recorder increases his sense of the working of God in history ; it does not guarantee the exact historical truth of what he records." In such thoughts, and in Gore's lectures at Cambridge, in which he fearlessly welcomed the application to every part of the Bible of the criteria of scientific inquiry, Andrews found his intellectual anchorage.

IV

Almost simultaneously with *Lux Mundi* was launched the Christian Social Union, of which from the beginning Westcott was the President. It was "a union of Churchmen to study in common how to apply the moral truths of Christianity to the social and economic difficulties of the present time." Its members set themselves to study facts and educate the conscience of the Church on such matters as dangerous unguarded machinery, and phosphorus and lead poisoning in industry. They declared that the doctrine of the Incarnation was shorn of its splendour if it did not mean a hallowing of the social and industrial as well as the individual life of men.

Andrews threw himself wholeheartedly into the work of the Cambridge branch of the Christian Social Union, of which he

* *Lux Mundi*—"The Light of the World" ; the word Catholic is used in its proper sense of "universal."

MR. AND MRS. J. E. ANDREWS AND THEIR CHILDREN, ABOUT 1890
(*C. F. Andrews standing on the left*)

became secretary. There was no intellectual conflict here to mar his happiness. Westcott's concern for the downtrodden and exploited labourer was of a piece with the impulse which had driven him after his conversion into the Camden Street slums, and his contact with the poor helped him now to keep his faith in God. During term time he taught a Sunday School class of poor Cambridge boys, visited their families and entered into their troubles. He spent many vacation week-ends at the Pembroke College Mission in Walworth, South London, and was an enthusiastic member of the College committee responsible for its support. The subject of the essay which won him the Burney Prize at Cambridge in 1895—*The Relation of Christianity to the conflict between Capital and Labour**—was directly inspired by Westcott and the Christian Social Union.

It would be difficult to overestimate the greatness of Bishop Westcott's formative influence on Charles Andrews. Mrs. Prior, in whose home he was soon a welcome guest, was the Bishop's daughter, and his youngest son Basil, who was an undergraduate at Trinity College, became Andrews' intimate friend. In the summer vacations he visited the Westcotts' home at Bishop Auckland, and shared their family holidays at Robin Hood's Bay on the Yorkshire coast. There Dr. Westcott spent the mornings in his literary work and in the afternoons tramped the moors with the young men, talking, talking. "Remember, Andrews," he would say, stopping in his walk to emphasize his point, "nothing, *nothing* that is truly human can be left outside the Christian faith without destroying the very reason for its existence." Sometimes he would speak of his dream of a new kind of Christian community life, through which a renewal of the social ideals of the nation might be brought about. It would follow, like the ancient monastic communities, a discipline of simplicity—perhaps a threefold rule of poverty, study and devotion, but the units of which it should be composed would be Christian *families*, not individual celibates. He was never able to realise his dream, but he sowed a seed in Andrews' mind which was to bear fruit later.

Another topic on which Andrews eagerly questioned Westcott

* Published by Methuen, 1896.

C

was that of the Christian attitude in industrial conflicts. There had been a coal strike in Durham which involved eighty thousand workers and lasted three months. Westcott had intervened ; he knew and loved the miners, and both they and the owners trusted him. He was able to bring them together in conference at Bishop Auckland, and under his chairmanship an agreement was reached and the strike ended. Machinery of arbitration was set up to deal with any future disputes.

This concern with all secular life was the fruit of Westcott's discipleship of the Greek Fathers. It was he who inspired Andrews with his enthusiasm for Clement of Alexandria and Origen, and taught him the legends, epigrams, and anecdotes of the Fathers which Andrews used again and again in his own books. It was he who drew the great parallel between Greece and India which inspired the Cambridge Mission to Delhi.

> He placed India side by side with Greece—these, he said, were the two great *thinking* nations who had made the history of the world. As Greece had been the leader of Europe, India would always be the leader of Asia. One of his great hopes was that Indian thinkers would be able to interpret fully the Gospel of St. John.*

The immediate result of such talks was that Andrews added to his multifarious College interests an enthusiasm for the Cambridge Mission to Delhi. He wrote to the Principal of St. Stephen's College to ask for information which might help him to interest other undergraduates in its ideals. In the spring of 1893 he held a meeting and distributed leaflets about the principles and work of the Mission. One of the men who attended was deeply impressed ; he kept the papers, and a few years later he joined the staff of the College. His name was Hibbert Ware.

In the summer of 1893 Andrews took a first class in the Classical Tripos, but not, as he had hoped, in the first division. His absorption in a hundred and one other concerns had prevented him from obtaining the distinction which his ability might otherwise have won. He realised soberly that he must achieve nothing less than the highest rank in the theological studies to which he now turned, if he was to have any chance of a Fellowship. Never-

---

* Unpublished reminiscences ; cf. a similar tribute in Andrews' speech at St. Stephen's College, Delhi, March 1939 (reported in *The Stephanian*).

theless, he led the same full varied life as before, and it would be misleading to picture him as concerned solely with religious activities. He was an energetic and very companionable lad with plenty of ordinary human interests ; he joined the crowd of adventure-loving undergraduates who flocked to Professor E. G. Browne's rooms in the Ivy Court of Pembroke, and listened far into the night to tales of his wanderings in Persia, and of the faith of Islam ; in the vacations he acted "Santa Claus" for children's parties, recited with zest and facility *The Hunting of the Snark*, and collected his Birmingham friends at home for uproarious evenings of dancing and music-hall songs.

There still exists, however, an intimate diary of 1894 in which one may catch glimpses of his deeper thoughts. It reveals a man of very tender affections ; records of private intercession are filled with the names of his family, his Sunday-school boys, and scores of his Cambridge friends. But he experiences the Christian life mainly as a strenuous and unremitting warfare ; it has not yet become also a secret spring of inward peace. He strains to "fill the unforgiving minute," and reproaches himself for lack of energy and zeal. He wars on his own shortcomings—his presumptuous sins, "especially when arguing" ; his conceit which "does things for show and says things for applause" ; his "boastful sense of success at every triumph in Thy name" ; his "arrogant fault-finding, contemptuous, unkind words." It is a tempestuous nature, now exalted to the heavens, now humbled to the dust. The knowledge of estrangement and misunderstanding at home is an underlying anxiety : "Bless my homecoming ; may it bring joy and peace . . . Oh if I *have* to offend, Lord, grant me no bitterness, no shirking, but loving kindness and truth." But at the end of the vacation he confesses : "I have been very neglectful. I have hidden from my father and not taken his confidence."

In 1895 the religious issue had to be squarely faced. For nearly five years of crowded Cambridge life the Church of England had given him new religious insight, intellectual integration, practical purposeful service, contact with new kinds of Christian holiness. Conflicts had been resolved, new vistas opened, nourishment provided for the soul. Did not Truth itself demand that he should openly and formally become a member of that Church ? Every instinct of family affection fought against the breach which such a decision would entail. The arguments at home were very painful ; the father, sure of the reality of his own religious experience, feared that his son's difficulties were a sign of pride of the intellect ; the mother did not argue—her own faith was very simple—but her eyes grew dark with pain. Andrews turned for advice to Srawley, to C. H. Prior, to Basil Westcott. The Tripos examination was drawing near. Could not the whole agonising decision be set aside till it was over ? Basil was clear that it could not. "You must seek *first* the Kingdom of Heaven," he said. "I feel it very strongly. If you shirk the decision now, our friendship must come to an end." Andrews left Cambridge—Prior, understanding, gave him leave—and for six weeks he remained alone in the country, thinking out his beliefs. When he came back the examination was only three weeks ahead, he had missed important lectures, but his decision was taken and his mind at peace. He took a first-class with special distinction : only once in the last ten years, he was told, had his papers been equalled in the University. A Fellowship was only a matter of time.

Srawley arranged for his Confirmation. Once more he knelt in Lichfield Cathedral, but there was no repetition of the joyous ecstasy he had once known there. There was instead the inevitable reaction after long-continued tension, and the misery of family estrangement.

Andrews spent much of the summer in Cambridge with Charles Prior. Cut off by his own act from the Church of his youth, he clung to the Church of his adoption, and each day strengthened his resolve to seek ordination as a priest and to find his lifework among the poor. Charles Prior welcomed this resolution and suggested a preparatory period as a lay worker in some industrial district. The district he chose was the parish of St. Peter's, Monkwearmouth, in Bishop Westcott's diocese of Durham, a few miles only from Andrews' own birthplace at Newcastle-on-Tyne.

CHAPTER III

APPRENTICESHIP

1895-1904

I

LONG before recorded history the mouth of the River Wear had been a refuge from North Sea storms. In A.D. 674, in the earliest years of Christianity in England, the monks built a priory on the little promontory of high ground on the north bank of the river, looking out over the grey seas towards Norway, and year after year they trimmed the beacon light which guided their people's tiny ships in safety to the anchorage below. By 680 a child novice was serving in the Priory Church of St. Peter whose name was to be revered throughout Europe as the first great scholar-saint of England—the Venerable Bede. Centuries passed ; marauding Danish pirates set fire once and again to the tiny church, warfare engulfed it, but the faith survived. Vast changes have swept the face of the country ; the industrial revolution has transformed the Sunderland shipyards, but the grey stone church in its green churchyard watches over them still.

The ancient battered little building, which had been the centre of so much patient fortitude, so much undaunted faith, spoke to Andrews in an altogether new and vivid way of the reality and majesty of history and of the spiritual riches of the Communion of Saints. In his childhood, religious impulse had been concerned with the future ; at Cambridge, with the strenuous present ; now, as he knelt on the stones where Bede had worshipped, he experienced the power of a great religious past. The whole valley of the River Wear was rich in Christian story ; the noble strength of Durham Cathedral dominated its middle reaches, and a few miles higher up the valley lay Bishop Auckland, Basil Westcott's home. The two friends made pilgrimage together to places of

21

old and sacred memories, Durham and Jarrow and the Holy Island of Lindisfarne.

C. G. Hopkinson, Vicar of Monkwearmouth and a college friend of C. H. Prior, welcomed the young lay-worker with great friendliness, and set him to tasks which brought him face to face with the grim problems of the present. Below the little green churchyard, along the blackened river, the redhot rivets were being hammered all day long into the giant steelplated ships. Twelve thousand men were employed at one shipyard alone, and "overtime" work might go on far into the night. Speed, and yet more speed, was the cry ; skilled workmen earned big wages, and every monetary inducement was used to tempt them to a more furious pace. In the rush to "capture the trade," time was money, and "efficiency" in production brought ever-increasing dividends. Andrews looked on. He saw the inhuman pressure, he watched the men, consumed with thirst and fatigue, pour out of the yards. The flamboyant drinkshops, clustered outside the gates, shamelessly exploited them. With desperate recklessness they found relief from soul-destroying labour in fighting and gambling.

Andrews saw, too, the less spectacular tragedy of the unskilled labourer, driven by ruthless competition to work for starvation wages, and without either strength or brains to organise resistance to the system which oppressed him. He found homes whose only income was a precarious eighteen shillings a week. He himself had deliberately limited his personal expenditure to ten shillings, in order to share as far as possible the experience of the people among whom he worked. He found that this often meant going supperless to bed. Yet, he reflected, he himself was sustained by a high purpose, and had the educated man's knowledge of food values. What of the casual labourer, with a family of four or five to keep, whose work, though so cruelly insecure, drove him by its very monotony into outbreaks of wild extravagance ? Andrews learnt once for all in Monkwearmouth the bitter power of a brutalising environment. He doubted whether, in such conditions, he himself could have resisted day after day the devil of drink. "In Sunderland," he wrote, "I became very soon an out-and-out opponent of the capitalist system."*

* *The Modern Review*, February-March, 1915.

He made other friends quickly among the men and women who came to the Church. Jack Jobling, the burly, muscular door-keeper, had been a drunken prize-fighter not long before. The story of his sudden and lasting conversion was dramatic. He had come rolling drunk into a Sunday School gathering and grossly insulted one of the ladies, and the young curate had knocked him down. He got to his feet sobered, went out, and came back the next day to give his life to Christ. He became Andrews' trusty ally in running a club for working lads from the shipyards. They came when the day's work was over, played rollicking games, and then listened, tired but happy, while Andrews told them the stories of heroic adventure which his father had once told him. A brilliantly-coloured picture of General Gordon riding his camel across the desert and wearing a red fez cap, adorned the walls of their club room. The "General Gordon Club" had life in it, and was flourishing years later when its founder returned from India and revisited the town.

On the eve of Good Friday, Andrews spent the night in prayer, watching the great moon whose light had shone over the Garden of Gethsemane, and interceding for the sleeping parish round him. Next day, when the Three Hours Service was over, a woman sought him out—a good religious woman, a regular attender at the church—and poured out her inner doubts and fears. Andrews listened, with the story of the Cross in his heart, and then said very simply, "When Jesus uttered from the Cross these words 'It is finished,' did He not bring to an end your sins and mine ?" He saw the light come streaming into her eyes, and knew that she had "seen the Lord." God had used him, Charlie Andrews, as His instrument. A few days later, with that memory singing within him, he had left Monkwearmouth, for C. H. Prior had need of him elsewhere, and he could not refuse the call.

II

The call came from the Pembroke College Mission in South London. It was only after long hesitation that the Rev. R. H. B. Simpson, the missioner, had posted his letter in the pillarbox outside the little house at 207A East Street, Walworth. He

realised that he was asking Prior and the Pembroke Committee
to take an unprecedented step ; he wanted Andrews as his
successor in the Mission, and Andrews was as yet unordained.
But what was to be done ? He himself was a very sick man, and
his only assistant was leaving for missionary work in Uganda.
The committee agreed that there was no alternative, and on
April 21st, 1896, Andrews arrived to take up his new duties. Six
weeks later, on Trinity Sunday, he was ordained deacon by Dr.
Edward Talbot, Bishop of Rochester, in Clapham Parish Church.

His surroundings were already familiar and beloved. The
mission district is off the Old Kent Road, not far from the
"Elephant and Castle," and though it did not contain any of the
very worst London criminal areas, many of its five thousand
people were desperately poor, and shamefully oppressed by landlords and brokers. The degradation was the same as at Monkwearmouth, but the people themselves were very different. The
northern shipwrights were rough, hardy, almost surlily independent ; the costermongers and dock labourers who formed the
greater part of Andrews' new parish were careless, thriftless,
happy-go-lucky, entirely lovable ; there was a strong Irish
element among them.

He plunged into the work, full of enthusiasm, energy, and ideas.
He founded and coached a men's cricket club which won six out
of its eleven matches in the summer of 1896 ; he collected a
Sunday School class composed of all the young pick-pockets of
the district. He hardly knew their real names ; to him as to each
other they were "Ginger," "Nipper," "Dodger," "Smiler," and
so on. They were very much like the General Gordon Club,
and he kindled their boyish imaginations with stories of adventure
in Central Africa or among cannibals in the South Seas. He was
soon voted a "gentleman," and won their complete confidence,
for he never scolded, never "preached," and never betrayed a
secret. With him they were entirely trustworthy ; but on rare
Sunday School expeditions to the country, when thieving was
strictly forbidden, they would stand longingly before apple-stalls
and coax him with most persuasive tongues to allow them "just
this once" to show him how easily the thing could be done !

Andrews, however, remained adamant—these excursions were harassing enough in other ways. There were so many horrible possibilities involved when three hundred children were let loose in the green paradise of Hampton Court or Epping Forest, and the anxious forebodings to which his temperament was prone were not decreased by the romantic imaginations of his charges : "Oh Mister Andrews, our Billy has been carried away by the gipsies"— "Oh Mister Andrews, our Mary Ann has fallen into the river." But there was ample compensation for these alarms in the excited pressure of confiding, sticky fingers and the ecstatic : "Oh Mister Andrews, aren't we enjoying ourselves, not 'arf !"

The first summer did not pass without difficulties. Some of them were due to his own inexperience and errors of judgment. He did not at first fully recognise the danger of popular or sensational methods which had the effect of trying to bribe people into religion by superficial "attractions." The energy with which he pushed on with new ideas and fresh arrangements of mushroom growth bewildered people who loved the old ways to which they were accustomed. But if his over-hasty zeal alienated them for a time, the frank humility with which he acknowledged his fault disarmed them completely. Rarely was a missioner loved as he was.

Other early failures were due to insufficient knowledge of the people's point of view, and especially of their profound suspicion of all officials.

> "Early in my Walworth days I had discovered a revolting case of cruelty towards a fatherless young boy. The neighbourhood was entirely on my side in wanting to get the boy away to one of the Gordon Homes, and all went well until I called in the officer of the S.P.C.C.,* who came in uniform. The sight of that official uniform ruined everything. The boy was off in a moment... We searched high and low but met nothing but sour looks. I asked the officer not to come again, and a few days later tried to find the boy myself. In a moment the whole neighbourhood was on my side again, and before the day was out the boy was handed over ... He went with me of his own accord to the country home of the Gordon Boys."† *Experientia docet.*

The uniform of the "copper" or policeman was, of course,

* Society for the Prevention of Cruelty to Children.
† *The Modern Review*, loc. cit.

most suspect of all uniforms, and Andrews usually had nothing to do with the police. But there were sometimes exceptional cases :

"One day a particularly odious theft occurred in Wapping. The ring-leader had escaped with £400 robbed from poor working-men's savings. The room where his wife was living could be overlooked from our mission house premises. There was a small unused cupboard room with a window from which a detective could watch. No one at all knew about it, not even the caretaker. On the eighth day the man we wanted came along the street with a hunted look, and went upstairs. The detective was down from his watch-tower in a moment. He caught the man from behind red-handed, just as he was handing over some of the spoils to his wife. The thief drew a revolver but it was too late. The handcuffs were on before he could fire . . .

When my conspiracy with the detective was all over I had to tell my own working men what part I had played in the capture. To my great relief they were one and all on my side. And when I put the whole case before my boys' club composed of thieves and pick-pockets there was no pity for the man who could rob the poor . . ."*

A few extracts from Andrews' own vivid reports will give some picture of community life as it then was in South London. Here is one, told with zest in the local vernacular, which incidentally reflects the same popular distrust of the "copper."

"Mrs. M., she was going to Ireland for a holiday and wanted to get her box to Euston, so she gets a man to say as he'd take it on his barrow. But when the day comes Bandanny (he's a fighting man) he comes and shows as he has a right to carry all boxes as is got to go to Euston, so he gets a barrow and the box and orf he goes. Dahn the street he meets Heffery, that's another fighting man . . . So they agrees as it wouldn't do for them two to fall out afore the neighbourhood, so they goes together with the barrow and the box. But when they gets about to the Bridge, they starts fighting and the coppers they runs 'em in for being disorderly and in unlawful possession of a box. Mrs. M. she goes to Euston, but no box ; the police they come to her house (being told by Bandanny and Heffery) to see if it was all right about her box, and she aint there and of course the neighbours they aint giving nothing away. So Mrs. M. she goes without the box, and Heffery and the other they stays at the Station until Mrs. M's husband he hears on it and goes and bails them out. So then they says to him it's all along of him and his old woman and his box, and he's to stand them drinks or there won't half be a rough house. So he stands 'em, and they all three comes back dahn the Walworth Road wiv Heffery on the

* *The Modern Review*, loc. cit., abridged.

barrow, a-singing Irish national anfems, and abaht a thousand people collects and the trams is stopped, and they gets run in again—Carter Street this time—and gets ten bob or a fortnight."

We laugh, and Andrews turns to the other side of the picture :

"One small room completely denuded of furniture, with damp peeling walls and rotten flooring ; one bed of dirty sacking for the parents and five children. An income of nine shillings a week of which four shillings goes in rent. The baby had died, being overlaid in the night ; two children suffering from diphtheria, and one from scarlet fever, were sleeping with the rest. There were three other families in the house. The Sanitary Inspector condemned the building, and when the children recovered the families moved, but the landlord left his property unprotected. Next day I watched while about five hundred children of the neighbourhood swarmed over it, tore it to pieces and carried away as treasure-trove pieces of wood or old iron which reeked with disease and vermin."

In Cambridge, he kept in close touch with Pembroke College. His pleas for help had their effect ; there was a large increase in the number of undergraduates who came to stay at the mission during the summer vacation. He set them a high standard of work ; gave them long lists of visits, often to cases of severe illness, and urged them to study the parish methods of St. John's College Mission, which he greatly admired, and the social planning carried on by Cambridge House. In the autumn of 1896 his old college friend, W. L. B. Parsons, joined him as Assistant Missioner, and such was the infection of Andrews' enthusiasm that two lady workers even followed him from Monkwearmouth to strengthen the staff. When Parsons left he went down to Cambridge and persuaded another college friend, W. Outram, to take his place, completing the arrangements with his foot on the pedal of his bicycle as he dashed off once more to the station. During the Christmas, Easter and summer vacations of 1897, 207A East Street was sometimes hard put to it to hold all the young volunteers who flocked to help.

"We have a Rabbit Warren at this Mission," wrote the Missioner in high glee, "whose capacity for beds is elastic ; and when its occupants swoop down into the bathroom in the early hours of a raw December morning there is a scene for a battle-piece. The tightest possible squeeze accomplished in the little dining room was a breakfast for seventeen and a dog—the dog subsequently died."

Andrews' description of the effect on the people of the undergraduates' presence is interesting in the insight it affords into his own mind. The doctrinaire socialism repelled him as much as capitalism did, and for the same reason ; a harsh contempt for human personality seemed to him to characterise them both.

"So-called Socialists are ranting at every street corner. One seems almost to be living on the edge of a volcano, so utter is the divorce between rich and poor. But the presence of the students has turned the sweeping condemnation of 'the rich' into a distinction between 'gentlemen' and 'money-grubbers.' 'We've no quarrel with the *gentlemen*,' they say . . . Loyalty, goodwill, chivalrous feeling, are slowly flowing back into the lives of our people through our touch with the College. Class feeling and that hard ungracious revolutionary spirit melt away, and something of the best old English generous respect between rich and poor is gradually taking their place."*

III

In June, 1897, Andrews was ordained priest at Southwark Cathedral. He had longed for this ordination with all his heart, yet as the time approached he was tortured by misgivings. As he studied the Articles of Religion appended to the Book of Common Prayer, he felt that he could not subscribe to some of them with complete intellectual conviction, but only "in a general sense." This was in fact all that was required by the rules of his church, and the longing for service finally overcame his doubts. But the conflict was not fully resolved, and the repressed misgivings had their revenge later.

The joy of ordination lay in the power it conferred to give his parish fuller religious service. Andrews no longer believed in "club methods" on a secular level. "There must be intensity before extension," he wrote in 1898, "slow seed growth before reaping, unsparing training of the small body and unceasing visiting of the multitude. You will win respect by showing the seriousness and sacrifice in religion."†

The life of the little church was renewed by his zeal. He changed the time of weekday Evensong from 5-30 p.m. to 8 p.m. so that the people could attend more easily ; and men and women began to drop in to the service in their shabby working clothes.

* Report of the Pembroke College Mission, 1897.

† *Ibid.*, 1898.

He gave a five-minute talk each evening, a little commentary on the Scripture that had been read, very simple, often extempore, but always telling and beautifully expressed. He encouraged weary mothers held by family duties to listen for the bell and be comforted by the knowledge that they were being remembered in prayer. The people responded. "As I lie here," said a parishioner lying ill in St. Thomas' Hospital, "I count the hours till service time comes. Now the bell's beginning—now they're all in church, and they'll be thinking of me and I'll be thinking of them."

There was no church building in those days. The east end of the large, bare, almost subterranean clubroom was screened off by a movable partition and arranged as the chancel of a church with its altar. When no service was being held, children's games, boxing, darts, and meetings of all kinds succeeded one another on the other side of the screen. It was Andrews who first set before his people the ideal of a real church building of their own, though his dream was not realised till years later.

Andrews also steadily encouraged his parishioners to give not only for their own needs, but for the work of Christ throughout the world. He told them the heroic story of the Baganda church in Central Africa, which his predecessor in Walworth was serving. He described the work which Basil Westcott was doing in Delhi. He asked them to set apart what they could during the seven weeks of Lent for the poor of India. At the end of the time one old couple brought him a little box. They were among the very poorest, struggling to live on a pension of five shillings a week. To his amazement the box contained three shillings and sixpence—sixpence for every week of the Fast. "We are sorry it is so little, Mr. Andrews," they said. Tears stood in his eyes for the wonderful generosity of the poor.

This little body of simple, affectionate Christians lived their lives in the midst of a still untouched multitude of men and women degraded by poverty and want. Drunkards loafed at the street corners, thieving vicious youths and defiant hard-eyed girls lounged and idled in the alleys. During the solemn hush of the Good Friday service gangs of ruffians shouted drunken songs in

29

the street outside, and in his visits to the sick and dying Andrews might be confronted at any moment by vice of the coarsest type. Once a mutinous little boy of six years old threatened him with a knife. Sometimes, if he mentioned in the club that he was going to some specially notorious street, one or two of the decent working men would insist on going with him "for company." Andrews met the callous indifference or hostility as a challenge to his own faith and enthusiasm, and even in such places there were miracles of grace.

There came a time when the longing to seek these "lost ones" conflicted with another impulse. The Missioner of St. John's College Mission, whom Andrews so greatly admired, fell seriously ill. Andrews tended the sick man with the intense, almost extravagant personal devotion of his own nature. He spent himself, body and spirit, in the service of his friend. Yet he also fretted restlessly because he could not at the same time give to his parish visiting the spiritual energies which it demanded, and because his conscience accused him of neglect.

The mental tension was increased by the return in aggravated form of some of the doubts with which he had struggled before his ordination. In his 1898 Report he had spoken of the value he set on the Book of Common Prayer :

> "The Prayer Book so completely meets the deepest needs of our District, gives the very moral fibre we so long for down here—so sober and so reverent, so strong and so subdued—no sensation, no popular standard, no toning down of awful severity, no weak indefinite undenominational vagueness."

Of the deep sincerity of that tribute there can be no question. Yet there were nights when he lay awake hour after hour in misery because the Prayer Book services contained in some of the Psalms and in the preface to the Athanasian creed, words of imprecation upon the sinner and the unbeliever against which his conscience revolted. Had he been wrong after all in seeking ordination ?

The conflict was all the more distressing because Andrews could not then conceive for himself any Christian ministry outside the Church to which he had given his allegiance. Despite his missionary enthusiasm he would have nothing to do with the

Student Volunteer Missionary Union, because it was not exclusively Church of England. "I remember him walking me round the garden at Fulham Palace," writes Dr. Tatlow, who was its Secretary, "and saying to me, 'I am sure the S.V.M.U. is a devoted body of Christian men, but I cannot make any personal link with you in view of the fact that you include dissenters in your membership.' I thought him a very nice, but exceedingly obstinate and very narrow-minded High Churchman."*

Overwrought, he fell victim to sleeplessness and low fever. A complete physical breakdown followed, and even a holiday with the Priors in Yorkshire failed to restore his health. In the summer of 1899 he was obliged to resign his post, but he left Walworth with a more passionate regret than he was ever to know again.

College Missions at that time were still in their youth, policies were being formulated, experiments tried. Andrews' advice was much sought after ; he thought and planned for the whole vast enterprise, and he made a great contribution. But the greatest contribution of all was the power, to which his colleagues bore witness, of lifting everything he touched on to the plane of worship ; the impression he made of being utterly and naturally at home among spiritual realities. A Retreat for Southwark clergy, about 1896,† had been something of a landmark in his life, for there R. L. Ottley had first turned his thoughts to the much neglected treasures of Christian mysticism, and amidst all the turmoil of Walworth he was learning the secret of peace.

IV

During the years at the Pembroke College Mission, Andrews had refused offers of a Fellowship from three different Colleges because he was so happy in the work he had chosen. When his nervous breakdown made a change imperative, he accepted the post of Vice-Principal of the Clergy Training School (now Westcott House) and returned to Cambridge to teach theology. In November, 1899, he was elected to a Fellowship at Pembroke College itself. For the next few years the greater part of his time

* Letter to the authors.

† See *Christ in the Silence*, Chapter I. Canon Walter Moberly spoke of Andrews, even at this time, as "a holy man."

was spent in teaching and study, his special interest being the history of religion.

It was a period of little outward incident, in striking contrast to the crowded adventurous years at Walworth, but it was marked for Andrews by the new and searching experience of heavy personal bereavement. When he reached Cambridge, C. H. Prior was dying of cancer, and for Andrews his death was a very grievous loss. It was followed by others. In 1900 Basil Westcott died of cholera in Delhi, and the Bishop of Durham did not long survive his son. Pembroke College itself suffered heavily ; R. A. Neil, Andrews' old classical tutor, Dr. C. E. Searle the Master, and Sir George Gabriel Stokes who became Master in his place, all died within the next two years. All were men for whom Andrews felt a deep and reverent affection.

These bereavements opened new spheres of service. For twelve years Andrews' links with Pembroke had never been broken, and his intimate knowledge enabled him to serve the College in very valuable ways in the months that followed the death of two Masters in succession. He had been appointed Chaplain, and the new Master and his colleagues relied much on his advice. Moreover, his rowing enthusiasm had given him a happy entry into undergraduate circles, and he had become an acceptable "coach." "Andrews was always ready to coach any of the eights," writes a former Captain of the Pembroke College Boat Club,* "and he was most successful with some of the most inexperienced and roughest crews. He could get them to 'row together' as a crew as few others could, and this was mainly because he took such trouble to encourage even the beginners . . . This kind of thing brought him into much closer touch with undergraduates than was experienced by most dons. I never felt it strange that he should stroll into my rooms at any time to discuss some College problem or see what could be done to rouse some student who was careless about his work."

To the succession of bereavements at Pembroke was added the death of Andrews' sister Kathleen. It was the first break in a very closely-knit family circle, and it was natural that Andrews'

* The Rev. F. A. Chase.

Mr. J. E. Andrews and his Sons, Christmas, 1900
(*C. F. Andrews standing on the left*)

thoughts should turn much to the mystery of immortality and the unseen world of spirit. On a summer evening during the Long Vacation of 1903, when the college was quiet and solitary, there came to him an experience of such intensity that he found in it an anchorage of the soul for many years to come. He was standing alone in the still evening twilight in the college "screens," looking across the Old Court towards the Porter's Lodge. He saw a figure coming towards him, "clothed in Eucharistic vestments, bearing the sacred vessels in his hand." He was preparing reverently to stand aside to allow the priest to pass, when the figure turned towards a door in the Old Court and vanished away. The door was creeper-covered and unused ; centuries before it had led to the sacristy of the old Chapel. Long into the night he pondered the vision, realising slowly that with all its luminous objectivity it had risen up from within.

The undergraduates, recognising instinctively, like the humble old woman at Monkwearmouth, the reality of this man's religious experience, came to him with their own perplexities in ever-increasing numbers. So pressing and so important did this work seem that even after Basil Westcott's death in Delhi, Andrews could not feel sure that he was called to take his place. His ardent spirit had been attracted at one time by the thought of Central Africa, "where the hardest conditions have to be faced," but he knew when Basil died that it must be India or nothing.

Nevertheless he hesitated ; Cambridge had insistent claims, and great pressure was put on him to remain. It was Dr. Ryle, President of Queen's, who settled the matter. "You are thirty-three," he said, "and every year will make it harder to get away from Cambridge. If you are going to India, go at once. In five years you will be too old." Faced with the blunt alternative Andrews doubted no longer. He must go.

Farewells were difficult to his deeply affectionate nature. The men and women of the Pembroke Mission bade him God-speed at a service of benediction conducted by Bishop Talbot in Southwark Cathedral, assuring him in their simplicity that they would pray that the cannibals might not eat him ! At home, he knelt in prayer at his mother's knee as he had done when a little child.

33

He spent a last Sunday at Cambridge, and on February 28th, 1904, left London in a bitter snowstorm, wondering wretchedly whether he had done right after all.

The sun and beauty of Switzerland, and a warm welcome to Lugano by another Pembroke friend, revived his spirit. The last glimpse we have of him, as he leaves the soil of Europe at Trieste, is of a typical young English collegian, showing the Italian porters how to swing his golf-clubs, and smiling rather pityingly as he hears one German fellow-passenger explain to another, "Das ist crickets." But he is not *quite* typical, for in his pocket, to be studied on the voyage, is a Sanskrit dictionary.

At Port Said, five days later, a cable reached him from Pembroke ; it proclaimed the triumph of the crew he had coached for the "Lents."

Andrews exulted, and set his face to the East.

PART TWO

THE TWICE-BORN

CHAPTER IV

ST. STEPHEN'S COLLEGE, DELHI

1904-1907

I

ANDREWS had always kept commemoration days. Birthdays, and the festivals of the Church calendar, were full of meaning to him. March 20th 1904, the day on which he landed at Bombay, was kept as his "Indian birthday." It marked his entry into a new world of experience, and made him, as he delighted to say, one of the "twice-born." The first days in Delhi passed in an enchanted dream. In the early mornings he walked in the Qudsia Gardens, and watched the delicate beauty of colour and form as the women carried their trays of flowers to the shrine by the Jumna ghat ; till long after midnight he kept vigil under tropical stars which "seemed coming down to speak of eternity." The wonder faded by day, but sunset, darkness and dawn went by in a pageantry of mysterious and tender loveliness such as he had never known before.

The principal of St. Stephen's College was his Cambridge contemporary Hibbert Ware, who had joined the Brotherhood (though Andrews himself did not know it till long after) as a result of the meeting he had called in his undergraduate days. "Paddy" Day, a young Irishman who had joined the staff after Basil Westcott's death, had been one of his undergraduate volunteers at Walworth, and Andrews had once coached him in theology and rowing. The Head of the Cambridge Brotherhood in Delhi was S. S. Allnutt, who as principal of St. Stephen's in the closing years of the previous century had built the College buildings near the Kashmir Gate. Their Moghul style (adopted in defiance of conservative missionary sentiment) was a visible symbol of the appreciation of Indian traditions of life and thought which characterised the Cambridge Mission. Andrews had met

Allnutt in England, and had a great respect for the quality of his mind and spirit. Among such men he was quickly at home, but the man to whom he was most strongly drawn was Susil Kumar Rudra, the Vice-Principal of the College. Not only had Rudra been Basil Westcott's most intimate friend, but his three little motherless children appealed to all Andrews' maternal instincts. They reminded him of the fatherless Prior children at Cambridge, and before many days had passed he was spending hours in their home. Humanly speaking, the intimacy established in those first three weeks in Delhi was determinative of the direction in which Andrews' thought was to develop. "I owe to Susil Rudra what I owe to no one else in all the world," he wrote in 1923, "a friendship which has made India from the first not a strange land but a familiar country."*

On April 12th Andrews was formally admitted to the Brotherhood, and immediately afterwards went to Simla to study Urdu. The Chaplain, with whom he lived, was an old Pembroke acquaintance ; among the junior officials were Pembroke men who had once visited the hilarious "rabbit-warren" at 207A East Street ; Andrews himself was tutor for a time to the children of the officiating Viceroy, Lord Ampthill. He was thus in touch from the first with official and military circles, although Delhi itself was then only a comparatively insignificant provincial town.

One result of this was that within a month of his arrival in India Andrews was brought face to face with the havoc wrought in human relationships by pride of race. There is nothing in the record of his work either in Cambridge or in South London to suggest that racial prejudice had ever before presented itself to him as a specific Christian problem. The English universities at the end of the century were healthily free from it ; Andrews relates for example that while he was in charge of the Pembroke College Mission it was the custom that the most popular undergraduate of the year should be chosen to collect the college subscriptions, and that in one of those years the honour had been given by general consent to an Indian student. The state of affairs which he found in India contrasted painfully with this. The strength of caste

* *The Stephanian* : A tribute to S. K. Rudra on his retirement.

prejudices among some students of St. Stephen's was a shock to him, and the prevalence of the "white caste" spirit in Simla was an even greater shock.

The fact was that at the beginning of the twentieth century a number of factors had combined to widen the social gulf between English and Indian. Competitive examinations for the services had brought out men with little personal interest in the country ; improved communications and conveniences made it easy for their wives to accompany them ; and these women, bored and idle, created the extravagant follies of an artificial hill-station society. An arrogant and jingoist imperialism had taken the place of the sturdy freedom-loving conservatism in which Andrews himself had been brought up. Missionary circles themselves had not escaped the taint. In 1907 an English Christian layman who had spent a long lifetime in India publicly stated as his opinion that "the influence of the clergy is waning fast ; the great obstacles to its exercise are the Pride of Race with missionaries and the Pride of Place with Chaplains."[*]

Andrews from the very first regarded Indian caste- and British race-exclusiveness as fruits of the same spirit. He saw no essential difference between the *saheb* who refused to travel in an Indian railway compartment with "a crowd of natives" and the famished hill-boy whose little half-starved face had "kindled with indignation and contempt" when Andrews offered him bread. He himself, with his clear perception of moral issues and with Rudra's friendship behind him, was proof against the racial virus. He longed for more Indian friends, but the only Indian with whom Simla brought him in touch was his gentle old Urdu teacher, Maulvi Shams-ud-din. The two defied Simla conventions to the extent of going long walks together in the woods, on which Andrews had his first experience of intimacy with a deeply religious man of another faith.

The long evenings in Professor Browne's rooms at Cambridge had first awakened Andrews' interest in the faith of Islam ; Maulvi Shams-ud-din strengthened his desire to understand its inner

* Report of the Lahore Diocesan Conference, *Civil and Military Gazette*, 7th November 1907.

CHARLES FREER ANDREWS

spirit, and when he returned to Delhi he sought the company of men who could help him to do so. There were men still living who inherited the gracious traditions of the old Persian nobility of the Moghul court—gentlemen of the old school, who had shared in the brilliant "Delhi Renaissance" of the latter part of the nineteenth century. Maulvi Zaka Ullah and Syed Nazir Ahmed were of their number. They were both men in whom religious faith and a reverence for the past were combined with a belief in the beneficent power of modern knowledge, and who were in consequence staunch friends of the Muslim University at Aligarh. They belonged to an informal "club" which used to meet after sunset on the roof of the Old Library in Queen's Gardens, and at which the young Englishman was made welcome. They found his friendliness and humility irresistible, and would talk to him intimately of their own religious experience. "You will never understand it," they would tell him, "this power and warmth of religion among us, till you can feel in your own heart the poetry and music of the Quran Sharif. There was never music in the world before like that." "What is the use of argument and controversy ?" the gentle, saintly Zaka Ullah would add. "Tell me your *Beautiful Names* for God, and I will tell you mine."*

Every week after his return from Simla strengthened Andrews' affection and respect for Susil Rudra. The two men would take long evening walks over the historic "Ridge" from which Delhi had been stormed during the Mutiny, or stroll up and down the garden arm-in-arm in the moonlight, talking long and earnestly over the questions which Andrews' experiences in India were forcing on his notice. It was Rudra who showed Andrews that the bribery and corruption which English officials were apt to regard as the peculiar weakness of the Indian were in fact the universal weapon of the oppressed, and had no significant place in the natural social order of the country. It was Rudra the economist who convinced him that when Indian public men such as Gopal Krishna Gokhale charged the British administration with responsibility for "a fearful impoverishment of the people"† there

* See Andrews' delightful memoir, *Zaka Ullah of Delhi*.
† Presidential Address, Indian National Congress, 1905.

40

was much more truth in the charge than Andrews at first had been willing to believe. When the talk turned from politics to religion it was Rudra once more who opened Andrews' eyes to the beauty and strength of the traditional piety which gave so many humble lives their patience, simplicity and unassuming goodness. It was Rudra, finally, who made him see how utterly at variance with the spirit of Christ was the harsh sectarian exclusiveness which he had up to then maintained. Rudra felt the "exclusive" practices of the church as an almost intolerable burden upon his own churchmanship ; Andrews saw his suffering, and the effect was revolutionary. "The scales dropped from my eyes," he said once in describing the change. In December 1905, the man who had formerly refused to co-operate with the Student Volunteer Missionary Union, because it admitted "dissenters" to member-ship, was one of the foremost to plead with his Bishop to recognize and bless the newly-formed non-sectarian National Missionary Society of India.

Before that day came, however, Andrews' work in India had suffered an unforeseen and unwelcome interruption. He had suffered so persistently from an affection of the ear that in April 1905, he was ordered to return to England at once for medical advice, and was there for six months. He found that the spirit of racial pride had begun to play havoc in the Universities. A brilliant young graduate of St. Stephen's, Har Dayal, who had won a Government scholarship to Oxford, had been so embittered by the hopelessly friendless environment that he was on the point of throwing up his high academic prospects for the hard road of the revolutionary. Andrews had a long talk with him, and his speeches and sermons on Indian problems were full of burning condemnation of the race and colour prejudice that made such tragedies possible. The experiences of 1904-05 had turned him already into a passionate prophet of racial equality. No written records of his work that summer have survived, but some of those who listened to his sermons at Birmingham and Cambridge remember them still as landmarks in the development of their own Christian thinking.

II

At the time when Andrews first began to teach in Delhi, Japan had gained her histocic victory over Russia in the straits of Tsushima, and every magazine and newspaper in India was filled with the reverberations of that achievement. A lecturer voiced in St. Stephen's Common Room the general response in India to the news—"Japan has proved to the world that the East is not a wilderness of dying nations." A great wave of national aspiration swept over educated India, and inspired splendid schemes of national service. Gopal Krishna Gokhale founded the Servants of India Society, and its lofty idealism had a profound and far-reaching influence. Eager young men broke through the narrow confines of caste duty to serve Indians in the name of India ; one of Andrews' Hindu students went to work among "untouchables" in the Punjab plague camps of 1905, and in the same year there was a generous response in the College to an appeal for relief funds after the Dharamsala earthquake—the first time the students had contributed spontaneously to such a cause. The National Missionary Society, which was launched in December 1905, was the fruit of the same awakening of national consciousness among Indian Christians.

In such a period of ardent idealism and awakened aspiration a University teacher with vision and sympathy had an unparalleled opportunity for service—an opportunity which Andrews seized with both hands. He was well qualified to do so. In his later years at Cambridge there had been a great quickening and deepening of his sense of the significance of history. He owed much to Lord Acton, whose Lectures on Modern History were at that time one of the outstanding features of University life ; and as a teacher of theology, religious and ecclesiastical history became his own special field. Trained though he was in the methods of scholarship, his interest in the subject, like that of Acton himself, was far more than merely academic. He read the records of the past as the clue to the present and the key to the future ; and in India he sought to throw light on the situations of the immediate present from the experience of mankind in parallel situations distant in time and space. He showed that the Italy of Mazzini, the England of Shakespeare, the provinces of the Roman Empire in the days of its decline, could illuminate the problems of India in the twentieth century. Moreover, for him the record of mankind in history and literature was a pledge of the greatness of the human spirit. One of his students vividly remembered the flashing scorn with which he commented to the class on the saying "Honesty is the best policy"—that a mere ignoble prudence could never have achieved the past, and could never have power to inspire the future. The almost casual comment struck deep. There is no yard-stick to measure the impress of life on life, but there are men in high positions of influence in India today whose national zeal was kindled, and whose ideals of human life were formed, by Andrews' classes at St. Stephen's College. His teaching was a living force; in the skill with which he related it to the all-absorbing passion of nationhood lay the secret of his literally incalculable influence on the students of that decade, in Delhi and throughout India.

Andrews saw no inconsistency between his sympathy with India's desire for national self-expression and the belief in the essential beneficence of the British connection in which he had been brought up. He had as yet seen no cause to question it. "Do as you would be done by" was his principle : if England valued political self-determination she should be eager to see her partners in Empire enjoying the same privilege. "England and the English Church," he wrote, "owe too much to the struggle for national liberty in the past to grudge that liberty to India and Indian Christians in the present."* The white caste doctrines of which he had had such bitter experience had not made him lose faith in the ideal of the British Empire as such. They seemed to him an aberration. His position is well summed up in a lecture on Indian Nationalism which he gave at Lahore in December 1906:

> "My one great wish is to express to you how wholeheartedly, as a Christian missionary and as a loyal Englishman, I sympathise with the higher aspirations of Indian nationalism today. Can I say this and be absolutely loyal to my own country and Emperor ? I say emphatically Yes. The very constitution and foundation principles of the British Empire are such that there is room for fullest and freest development

* *The East and the West*, October 1905.

within its borders. I would urge you to hold the ideal of nationality in a loyal and constitutional manner, to establish it upon the solid foundation of the Queen's Proclamation itself."*

In Andrews' classes on English literature he set before his Indian students, as their own rightful inheritance, the words of the English poets and prophets of liberty—Shelley and Tennyson, Wordsworth and Milton, and above all Shakespeare.

We must be free or die, who speak the tongue
That Shakespeare spake

they read, and he encouraged them to make the words their own. "Shakespeare and Nationality" was one of his favourite themes, and *Henry V* one of his favourite plays. He delighted to expound the robust, freedom-loving patriotism of this and other historical plays. The students listened fascinated as he recited Henry V's speech before Harfleur, and then threw himself with equal zest into the comedy of Fluellen. College theatricals with Andrews in charge were a stimulus to thought as well as an experience of team-work and an opportunity for high-spirited fun. Romeo and Hamlet, he once suggested, were warnings to the nation's youth against an excess of weakening emotion on the one hand and of brooding speculation on the other ; and he urged on them the importance of disciplined thought and vigorous action in all that affected the national well-being.

Nevertheless, though he inspired them with his own enthusiasm for Mazzini's *Duties of Man*, he warned them constantly against a mere lifeless imitation of European ideas.

"Go back to your own history," he wrote, "for your picture of a free and spontaneous Indian life ; do not be content to take your ideals of freedom and liberty at second-hand from the west . . . Compare those times thoughtfully, carefully, scientifically, with your own, and ask the question for your practical life : What present bonds of custom can I unloose, what chain of impeding habit can I unbind, in order to take my share in building up a new India not unworthy of the old ?"†

Andrews' choice of the word *scientifically* was deliberate. The regeneration of India, he taught, needed not only the burning sense of national unity which would sweep away ceremonial barriers between man and man, but also a scientific study of the

* Reported in *The Indian Review*, January 1907.
† *The Stephanian*, November 1908.

facts. "Charity," he would say, "is the careful inquiry into the needs of one's fellowmen that enables one to give the *exact* help needed." He pointed out to his students how in Delhi, under their own eyes, drink and drug habits were spreading in a way which threatened the very foundations of national health and character. Year after year malaria and tuberculosis took their toll, undermining the stamina of the nation. Here were evils which men of all creeds could unite to combat by a common programme of action based upon thorough and objective study. Above all, he pleaded with all the eloquence at his command that the national idealism of the young should be poured into the despised, ill-paid, but vital work of the teaching of children. "If education is neglected," he declared, "the foundations of modern India will be built on shifting sand."*

Some of his Indian friends criticised his faith in these "western scientific" methods of progress. India, they declared, would advance when the time was ripe by other paths—by the personal devotion of her multitudes to a *guru* who should catch their imagination by the power of his self-sacrifice for an idea. It was a prophetic argument, and Andrews recognized its force, but he contended nevertheless that such an appeal to the imagination might run to waste and become abortive unless prepared for and supported by the prosaic and practical work of education, hygiene, and material advance.

In December, 1906, Dadabhai Naoroji gave a striking Presidential Address to the Indian National Congress at Calcutta. It marked a turning point in the political life of the Congress by publicly claiming for India, for the first time, "self-government or *swaraj* like that of the United Kingdom or the Colonies."†. Andrews' comment on the Address shows that he still believed India's own social divisions to be the chief obstacle to her attainment of this end. He pays homage to the greatness of the President's vision, but criticises the scant attention paid in his speech to social cleavages :

"He dismissed the social question almost in a sentence. This seemed the one weak part of the address. Surely caste and race divisions, through dis-

* *The Modern Review*, 1911
† *Sic.* "Dominions" rather than "Colonies" are intended.

appearing among the educated few, are still too overwhelmingly strong among the masses to be dismissed in a word. They seem the real crux of self-government to

'An English Friend of India'."[*]

Andrews had had his introduction to the slums of Delhi through the parish work for which the Cambridge Brotherhood was responsible among the Christian *chamars* and *chuhras*. He longed that the Christian students of St. Stephen's College should serve these poor Christian outcastes in the spirit in which the Pembroke College Mission had served in Walworth, while adapting their programme to Indian needs and conditions. The Christians were then a small minority in the college, and the more sensitive of them were troubled at the charge that it was "unpatriotic" to belong to a "foreign religion." Andrews urged them to seize the opportunity to show, by the readiness and faithfulness of their service to the poor of every caste and creed, what Christian nationalism could give to India.

> "In course of time," he wrote, "this connection and sympathy with our poorer brethren will be, I trust, to the non-Christian College student a living witness of the breaking down of the barriers of caste within the Christian church."[†]

In his eyes one of the greatest of such opportunities was afforded by sick-nursing, because of the menial physical service which it involved. He set the example in person. "If a boy in the hostel had a touch of malaria," writes a colleague, "he attended him even with tears, and with what seemed to us the fussy sympathy of a sentimental mother."[‡] The natural extravagance with which Andrews entered into any personal relationship, coupled with the "feminine" quality of his devotion, made it inevitable that his tenderness should seem to border on the sentimental ; but it was a genuine and practical tenderness nevertheless, and his colleagues were quick to appreciate the extent to which it inspired the Christian students. Under his leadership they tended an "untouchable" college scavenger, while the more "orthodox" looked on in amazement ; they went out, often accompanied by

---

[*] *The Bengalee*, 28th December 1906.
[†] St. Stephen's College Report, 1909.
[‡] Colin Sharpe, Esq., to the authors.

Hindu and Muslim students also, for temperance and health campaigns in the slums ; they demonstrated the elementary rules of hygiene and the care of the sick ; they organised a drive for *Pawitra Holi*, when they strove to lessen the drunkenness and licence which so often disfigured the *Holi* festival by the provision of counter-attractions such as team games and sports. "All these boys," wrote Rudra to Mr. Andrews senior, as he looked back over ten years of friendship, "learned how to love and serve from your boy Charlie."*

III

When Andrews returned to Delhi late in 1905 it was on the strict understanding that for health reasons he should spend each "hot weather" in the hills. From 1906 onwards therefore his teaching work was so arranged as to make this possible.

It happened that the Principal and Chaplain of the "Lawrence Military Asylum" (as it was then called) was due for furlough. This was a school for the sons and daughters of British soldiers at Sanawar on the lower slopes of the Simla Hills. It was arranged that Andrews should officiate, and the first weeks of his work there were very happy ones. The duties were not heavy ; Susil Rudra and his son Sudhir spent a short holiday with him, and there was leisure to sketch with his water-colours and to take Sudhir for long tramps on the hills.

Sanawar brought him into happy contact with the British "Tommies" who were stationed in the vicinity. He was on good terms with them at once, for they were drawn from the same levels of English society as his club boys at Monkwearmouth and Walworth. Sometimes Sudhir went with him when he walked over to Dagshai or Kasauli to preach in the Garrison Church. His sermons were short and pointed ; he would tell some story of St. Francis or Father Damien, and then describe the need of the poor in India and the call to Christians to serve them in the same Christ-like spirit. The good-natured soldiers had heard this kind of preaching only too seldom, and they listened eagerly. One Sunday Sudhir saw a Tommy who was sitting in front of him

* S. K. Rudra to J. E. Andrews, 24th June 1915.

open his belt and pour out every coin in his possession into the offertory plate.

One afternoon something very delightful happened :

"I was seated in the Principal's study," Andrews relates, "when a young soldier came up the steep garden path and stood before me, with a smile all over his face, and said, 'Hello, Mr. Andrews, don't yer know me ?'

"I looked at his red crop of hair, and then into his freckled face, and it all came back to me in a moment—the little study in Walworth, the class on the Sunday afternoons, the Epping Forest excursions. I rose in my chair and took him by both hands and said, 'Why, bless my soul, Ginger, what brings *you* here ?'

"He was more pleased than I can say to find that I had not forgotten him. He told me with all his old frankness of his own past adventures. Shortly after I left Walworth he had committed some particularly daring robbery. Then he had found that the police were hot on his scent, so he had made the best of a bad business and enlisted. Later on his regiment had come out to India and was stationed in the hot weather at Sabathu. Ginger was now in the band, and had already got his stripe for good conduct. He made me promise to go over and have a meal with the band. It was a great ordeal, but I survived it ! They fed me with everything the regimental cook could bring forward, and Ginger stood over me with his old coaxing manner so that I could never once say No. He told me many yarns of the old Walworth gang—a rather pitiful record, on the whole ; but to see Ginger there, a smart young soldier, a total abstainer, liked by all his officers and respected in his regiment, was in itself no little happiness. I shall never forget that afternoon in Sanawar when his cheery jolly face appeared before my study window, and his eager voice rang out, 'Hello, Mr. Andrews, don't yer know me ?' "*

A similar happy coincidence happened only a few months later, when "Smiler," another member of the old Walworth gang, found Andrews out in Calcutta. He had made good in the Royal Navy, and his clean, honest young manhood made Andrews very happy, especially as it was clear from the merry twinkle in his eye that the mischievous spirit which had once made "Smiler" notorious for his outrageous pranks was very far from dead !

Sudhir Rudra, as an Indian, had experienced some initial coldness at first among the English schoolboys at Sanawar, but his prowess at hockey and running soon broke down the barriers. Andrews looked on with delight as he made friends, and with his usual alertness saw the chance for another little attack on racial

* From reminiscences published in *The Modern Review*, March 1915.

prejudices. Sudhir brought the St. Stephen's hockey team to play at Sanawar, and some time afterwards two of the Sanawar boys joined the college.

Later in the summer, however, Sanawar was the scene of an example of racial discrimination which was all the more painful for its total unexpectedness. Andrews discovered that the attitude of one of his English colleagues would make it impossible for Susil Rudra to stay with him again in the Principal's bungalow during the Long Vacation. He had already invited Rudra, and he felt the shame of revoking the invitation so bitterly that only Rudra's own strong representations prevented him from sending in his resignation on the spot.

In a sense it was a trivial incident : the attitude it revealed was then only too common. But while it still rankled in Andrews' mind, the English-owned *Civil and Military Gazette* of Lahore published a particularly arrogant letter, which referred contemptuously to Indian nationalists as a handful of mis-educated malcontents who could and should be dealt with like ill-disciplined schoolboys. The cruel injustice of the latter was thrown into the strongest possible relief by the personal slight to Rudra under which Andrews was still smarting. He could contain himself no longer. He sat down and addressed the Editor, vigorously, yet even then with dignity and temperance. He signed with his full name, address, and official rank.

The publication of this letter at the end of September 1906, roused the liveliest curiosity among Indians everywhere. The great majority did not know his name, and eagerly speculated who their new champion could be ; a military chaplaincy in the Simla Hills seemed a most unlikely quarter from which to receive understanding and support. For Andrews himself the consequences were of the utmost importance. As a direct result of it he was sought out in friendship by two remarkable men, the Punjabi patriot Lala Lajpat Rai and the Bengali Ramananda Chatterji, who was just about to launch *The Modern Review*. Within three months he had met and won the confidence of almost all the leaders of political thought in Upper India. The second consequence was that he secured at one stroke a sympathetic reading public ready to pay friendly attention to what he had to say, and could place articles on subjects of national interest in newspapers and magazines throughout the country.

A great opportunity for increasing the range of his Indian friendships was presented by the meeting of the Indian National Congress in Calcutta in December 1906. Besides the President, Dadabhai Naoroji, to whom reference has already been made, he was deeply impressed by the veteran Christian nationalist, Kalicharan Banerji, and also by G. K. Gokhale, his acquaintance with whom soon ripened into a warm respect. The passionate nationalism of Bengal was a revelation to him, but he felt himself to have less in common with its leaders than with Tej Bahadur Sapru of Allahabad, with whom he talked far into the night when he broke his return journey there. Sapru confirmed his own estimate of the importance of social reforms. "So long as we remain in social and domestic bondage," he said, "we weaken our case for political freedom."

Nevertheless it was during this visit to Allahabad that an incident occurred which opened Andrews' eyes to the possibility that the injury inflicted on India by British domination was of a much more fundamental character than he had hitherto believed. At a meeting in Sapru's house he made an appeal for mutual frankness between the races. "That is impossible," said one of the older men present, bitterly. "We *must* say one thing to you and another to our official superiors. We cannot help ourselves. We are a subject people." To Andrews it was a terrible confession. If it were true, it meant that British rule in India had failed at a vital point. The experiences of the next twelve months left him reluctantly convinced of its truth.

At the Calcutta Congress, Dadabhai Naoroji had called upon Indians to agitate, "peacefully of course," for the recognition of their claim to Swaraj. British officials had no faith that the promised agitation was likely to be peaceful, and they viewed with apprehension the approach of the fiftieth anniversary of the Mutiny. When the year 1907 opened the political sky was stormy. The partition of the unwieldy province of Bengal, necessary as it undoubtedly was*, had been carried out in a manner which outraged Bengali sentiment and inaugurated an era of murderous conspiracy and police repression. In the Punjab, a Canal Colonies Bill which "more than savoured of bad faith"† was being pressed through in the face of the popular protests led by Lala Lajpat Rai. Most serious of all, resentment against the treatment of Indians in South Africa was everywhere reaching boiling point. The student population, as being by far the easiest to organise of the nationally conscious groups, was very susceptible to anarchist and terrorist propaganda, and the fact that most of the colleges were under British control meant that the unrest inevitably took a racial colour.

At this juncture the Cambridge Mission to Delhi took a step of tremendous significance. When Hibbert Ware resigned from the Principalship of St. Stephen's College in 1907, it appointed Susil K. Rudra Principal in his place. No Indian had ever before been made Principal of a Mission college, and the effect upon the Indian public was electrical. The act was a proof that Christian professions of racial equality could be sincere. No single factor contributed more to the happy stability of St. Stephen's in the difficult years that followed than the spectacle of a team of brilliant English scholars working with enthusiastic loyalty under an Indian leader.

Much of the credit for the fact that this magnificent opportunity was seized must undoubtedly go to Andrews. When, some ten years previously, J. W. T. Wright had appointed Rudra as his Vice-Principal, he had silenced the latter's protests by a gruff but friendly piece of prophecy : "You are to be Vice-Principal, and one day you will be Principal." But when Wright died in 1902 the appointment had not been made ; even in 1907 many hesitated to take the step, not because Rudra was an Indian, but because he was not a member of the Brotherhood which was responsible for the college. The Bishop of Lahore, whose views carried great weight, felt that there was still danger that some parents

* Before the partition it included the four later-delimited provinces of Assam, Bengal, Bihar, and Orissa.

† The phrase used in *The Rise and Fulfilment of British Rule in India*, by Thompson and Garrett.

would regard the appointment of an Indian as a "retrograde" step likely to weaken the discipline of the college. Andrews, with his finger on the pulse of India, knew that this attitude no longer prevailed and acted on his knowledge. He was strongly backed by another young English lecturer, the Rev. F. J. Western.* They argued, they pleaded, they threatened to resign on the issue, and at last they carried their point. It is only fair to the Bishop's memory to add that he afterwards generously acknowledged that his judgment in the matter had been at fault.

The effect of Rudra's appointment on the life of St. Stephen's is described by Andrews in his contribution to the College Report of 1909, a year when unrest among students reached serious proportions, and when lecturers in other Mission colleges confessed to him that they never knew when they might be faced with open mutiny.

> "There has been on all sides from our students," he writes, "an increasing desire to show friendliness which often ripens into affection. They are proud of their college, proud of the attitude we have taken up, and wholly loyal in following the lead we have given them. That lead has been on the one hand to declare as strongly as possible against the anarchist propaganda, and on the other hand to abate not one jot of our earnest appreciation for all that is good and noble in the nationalist movement . . . They (sc. S. K. Rudra and his Vice-Principal, P. C. Mukerji) exercise a far stricter discipline than we could do without giving offence, and nothing can ever be made into a racial difference when the ruling is done by Indians themselves."

An Englishman who visited Delhi about this time emphasised the part which Andrews himself had played in securing this happy result. "At St. Stephen's," he writes, "I found case after case where something which might easily have become sedition, under the control of less-enlightened Englishmen, became an earnest enthusiasm for a fuller national life."†

The college was less happy, however, in its relations with the Punjab Government, which was slow to appreciate the value of this aspect of its work. In 1907 a famous official document was issued, known as the "Risley Circular," which prohibited all Government or Government-aided colleges from so much as

* Later Bishop of Tinnevelly.
† Letter to *The Church Times*, 5th December 1913.

mentioning political questions before their students. Such instructions were a contravention not only of the academic freedom of the college, but also of the elementary educational principle that adolescents should be allowed free discussion of the national questions which naturally and rightly occupied their minds. St. Stephen's decided to ignore the circular, "at the cost of considerable official disfavour."*

One of the consequences of the "considerable official disfavour" was that Andrews discovered with a shock the extent to which secret service methods were being employed against those suspected of nationalist sympathies. Several members of the college staff had reason to believe that their correspondence was being tampered with, and Andrews was very angry when his weekly home letters were delayed and his mother given needless anxiety. Then one day he caught a man red-handed, rummaging among the private papers in his desk at Maitland House. Many years later, when challenged to produce authentic evidence of the existence of spying, he published the story.

> "The man confessed that he had been sent by the police. I was naturally indignant, and sent at once to the Deputy Commissioner, who was at Cambridge with me and a personal friend, demanding an instant apology. A mounted policeman came back post-haste with the following words in a letter : 'My dear A., it's nothing to do with me ; it's those d——d C.I.D. people.' The adjective he used made any further apology on his part unnecessary."†

This was not the only incident of the kind. A young English police officer, with whom Andrews was friendly, and who had been greatly attracted by his ideals, told him that he had subsequently been invited to spy on him (and had indignantly refused). At a dinner-party at which Andrews was present, a British official began to boast of his own cleverness in getting Keir Hardie, the Socialist leader, who was then on a visit to India, to take on as his personal servant a man who was really a Government spy. Not all the claims of social courtesy could make Andrews swallow this in silence. "You cad !" he exploded wrathfully. But what hurt him most were the authenticated cases of students in St. Stephen's

* See F. F. Monk, *History of St. Stephen's College.*
† Letter to *The Statesman*, Calcutta, 20th April 1919.

53

and other colleges being tempted to spy upon each other. Such experiences wounded him very deeply ; he found it impossible to speak calmly of this poisoning of the springs of friendship between fellow-students at the university. The men who stooped to such methods undermined his faith in the honesty of purpose of his own beloved country, and the pain of it was more than sufficient to account for whatever "bitterness" or "one-sidedness" there may have been in his attitude at this period.

The experiences of 1907 brought home to Andrews the extent of the gulf between the officials of Government and the people whom they ruled. He knew that the agitation against the Canal Colonies Bill was justifiable, and he pleaded with his civilian friends to get into touch with the people themselves and learn their real needs at first hand. One of them shrugged his shoulders expressively by way of reply. "Just look at all those files," he said. In Andrews' eyes there could have been no more eloquent condemnation of the system of "government by file" which was making personal contact impossible.

In May 1907, Lajpat Rai was deported from the Punjab, and Andrews chafed against the restrictions imposed upon his freedom of comment by the discipline of the Brotherhood and by his position in the college. "I can hardly express," he wrote to Gokhale on June 24th, "the restlessness I feel at being compelled as it were to be silent in the face of what has happened recently." But the Viceroy, Lord Minto, rightly refused to sanction the Colonisation Act, and on November 9th news at last came through that Lajpat Rai was free. Rudra happened to be away, and in his absence the students came to Andrews for permission to illuminate the college buildings in token of their rejoicing. "Make it a regular *Diwali !*"* laughed Andrews, and putting his hand into his pocket contributed generously to the expenses. All Delhi came out to admire the magnificent display, but possibly it gave the "seditious" college another black mark !

As a matter of fact the accusations of "disloyalty" which were levelled at Andrews at this time were ridiculously exaggerated. A letter of his published in the London *Spectator* in October 1907,

* Diwali is a November festival celebrated with many illuminations.

caused a *furore* in India, but it was supported in England by more than one experienced "Indian civilian."* In it Andrews drew attention to a judicial scandal in Bengal, and demanded as a remedy the separation of the judicial and executive functions of Government. The independent Calcutta High Court, on appeal, had quashed a verdict by which one man had been sentenced to hanging and two to transportation for life, declaring that in their judgment the civilian judge was ignorant of law, that the evidence for the prosecution was worthless, and that European witnesses who might have given evidence unfavourable to the prosecution had been withheld. Andrews' comment on this indictment is a temperately-worded suggestion that "no expense is too great at the present critical juncture to remove the impression of unfair treatment."†

In writing to the *Spectator* Andrews was appealing "from Philip drunk to Philip sober"—from hysterical Anglo-India to the average Englishman's sense of fair play. The same appeal proved effective in another case in which Andrews himself was the central figure, and in which, as in the affair of the Risley circular, the issue of academic freedom was at stake. "The Rev. C. F. Andrews, Fellow of Pembroke College, Cambridge, was struck off a list of nominees for fellowships of the Punjab University by the Lieutenant Governor's own hand, and a man of no educational attainments put in his place, for no other reason than that he is a friend of Indians." That sentence, published in Ramsay Mac-Donald's *Awakening of India* a couple of years later, provoked insistent inquiries from Lord Morley, the Secretary of State. The result was that the nomination of Andrews was accepted ; he was immediately elected to the Syndicate, and his ability and scholarship left a permanent mark for good on the courses of the University.

IV

For St. Stephen's College the stormy and critical year of 1907 closed in a scene of delirious rejoicing wholly unmarred by the shadow of political strife. Late in December the St. Stephen's

* A former British Administrator in India.
† *The Spectator*, 26th October 1907.

cricket team met the hitherto invincible Government College of
Lahore in the final match for the Punjab University Cricket Shield.
All day they fought gallantly, but when the last man went in to
bat they still needed twenty-two runs to win. It seemed a
desperate chance, but the two batsmen were plucky and determined. Steadily the score mounted ; only ten runs needed . . .
only four ! A great hush of excitement settled over the field.
Watchfully the batsman faced the bowling—in another moment
he had driven the ball to the boundary, and friend and foe alike
arose to cheer. "All Lahore praised the excellence of our team,"
wrote Sudhir Rudra in high glee, "and all Delhi praises Mr.
Andrews for making the team so."*

The winning of the University Shield was the crowning
triumph of that generation of college cricketers. From the very
beginning Andrews had thrown himself into the game. His first
evening in Delhi had been spent in visiting the college playing
fields with Paddy Day and after that "his slim and slightly stooping
figure in flannels"† could be seen evening after evening on the
cricket pitch outside the Kashmir Gate. Mediocre as a player, he
was an excellent coach, as he had been on the river at Cambridge.
His buoyant youthful comradeship dispelled the last shreds of
shyness or reserve, and lecturer and students laughed, joked and
chased each other round the field in merry rivalry. "On the
cricket field we never thought of him as a teacher," says one of
them. "He was one of ourselves ; a real friend."‡ In such an
atmosphere they learned all the more quickly the spirit and
standards of the game. Andrews' ready and generous appreciation fostered every development of team loyalty and unselfishness;
a quiet friendly word from him in private checked each failure in
sportsmanship. Praise and rebuke went home, and were not
forgotten.

While Andrews was in Delhi he lived with other bachelor
lecturers in Maitland House, close to the College. His door and
Day's stood always invitingly open to a verandah which connected

---

* Sudhir Rudra to J. E. Andrews, 26th December 1907.
† The phrase is Sudhir Rudra's.
‡ Mr. Saharia of Tikamgarh, C.I., to the authors.

directly with the college hostel, and the students came in and out constantly. The completeness with which he had won their trust is illustrated by a small but long-remembered contretemps. It was the custom of St. Stephen's to have a College "outing" or picnic on the last day of each term at some place of interest near Delhi. On one such outing Andrews and Western happened to offer their sandwiches to the Christian students ; one or two Hindu boys also, whose own meal was not yet ready, unthinkingly helped themselves. Then it transpired that the sandwiches contained beef, the forbidden food. Consternation reigned ; one or two men began to mutter angrily that Andrews had offered them an intentional insult. In many colleges they might have found a ready following ; not so in St. Stephen's. At once the whole body of students turned indignantly upon the authors of the ill-natured suggestion. "It was entirely our own fault," they declared. "We should have been more careful." Andrews and Western, on their part, saw to it that neither beef nor pork was used in Maitland House again.

As early as 1905 Hibbert Ware and Rudra had recognized the value of Andrews' literary gifts and of his genius for personal friendship, and tried in the allocation of routine duties to give him time to use them, though in years when the college was short-staffed it was not always possible. To Maitland House came an endless stream of visitors, Indians of every religion, rank and occupation, attracted by Andrews' friendliness and zeal for justice—"so that to live with him was in itself a liberal education."* Students in every part of India turned to him as an oracle. He kept up an enormous correspondence with them, setting aside a period each day for this work alone. An early riser, he would sit through the cool morning hours in the verandah writing his articles—paragraph after paragraph in his fluent style with scarcely a pause, scarcely a correction. "The amount of work he got through was amazing—writing, study (Indian newspapers and magazines, theology, etc.), and at any rate in some years a heavy programme of College teaching."† In every spare hour he coached some of his students, brilliantly, untiringly. So wholly

* Colin Sharpe, Esq., to the authors.
† Ibid.

was he caught up in his vocation that he gave to more than one colleague the impression of being without close home ties, though never in all those years was his mother's weekly letter missed.

He travelled a great deal—Lahore, Allahabad, Cawnpore, Calcutta. Wherever he went he stayed with missionaries, introduced them to his Indian friends and brought them into touch with the national movement. Those who were left behind in St. Stephen's did not always find it easy. Andrews could never, either then or later, conform with any measure of success to a regular institutional routine. He would preach with the utmost sincerity of the vital part that must be played by hard, unspectacular daily grind in the building up of the nation ; but when the round of his own college teaching came into conflict with the unpredictable claims of personal friendship or of national emergency, it was the latter that seemed to him to be of the more pressing importance. His judgment of his own duty was probably right, but it was none the less embarrassing. Looking back, one can but pay a tribute to the insight and generosity of the colleagues who understood, so early in his career in India, the essentially *prophetic* nature of his vocation and made it possible for him to follow it. Casually he would drop into a neighbour's room : "I have to go to Lahore tomorrow. You will take my B.A. English for me, won't you ?—they are reading *Pendennis*." A newcomer from England found the whole of the college English teaching thrust into his hands within two or three days of his arrival, while Andrews and Day went to a Retreat at Cawnpore. "But how am I to manage ?" he asked in alarm. "Oh," said Andrews, "read these answers by Dinanath, give him full marks, mark other written work in that light. Here are the text-books for the other classes."

Personal foibles were in evidence. It was not only Andrews' later self-chosen poverty that made him so often a wearer of other men's shoes ; it was also a genuine lack of interest in a matter of such secondary importance as clothes, and an innocent (but sometimes exasperating) clarity of vision which regarded the claims of property as utterly unimportant. "I couldn't find my sweater," relates one victim, "asked everyone including C.F.A., caught a

chill for lack of it after hockey—and then found him wearing it !"
To attempt to cure him of this carelessness by the methods of
Mrs. Be-done-by-as-you-did would have been quite useless ; he
would probably never have noticed his loss, and if he had he would
certainly never have suspected anyone but himself. He would
similarly fail to conceive that anyone might wish for variety in
food, so long as the food was clean and sufficient. When the
household lived for weeks on "some sort of sago for breakfast,
dal for dinner, and goat chops for the evening meal," they were
inclined to "admire his devotion but not his housekeeping."

Another personal trait probably contributed as much as his
heterodox political opinions to the suspicion with which the
average European then regarded him. When his emotions were
aroused he could be demonstrative in the extreme. All his heart
went out to the underdog, and in India, socially, politically,
economically, the Indian was the underdog. More than one of
his Indian friends have described how the "gushing" affection
with which Andrews approached them at the time of their first
meeting led them to suspect his motives ; and if this was so among
Indians, it was even more so among Englishmen. Yet even those
who were most exasperated by his "extravagances" were constrained, if they knew him at all as a man, to recognize his
sincerity, and the most "hard-boiled" officials retained for him
their affection and respect. It is related that on one occasion an
English visitor, with a wholly insufficient knowledge of the
subject, began in his presence to make drastic *ex parte* criticisms
of Anglo-India, upon which Andrews spoke up, suddenly and
startlingly, in defence of his own fellow-countrymen. If the
British were even temporarily and in conversation the under-dogs,
he would back *them !*

CHAPTER V

THE CHRISTIAN CHURCH IN INDIA

1907-1912

DURING the latter part of Andrews' time at St. Stephen's his campaigns against racial exclusiveness and social injustice were continued without intermission. He protested against the political injustice of deportations without trial and of the invidious working of the Press Act. His study of the Indian scene was leading him slowly but steadily towards the conviction which he reached in his own thinking in 1910, though he did not put it into writing until years afterwards—the conviction that nothing less than the fullest measure of national independence could restore India to a healthy national life.

Nevertheless there was after 1907 a change in the balance of his interests. One may define it in part by saying that during the first three or four years in Delhi, Andrews had accepted his position in a missionary Brotherhood and on the teaching staff of a Christian college as offering him all the scope he needed for his personal Christian witness. From 1907 onwards he grew increasingly dissatisfied with these conditions. The Gospel of Love burned within him, and he longed to be free to give it expression, untrammelled by the demands of a prescribed round of college duties or by the accretions of a foreign religious tradition. The most significant of his experiences during this period were those which led him into new ways of Christian service and new categories of Christian thought. India drove him to seek a new integration of theology and religious experience ; the quest, uncompleted but not unrewarded, is the key to the understanding of these years.

I

It was natural that Andrews, with Bishop Westcott as his teacher, should from the beginning regard Christianity, not as the enemy of the highest Indian religious thought, but as its glorious

60

fulfilment. The spirit of the battlefield, which pervaded so much of the missionary writing and preaching of those days, was as repugnant to him as the wholesale repudiation of Indian customs, traditions and even dress, which had made many Indian Christians foreigners in their own land. There is a verse in the *Revelation of St. John* which he greatly loved, which describes how "the glory and honour of the nations" shall be brought into the Holy City of God. He had seen the "glory and honour" of India in the simple piety of her village people ; he saw the same Divine glory in the work of her non-Christian saints and prophets. "The indiscriminate use of the phrase 'Missions to the Heathen' jars upon me," he would say ; and he would go on to quote two passages which became for him almost as familiar and beloved as the New Testament itself :

> Farid, if a man beat thee,
>   Beat him not in return, but kiss his feet.
> Farid, if thou long for the Lord of all,
>   Become as grass for men to tread on.
> Farid, when one man breaketh thee,
>   And another trampleth on thee,
> Then shalt thou enter the Court of the Lord.

> Let a man overcome anger by love,
> Let him overcome evil by good,
> Let a man overcome greed by liberality,
> Let him overcome the liar by the truth.*

In such affinities between the teachings of Indian sages and those of Jesus Christ, Andrews saw the working of the Spirit of God preparing the way for the Christian evangelist. But he believed also that much *bhakti* literature owed something of its insight to direct Christian influence such as that of the old Nestorian missionaries.

> "There appears to be," he wrote, "a considerable amount of evidence that from Kabir onwards the *Bhakti* school of the north had access to Christian teaching . . . that Asia had been sown, centuries ago, with the seed of the Word, and that it had taken root in the religions which were there before it, and prepared the way for the advent of the full Christian message in our own times."†

* The quotations, from the *Granth Saheb* and the *Dhammapada* respectively, are given by Andrews in this form in *The Student Movement*, October 1909.
† *The Renaissance in India*, Appendix VII.

It seemed to Andrews at this time that India's national aspirations also owed much of their vigour to "the transplanting of Christian thought in Eastern soil." "Nationality, enlightenment, the raising of the multitudes," he wrote, "have come today to the East from the Christian West."* The Indian National Congress, he pointed out, began its sessions "with what is almost word for word a Christian prayer."† His writings reflect his conviction that these national aspirations, like the religious aspirations of the *bhaktas*, would find their true fulfilment only in the acceptance and practice of the Christian faith. In articles in *The Stephanian* and elsewhere he appealed to the witness of history to prove that this Christian faith, so far from being a denationalising factor, might in fact inspire the highest patriotism and act as a purifying and unifying force. He described how it had awakened the provinces of the Roman Empire (of whose history Andrews was making a special study at this time) from a colourless uniformity to a vigorous and varied life ; how it had inspired Mazzini in Italy and Kalicharan Banerji in India, and how it had won the respect of modern nationalist Japan. He illustrated from the history of Europe its power to "reach down to the foundations of society," and quoted what "one of the most ardent Indian nationalists" had said in his hearing : "After all, when it comes to practice, Christianity alone is effecting what we nationalists are striving for—the elevation of the masses."‡

Finally, he saw Christianity as a faith that could reconcile, by transcending, the rival religious groupings of India. He suggested that the living religions of the world fell naturally into two groups, the "static" whose type was Islam, and the "dynamic" represented by the Hindu-Buddhist tradition. Between these two, he said, Christianity is the bridge, "static" because it is centred in the unchanging Christ, "dynamic" because of its faith in the living power of the Holy Spirit.

The most complete single statement of his whole position is in a

* *The East and the West*, October, 1905.

† *Ibid*, July 1907. This enthusiastic description is slightly misleading. The phrasing of the noble prayer for the nation used at the Calcutta Congress is in harmony with Christian usage, but is in no sense a reproduction of any existing Christian formula.

‡ See *The Stephanian*, May 1908, and *passim*.

pamphlet called *India in Transition* which the Cambridge Mission published in 1910. It is doubly interesting because it contains a long quotation from Rabindranath Tagore, whose diagnosis of India's needs Andrews reproduces with warm admiration. He then goes on :

> If Christianity is to succeed, it must not come forward as an antagonist and a rival to the great religious strivings of the past. It must come as a helper and a fulfiller, a peacemaker and a friend. There must no longer be the desire to capture converts from Hinduism, but to come to her aid in the needful time of trouble, and to help her in the fulfilment of duties she has long neglected.

> Rabindranath Tagore has given us in his own words what India requires of us. "Do we not need," he cries, "an overwhelming influx of higher social ideals ? Must we not have that greater vision of humanity which will impel us to shake off the fetters that shackle our individual life ? We have begun to realise the failure of England to rise to the great occasion, and so we are troubled with a trouble which we know not yet how to name."

> If ever there was a claim upon the Church of Christ to come forward in the name of her Lord, it is to be found in words like these. Has she not to offer that "influx of higher social ideals," that "greater vision of humanity" ? If England has failed to rise to the great occasion, may not the Church of Christ succeed ?

> No ! She cannot succeed, so long as she allows within her own fold those very racial and caste evils from which India is struggling to be free . . .

> The final victory of the Christian faith in India depends upon the spiritual power manifested in bringing about the union of the English and the Indian, as Christians ; the union of the Brahmin and the Pariah, as Christians ; the union of the Hindu and the Musalman, as Christians, Then and then only will the heart of India respond fully to the Christian message, and a new Indian nation arise, enabled and strengthened to fulfil her great destiny in the world.

The passage bears the marks of a mind struggling with vast unresolved problems. How, one might ask, is "the union of the Hindu and the Musalman as Christians" to be achieved if at the same time "the desire to capture converts from Hinduism" (and presumably from Islam also) is to be renounced ? For there can be no doubt that by "Christians" Andrews here meant members of the visible organised Christian church. There is a similar ambiguity in his references to "Christianity." In a paper called *Christ in India*, written about 1910, he speaks of the sympathy and understanding he had found in intercourse with men of religious faith among non-Christians, and of how he had found the clue to his experience in the thought of the "Son of Man" :

> Because Christ is Son of Man, Christianity must be all-comprehensive, larger far than the church of the baptized. The Christian experience must be one of an all-embracing sacrament, in which Christ is seen and revered in all men.*

But when he turns to another aspect of his experience and seeks a basis upon which the various Christian churches might co-operate in their missionary work, he insists on baptism as essential, and declares that :

> The pressing danger to be avoided in India is the growth of a roving unattached Christianity which does not recognize the primary Christian duty of church membership at all.†

It would be profitless to attempt logically to reconcile these and similar statements. Andrews had started on his quest, and his keen mind focussed on first one aspect and then another of his problem. The old integration of thought had been dissolved by the acid of his Indian experience, and he had not yet achieved a new one.

His moral insight, on the other hand, was swift and penetrating. In his first years in India he sometimes made public criticisms of non-Christian religious movements which later he would have scrupulously avoided, as leading only to barren and uncharitable controversy. He would not wish these criticisms to be reproduced, but the things that earned his condemnation were always those which seemed to savour of intellectual or moral dishonesty. With genuine spiritual faith, no matter how alien were the forms of its expression, he was always and everywhere in sympathy ; but any attempt to exploit such faith, whether for political or for sectarian ends, at once aroused his anger.

It was moreover by the same path of moral insight that he drew closest to the heart of non-Christian India—to the saintly Maulvi Zaka Ullah on the one hand and to the saints of modern Hinduism on the other. One of the greatest of these, Swami Rama Tirtha, Andrews never knew personally, but there was much in his

* Place of publication not traced ; extant in typescript.
† *The East and the West*, July 1912.

writings which profoundly attracted him. There was, for example, a comment on the Lord's Prayer which pierced direct to the heart of the matter. *Give us this day our daily bread,* said the Hindu teacher, is not the prayer of greed, it is the prayer of renunciation, of humble acknowledgement that for prince and pauper alike the needs of the present and the future are in the hands of God. Andrews' heart went out to such teaching, and when he was asked in 1911 to write a preface to a volume of Swami Rama Tirtha's collected writings, he very gladly did so. His essay shows the same intellectual uncertainty, the same sure moral judgments of value, as characterise his other writings of this period :

> With the philosophy of the Advaita Vedanta I confess I have only a faint and distant sympathy ... The West insists on the eternal quality of human personality and rebels against the thought of the loss of personal identity, as in the noble sorrow and faith of Tennyson's *In Memoriam*. I recognise the danger in this emphasis of self-assertion and selfish individualism ; I recognize that it may need some balance and correction from the East ; but the West will never accept as finally satisfying a philosophy which does not allow it to believe that love between human souls may be an eternal reality.
>
> ... There are many things in Rama to which my heart goes out, his passages on renunciation as the law of eternal life, his intense appreciation of beauty in nature, and his ideal of married life. I trust that in any criticisms I have set down in order to make clear my own position I have not departed from that spirit of wide-hearted charity and kindness which was so marked a feature of the author of the book himself.

The reference to Tennyson's *In Memoriam*, which was the starting point of so many of his intimate personal talks on faith with the senior students of St. Stephen's, is significant. Perhaps the most abiding intellectual insight of those years was the thought which he expanded in the book which he was then preparing, *The Renaissance in India* :

> "The naturalization of the Christian message," he wrote, "amidst Indian conditions of life and thought, will take place through the medium of *art, music and poetry*, more than through the channels of controversy and hard reasoning."*

* *The Renaissance in India*, p. 220 (italics *ours*).

II

One of the first of the many cruel and baseless accusations which were levelled against Andrews in the course of his life was that in his zeal to show sympathy with the aspirations of non-Christian Indians he "neglected" the little group of Christian students in St. Stephen's College. Nothing could have been further from the truth, and when the charge was made in print both Rudra and Allnutt wrote warmly in his defence.* His care for the Christian students was both intimate and far-sighted. While he regarded them, as we have seen, as the potential spear-head of the nationalist attack on social injustice, he saw that it was not in their true interest to be segregated from other students in a separate "Christian hostel," and he worked for and obtained its abolition. His greatest gift to them, however, was made in the field of personal friendship. In 1906 he had been very deeply moved by the posthumously published *Letters* of Forbes Robinson, whom he had known at Cambridge, and especially by their revelation of the intense personal affection and intercession with which he surrounded his friends. He felt at once that they had a special message for the church in India :

> "We are so wrapped up in our organisations, schemes, and institutions," he declared, "that we may lose the one thing needful, the personal touch. The one great need is sincere and wholehearted personal friendships within the Christian body, *between men of different races.*"†

In accordance with this principle, Rudra and he would invite small groups of students, Christian and non-Christian, to join them for part of the Long Vacation in the Simla Hills, where they worked and played together in the leisurely atmosphere of a family holiday. There they learned to care for one another as a family in sickness as well as in health, and there were many opportunities on their rambles over the hills to give the same practical service to the needy which Andrews had taught them in Delhi. The story of one such incident reads like a modern Indian version of the parable of the "Good Samaritan" :

> "Mr. Andrews and I," relates Sudhir Rudra, "were walking one day between Kotgarh and Simla when we came upon a coolie doubled up with

* In *the Church Times*, February-March 1914.
† Speech at the Lahore Diocesan Conference, November 1906.

pain by the roadside—the result of eating snow to appease his hunger. We were only some ten or eleven miles out of Simla, and there were plenty of passers-by. We stopped one after another and begged for the loan of a rickshaw for him, but no one was willing to help. The very muleteers hurried on their way. We had just had tea with a British military officer at the Rest House at the twelfth mile, so Mr. Andrews went to ask for his help, while I stayed with the sick man, massaging him and doing what I could. Mr. Andrew's came hurrying back to us with brandy and blankets which the officer had sent ; the officer himself followed a little later, bringing a rickshaw, and the poor fellow, warmed and comforted, was sent back to Simla."

The students who shared in such adventures might well have used of Andrews the words in which he himself expressed his debt to his own Cambridge teachers—"whose friendship is inspiration."*

In the summer of 1906 Andrews had gone with Bishop Lefroy to Kotgarh, some fifty miles beyond Simla in the mountains, where the Bishop conducted a Confirmation Service. On the following morning the two men had climbed the heights of Mount Hattu. Before they reached the top the clouds descended, and they stood together in the mist and recited Morning Prayer. As they reached in the *Te Deum* the words "the Holy Ghost, the Comforter," the sky suddenly cleared. Across the clouds that filled the valley a steep pathway of dazzling light led up and up, as it seemed from their very feet, to the eternal snows that towered above them. In silent wonder they watched that marvellous scene ; then as the mists closed in once more they took up with a new fervour the great words of adoration : "Thou art the King of Glory, O Christ." For Andrews that day had made Mount Hattu a sanctuary, and each year he would lead the little company of Christians to the summit, where with a cool sunlit rock for altar and the majestic silences around, he celebrated with them a service of Holy Communion. As Andrews read the stately and beautiful sentences of the Prayer Book, they came home to his companions with the power of a fresh revelation ; for the artist-poet in him leaped in response to the poetry and wonder of the Gospel, and he led them with him into the depths and heights of worship.

* See Andrews' Convocation Address to the students of Calcutta University, March 1939. The phrase is from A. N. Whitehead.

The eagerness with which young men responded to this intimate friendly companionship made him feel very keenly the need for teachers of the right quality by whom such work might be extended throughout India. In 1907 he united with V. S. Azariah of the National Missionary Society* and J. Carter of the Y.M.C.A. to send a famous cable to the summer conference of the British Student Christian Movement in which, in the name of the Christian students of India, they appealed for help to the students of England. He and Rudra followed this up with a plan for a "short service" scheme whereby young English graduates, who were as yet uncertain of their life vocation, might work as laymen for two-year periods on the staffs of the Christian colleges of India. "It is the Christian student spirit from England that we ask for," they wrote. "It is that fresh, glorious enthusiasm of men that we need."†

On the men who came to India in response to these appeals Andrews' influence was very great ; sooner or later many of them sought him out at Maitland House or in Simla. "I had the inestimable privilege of having talks with him about the relations of missionaries and Indians in a way that was, I think, formative of my own outlook," writes one.‡ "He transformed all our thinking," says another.§ "To me he was veritably a *guru*," writes a third.‖ At St. John's College, Agra, some of these young English recruits, and some of Andrews' own old students who were also teaching there, lived together in a bachelor "chummery" which formed a pattern for other similar experiments in interracial comradeship elsewhere.

S. K. Datta, the great Indian Christian leader, was on the staff of the Student Christian Movement in Britain when the "short service" scheme was launched. When he returned to India he and Andrews gathered their little band of pioneers in friendship for a memorable Retreat at Okhla on the river Jumna, a few miles from Delhi. Andrews himself felt it to be one of the deepest

---

* Later Bishop of Dornakal.
† *The Student Movement*, 1907.
‡ Arthur Davies, now Dean of Worcester.
§ Bishop Norman Tubbs, now Dean of Chester.
‖ Father J. C. Winslow, formerly of Poona.

moments of his own life in the East. He was reading P. C.
Mazoomdar's *Oriental Christ*, and Mazoomdar's phrase, "the dim-
ness breaks out into glory," seemed an echo of his own experience
as he led his young companions in meditation. His talks were
based upon the words of Christ in St. John's Gospel, "Let not your
hearts be troubled." In his devotional reading he was now turning away from St. Paul's *Epistle to the Romans*, where at first he
had found the supreme warrant for his missionary work, to the
Hymn of Love in the *First Epistle to the Corinthians*, the Sermon
on the Mount, and the great parables of Jesus. Most frequently
of all he turned to those five immortal chapters of John, whose
power over him went back to the days when he had listened to
them as a child of seven at the Holy Week services in Birmingham. The men who gathered at Okhla were the first of many
hundreds to whom his talks on John's Gospel at student conferences and retreats gave a deeper understanding of the life of prayer.

Another long-remembered gathering was the "summer school"
inspired and led by Andrews, which was held at Bereri in the
Simla Hills in May and June, 1911, and was attended by young
missionaries from many churches and from many parts of India.
Andrews lectured brilliantly on Indian religious history, and his
own personality—the burning flame of his love of Christ, the
warmth of his human comradeship—made the days memorable.
Many felt that the seeds of a great hope had been sown at that
summer school—the hope of a United Church of Northern India.

A united church was then a distant dream, and Andrews was
gravely troubled about the ecclesiastical rules which restricted him
from sharing freely in the service of Holy Communion with
members of other Christian bodies. He knew now that Susil
Rudra's criticisms of these rules represented the mind of Indian
Christians generally, and it was not long before events compelled
him to make up his own mind on the issue.

"Once," he wrote, "we had asked one of the saintliest Indian Christians,
the Rev. Dr. Chatterji, who as a Brahmin had renounced caste for Christ's
sake and had been excommunicated for doing so, to conduct a Retreat for
Mission workers near Delhi. This Retreat was to end with the Holy
Communion service, and every Indian Christian present felt that the old
saint, Dr. Chatterji, who was a Presbyterian, should preside ; in all

humility and love he did so. How could I refuse to join at such a solemn moment ? If I had withdrawn, would there not have been something parallel to the scene at Antioch, when Paul rebuked Peter to his face for drawing apart ?

"A young Mahommedan convert was my godson. He was transferred to a district where there was no Anglican mission. Was I to tell him to stand aloof in isolation, just because he had been baptized and confirmed in an Anglican mission, and his fellow-Christians there were non-Anglicans? Who are we to lay on these young Christians a burden which neither we nor our fathers have been able to bear ?"*

Andrews had also become very friendly with the Rev. C. B. Young, a Baptist missionary who came to Delhi in 1908. At his suggestion Young began to help with teaching at St. Stephen's, and Andrews, who suffered a good deal from sleeplessness at Maitland House, often went to Young's home outside the city, where it was quieter and cooler, to spend the night. One Friday evening in 1910 he arrived to find Young down with malaria, and a little troubled about the service which he was due to conduct on the following Sunday. "I'll take it for you," promised Andrews impulsively, sure that the breach of church discipline would, in the circumstances, be condoned. Next day he found that his assumption was mistaken, and in fact he could not obtain the necessary permission. Fortunately, Young was well enough to take the service himself, but such incidents made Andrews deeply dissatisfied with the policy of his own church.

III

Very early in Andrews' life in India he had been walking through the streets of a Punjab town with an Indian Christian friend, when an Englishman drove by in a pony-trap, scattering the people to right and left. "Look !" said his friend, "there is your Christianity driving along ! That is how the local missionary goes about his work. Now come with me." They came to where a Hindu ascetic was seated on the bare ground. "I know," went on the Indian, "that there are many frauds and rascals living that life. But that man is a true *sadhu*, and people come to him from miles around." There was another such genuine *sadhu* who took up

* From an essay on Inter-communion written about 1937, extant in typescript.

his abode from time to time under a tree near St. Stephen's College. Andrews could watch him from the windows of his comfortable room in Maitland House. The contrast was profoundly disturbing; how could the Lord who "had not where to lay his head" be commended to India so long as his followers lived lives so much out of harmony with the national religious ideal :*

In the cold weather of 1906–7, while these ideas were seething in Andrews' brain, reports began to reach him of two young Christians, an American and an Indian, who were living a life of homeless poverty and menial service in the plague-stricken villages of the Punjab. Stokes, the American, had been wealthy. He had been wandering in the Simla Hills on a pleasure trip when he met Mrs. Bates, the widow of a retired Forest Officer. Through her simple goodness there had come to him an overwhelming experience of conversion, so that he renounced his great possessions and went out in the rough robe of a *sadhu* to serve the needy. Sundar Singh was scarcely more than a boy in years ; he had been driven from his orthodox Sikh home because of his determination to follow Christ openly, and after his confirmation by Bishop Lefroy (at that very service in Kotgarh to which Andrews had accompanied him) he had joined Stokes in his work in the leper camp at Sabathu and had been with him ever since.

The story of their venture of faith came to Andrews like an answer to prayer. He sought out Mrs. Bates, who was spending a winter holiday with friends in Delhi, and she promised that when he came to Kotgarh in the summer he should meet her modern Franciscans. So began a friendship which was fraught with far-reaching consequences. Andrews invited his new friends to Maitland House, where their joy in poverty made a deep impression upon boys who had hitherto accepted unthinkingly the somewhat materialist values of the average Christian home. His fertile brain, fired by the new enthusiasm, devised scheme after scheme whereby his own Cambridge Brotherhood might follow their example. Could not its members, while continuing their common corporate life at certain seasons, go out two by two during the remainder of the year like the first Franciscans or the

* See the last two chapters of Andrews' *North India*, published 1908.

71

first disciples of Jesus, "taking nothing for their journey" ? Was there no one who would dedicate himself for Christ's sake to the full life of Holy Poverty, extravagant with an extravagance which India would understand ?

"He was like an earthquake in the calm placid Mission House," wrote a friend*—and indeed Andrews himself was thinking in some such terms. It seemed to him that an explosive inner force, a volcanic Pentecost, was needed to burst the hard confining crust of Western forms and western methods and set the Indian Christian Church free for service. He made his appeal to the ardour of the young :

> "Christ bids you cast off the Western leading-strings," he cried, "and quit you like men, be strong in the faith. The one and only witness which will appeal to educated India is Renunciation. It is not our money, not our organisation, that is being weighed in the balance. It is the intensity of our spiritual life."†

Before the end of 1907, Stokes, Andrews and Western were dreaming of a new international brotherhood of renunciation and service. The next year Stokes travelled in England and America, telling his story and rousing very great sympathy and interest. When he returned, the plans for a "Brotherhood of the Imitation of Jesus" were earnestly discussed. It was soon clear that Sundar Singh should join no Order, but should follow the path of his own wayward genius as a solitary Christian *Sadhu*. Andrews however would not have been Andrews if he had not longed with all his heart and soul to throw in his lot with the gallant new venture. He dreamed of making his home among the *chamars* and *chuhras* in dusty sordid Sabzi-Mandi, on the outskirts of Delhi, while he continued for the time being to fulfil his obligations to the college. Allnutt and Rudra however would not hear of it— it seemed to them only too likely that his always uncertain health would have broken down completely under the strain. Stokes and Western went forward without him, and on February 22nd 1910, the new Brotherhood was solemnly inaugurated by the Bishop of Lahore.

The following year Andrews contributed to *The East and the*

* Bishop Norman Tubbs.

† Address at the Christian Endeavour Convention, Agra, 20th November 1909.

West an essay on Brotherhood ideals which shows a profounder understanding of what the "fulfilment" of Hinduism by Christ might mean than anything he had written before. The missionary, he says, must discard the western trappings of Christianity, but he must not seek prematurely to clothe it in Hindu dress.

> "Christ's fulfilment of Judaism," he points out, "was no smooth, graduated evolution. The Jews crucified Him. He is the fulfilment of the Law, yet Paul knew that he must die to the Law in order to live to Christ. Even so, Hinduism, great and lofty as it is, must die and be reborn before it can live to Christ."

The true way, he argues, is "to empty ourselves of the west, to be the citizens of no country, but Christians pure and simple, like the first disciples."

> "Once let there be the real and unmistakable birth of the Christ life in India," he goes on, "and we may say to the Indian church concerning the treasures of Indian spiritual life, past, present and future, 'All things are yours, for ye are Christ's'."

In the summer of 1911, while Andrews lay ill at Simla, his physical frame wasted by the very intensity with which he lived, Stokes and he talked for hours over a new problem. People saw in the Brotherhood, said Stokes, not a means of sharing the burden of humanity, but a way of escape from the problems which beset the common man. That being so, might it not be a higher discipleship to uphold the supreme standards of Christ amid the daily perplexities of the householder ?—not the Christian friar, but the Christian family, was India's greater need ! Andrews' mind flashed back to the walks on the Yorkshire moors when Bishop Westcott had talked of the Christian family community which he believed might regenerate the west, and he warmly supported Stokes in his decision to marry an Indian Christian lady.

With Stokes' marriage the Brotherhood of the Imitation came to an end, but short-lived as it was it had done its work. In the ranks of the National Missionary Society in the Punjab were some of Andrews' own Christian students, and they too sought to live in the spirit of the first disciples and to naturalise their Christian witness in the village surroundings where they worked.* The influence of the Brotherhood ideal, and of Andrews' preaching of

* For an account of these experiments see Ebright, *History of the N.M.S. in India.*

it, spread far and wide. In April 1912, at a meeting of the National Missionary Society, Andrews made the suggestion which has brought new Brotherhoods into being through the length and breadth of India. "There is a great future," he said, "for Christian ashrams."

I V

"A Christian pure and simple, like the first disciples." The following pen-picture of Andrews as he was in 1911, written for *The Delhi Mission News* by an anonymous English visitor, shows how close he lived to his ideal. The scene was a Convention of Religions held at Allahabad.

> "There was to be no controversy, only statement. The Maharajah of Darbhanga presided, chewing betelnut. All kinds of -isms were there, including naturally much eclecticism. Then came S. K. Rudra, very strong, very dignified, clinging to his country and his people, quoting St. John. Then Andrews—he is a saint and an ascetic, though he looks chubby enough—preaching the Cross. His voice was very weak, his words intensely simple. 'I am here as a Christian to tell you about the Lord I serve.' He repeated the Lord's Prayer. He spoke of the God Who is Love and so came Himself into the world—'that is why we can never, we Christians, put our Lord on a level with any other prophet.' He went on to speak of the Cross, the suffering of God and the sin of man. And they listened anyway, and I felt that I had heard the Gospel preached at last, *with the simplicity of itself, and one thought of St. Paul on Mars Hill.*"*

V

Andrews in these years was not only a saint and a pioneer, he was also a Christian statesman whose intellectual mastery of certain lesser but still important problems left its mark upon the church. One of these was the controversy provoked by a suggestion made by Bishop Whitehead of Madras that men and money should be withdrawn from the "unremunerative" work of higher education in order to strengthen Christian missions in "mass movement" areas. With the Christian service of the simple primitive peoples Andrews had a deep sympathy. *North India* contains a keen discussion of its problems, which should be studied, he says, "from a critical, not an emotional, standpoint."

* Italics ours.

He points out that Jesus Himself, out of his very compassion for the multitudes, had turned aside to train disciples to carry on his work, and that the Church in India, through its colleges, should do likewise. He boldly suggests that though the colleges should be strengthened, the Christian elementary schools might be abandoned with benefit to the Church. India, he says, might consider the example set by the church in the Roman Empire, where

> Christian children were not segregated, but were educated with others in the public schools, while Christian learning and philosophy received the greatest stress, as in the school of Origen at Alexandria.*

Andrews' ideas about the training in "Christian learning and philosophy" which should be given to Indian candidates for the priesthood were far ahead of his time. He ascribed the dearth of indigenous, original Christian thought in India to the deadening weight of a curriculum so remote from the Indian Christian's daily life as to make theological study utterly unreal. His own proposal was that the whole accumulation of peculiarly Anglican and western subjects should be swept away, and the students' attention centred on the Bible itself, the early formative period of Christian history, and the relation between Christian doctrine and the living currents of Hindu and Islamic thought among which Indian Christians passed their lives.†

He devoted much thought also to the Christian instruction given in his own college. He was too great a teacher to regard religion as merely one subject of the curriculum, to be added or subtracted at will. The religious view of reality must permeate the whole life of the college, or it was nothing. To him, the maintenance of religious instruction was "the assertion of a fundamental principle of education, namely that it should be rooted in religion." At the same time, his sensitive spirit was deeply concerned with the question of how far this religious teaching ought to be compulsory for all students, how far voluntary. It is a tribute to his greatness that he found no easy, superficial answer that could be applied ready-made to any situation ; but the essays in which he discussed the problem are a valuable contribution to

* "The Indigenous Expression of Christian Truth," *Young Men of India*, 1911.
† See *Ordination Study in India*, Cambridge Mission to Delhi, 1910.

thought on a subject which has a relevance in India far beyond the borders of the Christian community.*

Under his leadership, St. Stephen's College was one of the first Christian colleges in India to associate its non-Christian with its Christian staff in the religious life of the college ; staff and students alike valued the *esprit-de-corps* and confidence which were thus maintained at a time when much Christian work was an object of the bitterest suspicion, and their respect for and interest in the Christian inspiration of the college increased.

VI

Andrews was present at the Delhi Durbar on December 12th, 1911, when King George rose and announced a decision whose secret, till that dramatic moment, had been supremely well kept— "the transfer of the seat of the Government of India from Calcutta to the ancient capital of Delhi," and the simultaneous restoration of the unity of Bengal by its separation from Assam on the one side and Bihar and Orissa on the other. Andrews at once pointed out the tremendous possibilities inherent in that "truly royal announcement," and prophesied, with an almost startling accuracy, how the provinces and the provincial capitals were likely to grow in number and significance. He urged that the church should bring its own organisation into harmony with this regional development, and that ecclesiastical provinces should be planned to correspond with the temperamental differences between the practical, austere north, the colourful, emotional south, keenly speculative Bengal, and eventually central and western India also. The Metropolitan or Primate, he suggested, might be bishop of a small diocese of Delhi where he would not be burdened with too much purely local work.†

Small wonder that many people regarded it as virtually certain that Andrews would succeed Lefroy as Bishop of Lahore, and would one day himself be Metropolitan of India !

The King's Proclamation had an immediate importance for St. Stephen's College, for the change in the status of Delhi would

* College Report, 1909, 1910.
† *The East and the West*, July 1912.

immensely increase its field of service. In 1910 Rudra had formulated in a remarkable paper the principles on which he believed Christian higher education should be based,* and during the next two years he and Andrews were working at a new college constitution which should embody them. From the time of the Proclamation they aimed explicitly at a fully residential college on a new site, with limited numbers and a staff which should be a corporate unity. In April 1912, they sailed together for England to lay their proposals before the Mission authorities in Cambridge. (It is on record that a fellow-traveller on the Marseilles-Calais express, seizing a moment when Andrews had left the compartment, was heard to observe in a stentorian whisper, "Cast-offs ?" The trousers which Andrews was then wearing had been made for a colleague who stood six-foot-three in his socks, five or six inches taller than Andrews himself.)

The new college constitution was mainly Andrews' work. It was a masterly achievement, and it has stood the test of time. But it needed all the authority and persuasiveness of the two friends combined to carry the provisions for non-Anglican and non-Christian participation in management through the conservative and hesitant committees. In fact, both had to threaten to resign before they succeeded, and the revelation of the narrow sectarianism that prevailed in England was a shock to Andrews so great as to constitute "a moral revolution,"† and did much to prepare the way for the revolution in life which was shortly to follow.

Another controversy arose over Andrews' outspoken article *Race within the Church*,‡ in which he advocated full and generous recognition of racially mixed marriages (such as Stokes') as the crucial test of the Christian belief in human equality. His old friend Dr. Gore declared his arguments to be "unanswerable," and the interest which was aroused contributed to the phenomenal success of *The Renaissance in India*, which was published shortly afterwards. Few missionary textbooks have

* They were endorsed 20 years later by the Lindsay Commission on Christian Higher Education.

† Andrews uses the phrase in this context in a letter to Dr. Stanton of the S.P.G. in July 1913.

‡ *The East and the West*, October 1912.

made so great an impression upon the British student community. The book helped to attract a brilliant team of badly-needed recruits for St. Stephen's, though the spectacle, unique in pre-war Cambridge, of the close and loyal friendship between Andrews and Rudra (a pledge of the reality of inter-racial fellowship in the college) was possibly an even more powerful attraction. In the summer of 1912 it seemed as though their partnership was about to enter on its most fruitful phase of service. Yet the currents which were to sweep Andrews away from Delhi into even wider seas of thought and action were already gathering force.

PART THREE

THE PIONEER

CHAPTER VI

UNKNOWN SEAS

1912-1914

I

IN June 1912 Andrews went up to London from Cambridge to attend the Congress of the Universities of the Empire. There he saw Henry Wood Nevinson, the writer and journalist, who had been his guest in Delhi. "Would you like to meet Rabindranath Tagore ?" asked Nevinson. "William Rothenstein, the artist, has invited me to go over to his house in Hampstead on Sunday evening. Tagore is to be there ; and William Yeats, the Irish poet, is to read some English translations of his work. Why not come along too ?"

Andrews needed no second bidding. Ever since the news had reached him in Cambridge, a short time before, that Rabindranath was in England, he had been casting about for some way of meeting him. The Sunday evening in Hampstead was one of the landmarks of his life. When Rabindranath heard his name announced he came forward eagerly, for though the two men had never before met, he had been attracted by Andrews' writings as strongly as Andrews had been attracted by his. Common ideals and aspirations for India's national destiny had drawn them together. Andrews admired Tagore profoundly as a political thinker ; but he knew of his greatness as a poet only by hearsay, for none of his poems had as yet been published in English translation. The meeting at Rothenstein's house was to introduce them to the English literary world.

As the historic reading from *Gitanjali* began, Andrews sat by the window in the long summer dusk. Below in the valley twinkled the myriad lights of the great city ; around him was a growing stillness, for this poetry was opening a new world of beauty to the men and women gathered in the room. All

81

Andrews' enthusiasm leaped out to salute the lovely simplicity, the universal humanity, and the lofty faith which breathed through the poems. Here was a message which could win its way across thousands of miles of distance and countless ages of tradition, into the hearts of the English people. He had contended often that the key to mutual understanding between East and West in the realm of religion lay in music, art and poetry. He had then been thinking chiefly of the appeal of English poetry to India ; here was Indian poetry with a supreme appeal to the west.

With such thoughts as these rising in his mind Andrews sat and listened till nearly midnight. As time went on all thought was swallowed up in the aesthetic and emotional response of his nature to the poems themselves.

"I walked back along the side of Hampstead Heath with H. W. Nevinson," he wrote, "but spoke very little. I wanted to be alone and think in silence of the wonder and glory of it all. When I had left Nevinson I went across the Heath. The night was cloudless and there was something of the purple of the Indian atmosphere about the sky. There all alone I could think out the wonder of it :

On the seashore of endless worlds, children meet.
On the seashore of endless worlds, is the great meeting of children.

"It was the haunting, haunting melody of the English, so simple, like all the beautiful sounds of my childhood, that carried me completely away. I remained out under the sky far into the night, almost till dawn was breaking."*

There, perhaps, is the secret of the spell that bound him. *Gitanjali* sang to Andrews, not of India only, but of the mother-love which had cradled him and the music of the far Northumbrian seas.

Rabindranath himself, a stranger to London, and bearing in his face the marks of recent ill-health, seemed to Andrews a very frail and lonely figure. Back in Cambridge he was haunted by anxiety lest the poet's strength should be unequal to the honours which were heaped upon him. He could not rest without seeing him again, and towards the end of July he made a special journey to London to do so. It was as he feared. Rabindranath was worn with the strain of publicity, and longing for quiet.

* *The Modern Review*, January 1913.

Susil Rudra and his daughter Ila were staying with Andrews' old Pembroke friend "Bill" Outram at his quiet country vicarage at Butterton in Staffordshire. At Andrews' request, Mr. and Mrs. Outram made the poet welcome also, and Andrews took him to Butterton early in August. The days of relaxation marked the beginning of a friendship in which, on Andrews' side, there was both the mother's protective tenderness and the disciple's reverent devotion to a master. During September and October, when Rabindranath was back in London, Andrews went up again and again from Cambridge to see him. They would spend the morning together, going over the proofs of *Gitanjali* which were then coming from the press. In the afternoon they would meet again at Rothenstein's house, where Rabindranath was sitting for his portrait, for more talk.

At the end of such a day, as the train carried Andrews back to Cambridge, his thoughts would race ahead through the vistas which Rabindranath's friendship had opened before him. He would learn Bengali ; he would help the poet with the further translations which would soon be demanded, and which might so nobly interpret India to the world. He would study more intimately, under Tagore's guidance, the great heritage of Indian religious thought. But he had no expectation of any break with St. Stephen's College. Rudra had named him Vice-Principal, and when he returned to Delhi in November 1912, it was with a renewed enthusiasm for the great contribution that a Christ-inspired education might make to the future of India. "My own hope lies more and more in education," he wrote to Tagore, who had gone on from England to America. "My own missionary work would be impossible in any other sphere, but along this line I feel I can fulfil my highest Christian instincts and fulfil also the highest service to India."*

Another passage in the same letter is of great interest because in it Andrews gives expression for the first time to those convictions about the true goal of Indian nationalism which, he says, had been formed in his own mind as early as 1910 :

"My thoughts turn more and more to an India that shall be really

* Letter dated 20th December 1912.

83

independent. And yet one knows that this can hardly be at present. Only how to get out of this vicious circle of subjection leading to demoralisation (both of rulers and ruled) and demoralisation leading to further subjection?"

Independent India. Was Andrews the first man in the century to make the claim ?

II

In spite of the belief in his missionary vocation expressed in the letter to Tagore, Andrews had nevertheless a deeply-divided mind. From the moment he returned to India he was faced with racial barriers in the Punjab church. Over and over again he made the wearisome night journey from Delhi to Lahore, as peace-maker in some misunderstanding between Indian and English clergy, or to try to set right such tragi-comic wrongs as the perpetuation of separate burial-grounds for Indian and European dead. Always at the back of his mind was the knowledge of the divergence in outlook between himself and the mission committee members with whom he and Rudra had argued and pleaded in England. He would lie awake at night wondering whether he had any right to accept a salary from people whose ideals of Christian service were so remote from his own.

Then came Christmas Day. Andrews went to church with a heart filled with love and worship. But as the service went on, the Indian choir-boys began to chant the first phrases of the "Athanasian Creed," which had troubled him so much even in Walworth—"which Faith except every one do keep whole and undefiled, without doubt he shall perish everlastingly." Andrews listened with a greater revulsion of feeling than he had ever felt before. In the eyes of a church which accepted such a creed even Rabindranath Tagore was shut out from the mercy of God—Tagore, whose poetry had brought him new religious inspiration, and in whom from their first meeting he had recognised one of the pure in heart ! And that the terrible words should be put into the mouths of young, uncomprehending children like the little choir-boys—children of whom Tagore had written with such delicate understanding—seemed the final blasphemy.

As so often with Andrews, his moral revolt led to a questioning

84

of the credal statements with which the offending phrase was associated. After he had met Tagore, he had begun to study the Hindu and Buddhist Scriptures with new appreciation. Was this highly speculative doctrine of the Trinity, he asked himself, really as essentially Christian as the *bhakti* doctrine of Unification? Was the Virgin Birth of Christ anything more than a legend which symbolised the reverence of the common people for one who was supremely great, like the similar stories told of Lord Krishna and the Buddha? Might not the Gospel story itself be a myth, as so many believed these other tales to be? His distress of mind drove him into a certain isolation, such as he had not known before, even from those old friends who most wholly shared his ideals of racial equality and of Franciscan service.

So it came about that new friends were cherished with a specially warm outpouring of affection. In January, 1913, in the midst of his loneliness and doubt, Andrews first met in Delhi that great and magnetic personality, Mahatma Munshi Rama of the Arya Samaj.

Before this time his attitude to the Samaj had been one of impartial and dispassionate appraisement. As a whole, it was bitterly anti-Christian, and Andrews did not conceal his opinion that the attacks on the Christian faith in its chief scripture, the *Satyartha Prakash*, were ignorant and biassed. But early in 1910 his sense of fair play had been outraged by some equally biassed attacks on Sri Dayanand Saraswati, the founder of the Samaj, and on the *Satyartha Prakash* itself, and he had at once spoken out in their defence. The accounts which he had heard of Mahatma Munshi Rama and his educational work at the Arya Samaj Gurukula at Kangri near Hardwar were such as to win his respect, and when he met the Mahatma he lost no time in arranging to visit the Gurukula. During the early months of 1913 he went back to it more than once, and spent week after week in the little house by the Ganges where Munshi Rama lived among his boys. Their intimacy grew apace, for Andrews looked up to the Mahatma as to a loved elder brother, admiring his magnificent manhood, his energy, his humour, his simplicity of life. He began to understand his passionate love for the sacred River and the sacred soil of India, and to enter into his thoughts of God the Mother. His own unquenchably youthful spirit responded to the youthful idealism which he found in the Gurukula, and he described the vision which it had brought to him in an enthusiastic article in *The Modern Review* :

> Here by the clear translucent waters was the ancient pathway of the pilgrims, the threshold of the great ascent, leading up and up to the eternal snows . . . the Motherland, not worn and sorrowful, but ever fresh and young with the springtime of immortal youth. Here in the Gurukula was the new India, the sacred stream of young Indian life nearest its pure unsullied source.*

Fellow-missionaries in Delhi looked askance upon this intimacy with their most formidable controversial opponents, and upon Andrews' encouragement of friendships between his own Christian students and the Gurukula boys. On the side of the Arya Samaj also there were some who called him a "missionary spy." He spoke of the pain of these misunderstandings in a letter to the Mahatma. Munshi Rama's reply brought him an over-whelming recompense of happiness, for he assured Andrews that his love had given him "a taste of pure joy," such as he had not known for many years, and had filled him with a renewed hope and faith in the Love of God. "I and you," he wrote, "sinners as we are, will in the end be able to convince our brethren that the Mother belongs specially to no country or sect, and that Her loving arms are open for all Her children."†

Andrews thanked God for that letter, and begged Munshi Rama to call him not only "Brother," but "Charlie"—"for Charlie means one who is very dear."

His enthusiasm for the Gurukula found practical expression. He sent rose-trees for the garden ; he worked out English courses for the school ; and he did very much to lift the cloud of official suspicion which then hung over it. This last he was able to do because of the warm friendship which had grown up between him and the Viceroy, Lord Hardinge.

The story of Andrews' friendship with the Hardinges is an

---

* *Hardwar and its Gurukula*, March 1913.
† Mahatma Munshi Rama to C. F. Andrews, 25th April 1913.

example of how inextricably his religion and his political influence were mingled together. In May, 1911, Lord and Lady Hardinge had attended a service at Christ Church, Simla, at which Andrews was the preacher. For them it was a time of personal sorrow, and something in his words and personality had so met their need that they asked him privately to lunch. From that time onwards he was a friend, though not at first a very intimate one. Then on December 23rd 1912, at Delhi, Lord Hardinge had been wounded, almost fatally, by a bomb thrown during his State Entry into the new Capital. But he would hear of no reprisals, strictly forbade any measures of repression, and kept his faith in the power of friendliness and trust. Andrews warmly admired his attitude, and his helpfulness to Lady Hardinge during the anxious days of nursing set the seal on their friendship. During Lord Hardinge's convalescence at Dehra Dun in February he invited Andrews to visit them to discuss the political situation.

A fund had been started in India as a thank-offering for the Viceroy's escape and recovery, and Lady Hardinge took the opportunity of Andrews' visit to Dehra Dun to consult him about how it might best be used. Andrews suggested that Lord Hardinge's birthday, June 20th 1913, should be celebrated by a birthday treat for children in hospitals and orphanages. "The Indian people would like it," he said. "They love children, and even the simplest and poorest would understand." Lady Hardinge took up the idea with enthusiasm, and all through May and early June Andrews was in Simla working hard to make it a success. Some sections of officialdom would have preferred a more "dignified" form of celebration, but in spite of their doubts it was a great success ; village after village entertained its own children on the happy day.

This work kept Andrews in close touch with the Hardinges and with Indian organisations of all kinds, including the Arya Samaj ; and it was in this atmosphere of friendly human co-operation that he arranged for Mahatma Munshi Rama to meet the Viceroy. He also persuaded Sir James Meston, the Governor of the United Provinces, to visit the Gurukula. Officials hesitated, fearful of more bombs. "Let the reforming movements of the country be *trusted,"* urged Andrews, "not patronised, but *trusted*. That would be worth all the police protection in the world."

Meanwhile, in early March, he had paid his first visit to the pioneer school founded by Rabindranath at Santiniketan in Bengal. Boys and teachers made him welcome as a friend of their Gurudeva, and with such men as the poet's eldest brother, Dwijendranath, and the scholar, Khitimchan Sen, he at once reached a deep level of intimacy. From Santiniketan, as from the Gurukula, he gathered into his hands the threads which he wove into his work of reconciliation. Lord Hardinge gave him an opportunity to lecture at the Viceregal Lodge at Simla on Tagore and the Bengal Renaissance. He took immense pains over the preparation of the lecture, which was given in May 1913, before a distinguished official audience, and repeated in substance on many later occasions. From that time onwards the English *Gitanjali* formed a common bond of appreciation between English and Indian to which he constantly appealed.

At Simla, in June, Andrews received a letter which gave him much delight. It was from his friend Sir Ali Imam, and it was a formal invitation to a dinner-party "for Indians only." "I told him," he wrote in narrating the story, "that it was the greatest compliment I had had paid since I came to India. He laughed and said, 'Well, you see, we can never look on you as anything else than one of ourselves.'*

So much was he one of themselves that without fear of mis-understanding he could now write to Munshi Rama about a crude attack on the Bible which had appeared in the *Vedic Magazine*, the monthly journal of the Arya Samaj. The attack had been based upon John Stuart Mill's criticisms, and Andrews was courteous but frank. "We who are struggling to maintain in the world *a living belief in God*," he pleaded, "ought not to attempt to destroy that belief in others, and to use as our weapons the accusations of atheists and agnostics. That is fighting with poisoned weapons."† To the young editor of the magazine he wrote in similar fashion, and promised him at the same time articles from his own pen.

* To Mahatma Munshi Rama, 14th June 1913.
† To Mahatma Munshi Rama, 28th July 1913.

On Holiday in the Simla Hills about 1909
(*with Principal Rudra and his two sons*)

This was in July, and Andrews was again in Santiniketan. He had been very greatly attracted by the freshness and spontaneity of the life there, and with Rabindranath's very glad consent he had returned to the school during the Delhi Long Vacation in order to give an elder brother's help to the young workers during the poet's prolonged absence. Through the Tagore family he came into close touch with the Brahmo Samaj in Calcutta, and was invited to address one of their public meetings. His speech, the writing of which he discussed fully in his letters to Mahatma Munshi Rama, was a plea for whole-hearted co-operation between the Brahmo Samaj, the Arya Samaj, and all earnest reformers, in order that the "mass weight" of Hindu orthodoxy and idolatry might be overcome. The *true* spirit of religion, he urged, was not to be found in hostile isolation, but in "a zeal that makes for harmony and peace."

During these weeks in Santiniketan the sense of an impending change in his own life grew stronger. "It is the call of the *sannyasin*," he wrote, "to give myself wholly into the hands of God, to go where He leads and to take up whatever work He gives me to do."* He pictured this work as the study of Indian thought and the endeavour to interpret it to the West, while "from a completely independent standpoint, not as a paid agent," he would also try to express Christian thought to the East.† He spoke or wrote of this to his most intimate Indian friends, Dwijendranath, Rabindranath, Munshi Rama ; one and all urged him not to act hastily but to wait prayerfully for an unmistakable call.

As he waited, his tormenting doubts about the historical reality of the Christ were swept away by a great book of Christian scholarship and devotion, Albert Schweitzer's *Quest of the Historical Jesus*. The last paragraph of that book so met his need that he named it ever after as his favourite Christian quotation :

"Christ comes to us as One Unknown, without a name, just as of old by the lakeside He came to those men who knew Him not. He speaks to us the same words, 'Follow thou Me,' and sets us to those tasks which He has to fulfil for our time. He commands. And to those who obey Him,

* To Mahatma Munshi Rama, 28th July 1913.
† To Rabindranath Tagore, 28th July 1913.

whether they be wise or simple, He will reveal Himself in the toils, the conflicts, the sufferings, which they shall pass through in His fellowship. And as an ineffable mystery they shall learn in their own experience who He is."

The flame of his devotion rekindled, he listened expectantly for the new call. It came.

III

For several years Andrews had watched the position of Indians in other parts of the Empire. It was too relevant to his own struggle against racial discrimination to be ignored, and it was one of those national causes in which Indians of every caste and creed could fight side-by-side on a clear moral issue. India first learned of South African Indian disabilities when Gandhi returned to India in 1896. In 1909, Henry Polak had come from South Africa to place before the Government and people the grievances and disabilities of the South African Indians, and to press for the termination of the system of indentured labour emigration to Natal. This system had been introduced in 1860 at the request of the *English colonists* and on their promise of equal rights and treatment for the immigrants. From Polak, India learned of the degrading effects of indenture and of the violation of the promises made to the labourers, and of Gandhi, who had become the leader of the Indian Passive Resistance struggle in 1907. The termination of indenture recruiting for Natal was the fruit of this visit and of Polak's collaboration with G. K. Gokhale. Andrews met Polak, and eagerly absorbed every detail that the latter was able to supply. Two years later when Polak visited India again, he met him several times, and followed with the closest interest the powerful campaign for the complete abolition of indenture which Gokhale and he were then conducting at Gandhi's instance.

In 1912 Gokhale visited South Africa and the lines of a settlement of the "Indian question" in Natal were then laid down. Gokhale had agreed, in spite of a storm of abuse from his own countrymen, to withdraw the Indian demand for free immigration and the political franchise, on condition that Indians already domiciled in South Africa should be justly treated ; and as a first

token of justice and goodwill he asked for, and believed he had
obtained, the abolition of a £3 poll tax which pressed heavily
upon the Indian labourer. The South African government
denied having made this promise, and when, shortly afterwards,
the Supreme Court declared Indian religious marriages to be
invalid in law, resentment came to a head. Mohandas Karamchand
Gandhi, who had led the South African Indians for nearly twenty
years, resorted to passive resistance in September, 1913. Preparations were made to challenge the laws restricting Indian entry into
the Transvaal, and on November 6th the "Transvaal march"
began. Five days later Gandhi and his leading associates, Indian
and European, were arrested and imprisoned.

Meanwhile, Gokhale was touring India in a strenuous campaign
for moral and financial support for the "resisters." When he
came to Delhi in November, Andrews threw himself heart and
soul into the cause. He worked literally night and day. He
brought the whole of his own little capital—£300—to offer to
the funds. Gokhale would not accept more than a thousand
rupees, but for such a sum to be given by a missionary of modest
means set a great example in Delhi, and St. Stephen's College
raised something like sixteen hundred rupees in addition. This,
however, was the least of Andrews' services. No one will ever
know how much he had to do with Lord Hardinge's famous
speech at Madras on November 28th, when the Viceroy declared
his "sympathy burning and deep" for the Indians of South Africa.
But when Gokhale spoke to him of his need of more European
support, Andrews at once undertook the thousand-mile journey
to Calcutta to ask his old friend Bishop Lefroy, now Metropolitan
of India, to give the weight of his authority to Gokhale's appeal.
He succeeded. Lefroy's generous contribution to the fund, and
even more his letter to the press, rallied Christian opinion in India
and England, and made its mark in South Africa.

As the train carried Andrews to Calcutta one thought filled his
mind—should he not volunteer for South Africa in person ? Just
as he left Delhi, news had come of police firing on Indians in Natal,
and his brain was on fire with shame and horror. Because he was
an Englishman, should he not atone ? And where the colour bar

was so strong, would not his English status itself be an asset to the Indian cause such as it could never be in India? Only a few days before Gokhale came to Delhi, Andrews had booked his passage to England for February, 1914, and written to his ageing mother that he would be with her by mid-March. But if he were needed at all in South Africa he would be needed immediately, and he could still reach his mother at the time he had promised by sailing from Capetown. The course of duty seemed clear. When he wired Gokhale the good news of Lefroy's support he added an offer to go out to South Africa if and when he should be needed.

Then he went to Santiniketan to consult Rabindranath, who had returned home early in October. The news that the poet had been awarded the Nobel Prize for literature had already reached India, and on November 23rd, while Andrews was with him, a large deputation of Calcutta admirers came to offer congratulations. A memorable scene followed. Tagore was very sensitive to the danger of insincerity in such a demonstration, and he replied to the somewhat fulsome speeches of his admirers with a searching demand for absolute truthfulness. Andrews watched his tall figure from the fringe of the crowd, and though he did not understand the Bengali, he sensed the stress of spirit in the words. His heart filled with a new rush of admiration : this was no longer the frail invalid he had seen in London, but a very king among men.

The meeting ended ; Tagore withdrew from the half-comprehending crowd, and Andrews went in search of him. Rabindranath was standing all alone in front of the old house that had been his father's *ashram*. With a great upsurge of devotion Andrews stooped down and touched his feet.* The older man raised him up and embraced him closely, and in that moment he knew that the call for which he had waited had come. Tagore left the *ashram* the same evening, and Andrews spent the night alone, sleeping little ; the next morning before he left for Delhi he wrote to the poet asking to be allowed to share his work at Santiniketan.

Gokhale met him at Delhi. "Your wire was like a gift of

---

* The Indian gesture of reverence to an elder or leader.

God," he said. "We need you in South Africa. When do you start?"

Maitland House hummed with preparations. Colleagues took on at short notice the whole of Andrews' teaching work, and took it gladly, for they had long recognised his special gifts and vocation. Jokingly they made good the deficiencies of his notoriously ascetic wardrobe—some socks came from one, a shirt from another, and so on. But Susil Rudra knew that what Charlie would need above all things was an understanding companion, and he set himself to find one. Lala Sultan Singh, an old friend of St. Stephen's, had at Andrews' suggestion employed a young Englishman, William Winstanley Pearson,* as tutor to his son. The three took counsel together. A little while later Willie Pearson walked in upon Andrews as he struggled with his packing. "I've brought you a present to take to South Africa," he announced, "—Myself!"

IV

On January 1st, 1914, the little ship struggled into Durban harbour, five days late, after storms which at one point had made observations impossible. For Andrews it had been a terrible voyage. To physical *malaise* (he was always a bad sailor) was added mental agony, when two days out of Colombo an Indian cook from Calcutta disappeared overboard. He was horrified at the weight of human misery the suicide revealed. It gave him ever afterwards a personal interest in the struggle to improve the conditions of work for Indian seamen. He was haunted too by a strong presentiment of danger and possible death, and as the danger became more real he tasted the full bitterness of the thought that perhaps he had stood on the threshold of new worlds of friendship only to be snatched from them for ever. When the ship came at last into the calmer seas outside Durban, he felt that the waters had indeed gone over his soul. There was a new

* W. W. Pearson had been for some years a missionary in Bengal, and Andrews had worked with him on the Y.M.C.A. Student Committee. He returned to England in bad health, and Andrews met him in London in 1912 and suggested cold-weather employment in Delhi as a solution of the health problem, such as he himself had found in 1905.

freedom, but also a desolating loneliness. The old anchorages of life had been left behind and he had launched at last upon the open sea.

Henry Polak, whom Andrews had met when he visited India on behalf of South African Indians, was waiting on the quay—he, with Gandhi and Hermann Kallenbach, had been released from prison twelve days before. Andrews greeted him eagerly. "Where is Mr. Gandhi ?" he asked. Polak turned to a slight ascetic figure, dressed in a white *dhoti* and *kurta* of such coarse material as an indentured labourer might wear. Andrews bent swiftly down and touched Gandhi's feet.

The Archdeacon of Durban took the two Englishmen to his home. He was a stranger to them, but the sight of *Gitanjali* on his table was the best possible introduction, and he opened for Andrews the doors of the "white" society of Natal. From the beginning it was clear that his path and Pearson's must diverge if the ground was to be covered. Pearson devoted himself to the investigation of Indian labour conditions on the Natal sugar estates ; Andrews partnered Gandhi in the immediate political struggle, the drama of which unfolded in one of those series of breathtaking eleventh-hour crises which sometimes make history less sober than fiction.

Far-reaching questions of principle had to be decided at once. In December, General Smuts had appointed an Indian Grievances Commission, and Gandhi and his co-workers had been liberated in order that they might give evidence before it. It was analogous to the commissions which had investigated the claims of Rand miners and of railway labourers during the previous six months. Although some of the miners and railwaymen had been guilty of violence, they had been allowed to nominate their own representatives to these commissions. The Indians, whose agitation had been non-violent, were denied this privilege. Gandhi had therefore notified General Smuts that it was not consistent with Indian self-respect to give evidence before the Commission. Was this decision to stand ?

From the point of view of expediency it seemed foolish. The Indian case was strong and well-prepared, but not to present it was to invite the taunt that there was no case at all. If negotiations should fail, passive resistance would have to be renewed—and that, as Natal Europeans frankly told Andrews, would mean shooting. Gokhale sent messages pleading for reconsideration of the decision, lest the Viceroy and other English supporters should be placed in a false position.

The Indian leaders met, Andrews with them. After a few minutes' talk he turned to Mr. Gandhi. "Isn't it simply a question of Indian honour ?" he asked. Gandhi's eyes flashed. "Yes !" he said vehemently, "that is it, that is it. That is the real point at issue." "Then," said Andrews, "I am sure you are right to stand out. There must be no sacrifice of honour." He and Gandhi were friends from that hour ; within two or three days they were "Mohan" and "Charlie" to one another.

A long cable of explanation was sent to Gokhale, and both he and Lord Hardinge accepted and upheld the decision. Would General Smuts negotiate ? Andrews went with Gandhi to his home at the Phoenix *ashram*, sixteen miles from Durban, to wait for the reply. There he had his own first personal contact with indentured labour, and his first glimpse of the compassionate tenderness of Gandhi's care for the downtrodden. A poor runaway Tamil *coolie*, with the marks of cruel beating on his emanciated body, had sought refuge in the *ashram*, and the tears came to Andrews' eyes as he watched Gandhi dealing with him. But the stay in this quiet and simple place was brief, for a few days later came Smuts' message asking Gandhi to meet him at Pretoria.

Once more an industrial crisis was threatening the country. The Station Master at Durban gave the two travellers a friendly tip. "Better take the 'European Mail'," he said. "There will be a big strike, and the 'Kaffir Mail' may not get through." They did as he suggested—it was the last train to reach Pretoria for a fortnight.

At Pretoria, the Editor of the *Pretoria News* greeted Gandhi in friendly fashion. "Are the Indians going to join the General Strike ?" he asked. "No, certainly not," replied Gandhi. "We are out for a clean fight. Passive resistance will be suspended."

"May I publish that ?"

"No—there is no need to do so."

The Editor turned to Andrews. "Do persuade him, Mr. Andrews," he said. "There will be Martial Law within twelve hours." Andrews took his meaning. Up and down they walked, outside the Editor's office, while he argued the point with Gandhi. "Of course you are right to suspend the struggle," he said, "but if no one knows till afterwards, all the good effect will be lost—people will say you did it out of fear." At last Gandhi yielded : the message went out, with all its power for good, to Capetown and the world. A few minutes later the strikers cut the telegraph wires.

Day after day they waited in Pretoria, but Smuts' whole attention was absorbed by the national crisis, and he could not see them. Andrews was not idle. He had known the Gladstone family in Cambridge. Lord Gladstone was now Governor-General, and his sister, Mrs. Drew, was in Pretoria. Through her good offices he met many of the Government leaders, and little by little cleared away their misunderstandings of the Indian position. From their luxurious homes he returned each evening to his own chosen quarters—the crowded squalid Indian "location" outside the city.

> "The *dhobis** of Pretoria became my great friends," he wrote. "Their great delight was to give me a *khana*, either a breakfast or a dinner. They also gave me clothes to wear ; they fitted me up with shoes and slippers , they were eager to wash and iron my white summer suits every day. It was like having possession of the magic ring in the fairy story, and it was such a real joy to them that I could never have the heart to refuse them."†

Then came days of anxiety. Mrs. Gandhi, who had not been released from jail until after her husband left for Pretoria, was seriously ill. Gandhi's courtesy and forbearance during the strike had won Smuts' regard, but the negotiations had reached a dead-lock because he could not agree to a phrase which Smuts desired to insert in the proposed agreement. A still more urgent telegram came from Durban, but Gandhi would not abandon his public duty to go to his wife. Andrews described the critical hours :

> That night we talked till 1 a.m. Finally, an alternative phrase occurred

* Washermen.
† *The Modern Review*, August 1914.

In South Africa, 1914
(*with M. K. Gandhi and W. W. Pearson*)

to me. The difference seemed to be very slight, but Gandhi found it acceptable. "If General Smuts will accept your phrase," he said as we went to bed, "then everything is finished." In the morning, saying nothing to Gandhi, I went to Smuts and at eight o'clock found him alone. I told him Gandhi's personal anxiety, and showed him the suggested wording. "I don't mind a bit," he said, "it makes no difference so far as I am concerned." "Would you make the change and sign it on the spot ?" "Certainly."*

The task was done : by eleven o'clock they were on the train. Just as they were starting a second wire came to say that Mrs. Gandhi was better. The long strain was over ; now it took its toll, and Andrews' latent malaria seized him on the journey. When he reached Durban, feverish and weary amid the scenes of enthusiasm, Willie Pearson was waiting with a letter which told him that his mother was dangerously ill as the result of a chill caught at Christmas, and was not expected to live. Next day came the news of her death. It was a very heavy and unexpected blow, but comfort came to him in a beautiful way from the womanly sympathy of Mrs. Gandhi and the other Indian ladies who visited him in his bereavement, saying, "We will be your mothers now." He knew that his own mother before her death had rejoiced to think of the work for the honour of Indian womanhood which was part of his task in South Africa, and in after years all his work for Indian women was invested with a peculiar sacredness for her sake.

"I had so often wondered," he wrote to Tagore on the day the news came, "what it was that made me love India with such an intense love. I can see now what a unique part my dearest mother's love and devotion played in quickening my love for India herself. I was so constantly being reminded of all that I saw and read and learned about Indian motherhood by what I knew of my own mother . . . I have been able to leap to the recognition of Indian devotion because it is so like my mother's. It has made India my *home* in a peculiar way ; and her death will make me find her in Indian homes. Her spirit will shine out at me through Indian eyes and Indian mothers' faces."†

Six months later the Indian Relief Act was passed in the Union Parliament by a substantial majority. The newspaper *Indian Opinion*, commenting on the spirit of justice and conciliation

* Unpublished Reminiscences.
† To Rabindranath Tagore, 27th January, 1914.

H

which had pervaded the debate, paid a tribute to the part played in the happy issue by Andrews' "mission of love." "His spirit," said the writer, "seemed to watch and guide the deliberations of the House." Yet months had then elapsed after Andrews left the country, and his whole visit had lasted barely seven weeks. "Mr. Andrews has won his way in South Africa," wrote an English journalist in Capetown, "by his transparent singleness of purpose and his utter humility." In a letter to Andrews' father, S. K. Rudra expressed his belief that "No other man in India could have done it, or in the British Empire either."*

V

Andrews' letters to Tagore vividly describe the atmosphere in which his work in South Africa was done. His own first act on landing in Durban—his gesture of reverence towards Gandhi—caused an uproar in the "white" press. One editor protested in person.

> I can see him still, holding up his hands in horror and saying, "Really you know Mr. Andrews, really you know, we don't *do* that sort of thing in Natal, we don't *do* it, Mr. Andrews. I consider the action most un-fortunate, *most* unfortunate." I felt like a little schoolboy in the Head-master's study, waiting to be whipped !
>
> . . . They boil over with indignation that I—an *Englishman* mind you !—should have touched the feet of an Asiatic. When I remind them that Christ and St. Paul and St. John were Asiatics they grow restive and say that things were altogether different then. If I go down the street talking with one of my new Indian friends, everyone turns round to have a big stare, and I am buttonholed afterwards by someone who tells me, "Look here, you know. This really won't do, you know. We don't *do* these things in this country." And when I say politely, "I am very sorry but I *do* do these things," they say "But only think of the bad effect it has on the Kaffirs !"†

A comment such as that in the last sentence was only one of many indications that the Indian question could not be separated from other racial issues in South Africa. At first, indeed, Andrews' pity for the Indian labourers, and his consciousness that he himself came as the representative of a great number of friends and supporters in India itself, tended to obscure from him the

* To J. E. Andrews, 12th March, 1914.
† To Rabindranath Tagore, 6th January, 1914.

larger issue. As he faced his first large Indian audience at the "welcome" meeting on his first Sunday morning in Durban, he tried "to bring the love of the Motherland to her far-off children on that alien shore." At Phoenix a scene took place which he loved to describe, and to describe as an epitome of the spirit of India. He might more truly have described it as an embodiment of the spirit of human brotherhood which was needed in every land alike :

> The strain of a long day of unwearied ministry among the poor was over. In the still after-glow of twilight, Mahatma Gandhi was seated under the open sky. He nursed a sick child on his lap, a little Muslim boy, and next to him was a Christian Zulu girl from the mission across the hill. He read us some Gujerati verses about the love of God, and explained them in English. Then these Gujerati hymns were sung by the children's voices. He asked me to sing "Lead, Kindly Light" as the darkness grew deeper, and in the silence which followed its close repeated the last lines :
>
> > *And with the morn those angel faces smile,*
> > *Which I have loved, long since, and lost awhile.*
>
> "What is India like ?" said a young Hindu to me with eager eyes. "India," I replied, "is just like this. We have all of us been in India tonight."*

It was one of the European supporters of the Indian cause who taught him to see more deeply than this into the realities of the present and the future. Miss Molteno was the sister of the Speaker of the House of Assembly, and she was one of the other speakers at the "welcome" meeting in Durban. "Only as you learn to call *Africa* your Motherland," she told her Indian audience, "can you become worthy children of her sacred soil." There was no future for them, she said, if they lived apart, as strangers "on an alien shore." Andrews saw at once the truth of her position. That same afternoon he spoke at the Indian mission church on St. Paul's Hymn of Love, with the eloquence of deeply-felt emotion. Miss Molteno came to him at the end with shining eyes. "While you were speaking," she said, "the vision of a united Africa came so close I felt I could touch it with my hand. You must go forward with *that* message—they are all thirsting for that, Boer and English and Kaffir alike—and one day Love will conquer."

* Composite from accounts in *The Modern Review*, *Mahatma Gandhi's Ideas*, etc.

Andrews went forward. It was not easy, and often he could not contain his burning indignation at the things he witnessed around him. Yet he saw clearly that denunciation only made division worse divided, and erected a barrier of cold hostility between him and those to whom he spoke. *Gitanjali* and *The Crescent Moon*, which he found in cultured Boer and English homes throughout the Union, broke down the barriers everywhere. Before every kind of audience—in Cathedrals and Universities, before the Governor-General and the *élite* of Capetown, from platforms in humble Kaffir churches, in bioscope halls, in the open air in squalid locations—he spoke of Tagore's personality and poetry, of Indian national ideals, of the Kangri Gurukula and its great-hearted leader, and of the living heritage of culture out of which these things had sprung. Gandhi told him laughingly that Susil Rudra, Munshi Rama and Rabindranath Tagore composed his real Trinity. He himself felt that his lecture on Tagore in the Capetown City Hall, in which he repeated much that he had said at Simla, marked the turning of the tide of public opinion in favour of the Indian cause.

He met Emily Hobhouse, the English lady whose protest against the scandals of the concentration camps for Boer women and children had made her one of the heroines of the Boer War. Her sympathy with the Indians was of great value, for she had influence with the Boer leaders and did much to pave the way to reconciliation. She quickened Andrews' interest in the Boers, with their strong religious faith and their love of home and soil. His meeting with her had a profound influence on his whole conception of the South African problem ; but even more profound was the memory of a night in Durban when a little party of Zulus had followed him from one of his meetings to the home of his Indian host. "We can see you are ready to die for the Indians," they said, "Are you ready to die for *us* ?"

He felt more and more sure as the weeks went by that only new religious insight could purge the old racial hatreds, and he sought for practical ways in which a new spirit might find expression. As a beginning, he suggested to his fellow-Christians an experiment such as his friend the Rev. T. H. Dixon had carried out as

Chaplain of Delhi the previous year—a united Holy Communion service on one Sunday in a month for all the Christians of a town or city, of whatever race, the other churches being closed for that occasion.*

The inward peace which gave him his own power to be a peace-maker was drawn from the hours of quiet prayer with which he began each crowded day. He would rise at half-past three and remain till six in meditation, watching the stars and the dawn ; but even so it was all too easy to lose poise in the intoxicating excitement of "going *at* things."†

One evening in Pretoria, while he sat under the stars outside his tiny room at the end of a busy day, relaxed but wakeful, the inner problem of his life took visible shape before his eyes. Instead of the bare wall before him he saw a low sandy plain stretching to the horizon ; in the midst of it tiny human figures were working with feverish haste, scarcely lifting their heads, as if on some gigantic ant-hill. They seemed to be building a city, yet as fast as they built, it came crumbling down again. He watched fascinated, sure that he could do the work better.

Then he looked up and saw the purple night with its wonderful stars. And as he watched, the sky was transformed into a calm and tender Face, that looked down in compassion on the feverish activity below. Then there appeared other faces, shining in and through the one Face, their eyes looking at him through the stars —the faces of those in India whom he loved. Then, luminously clear, the face of Tagore filled the whole vision, gently bidding him good cheer.

"I am still the restless Englishman," he commented when he described this experience to Tagore. "I experienced, even in this vision, a fierce desire to 'put things right.' But, but, is there not a more excellent way, a way of *being* rather than *doing* ?"‡ The question echoed and re-echoed through the next ten years of his life.

"South Africa will be a shock to your Christianity," Gokhale

* The proposal is outlined in a letter to the *Church Times*, March, 1914.

† "You have a good way of going *at* things, Charlie," a friend had commented in his college days.

‡ To Rabindranath Tagore, 28th January, 1914.

had said, and Andrews found it true. On the first Sunday evening in Durban, Gandhi had come with Willie Pearson to hear him preach, and had been turned away from the church door because he was an Asiatic. Seven weeks later, as the R.M.S. *Briton* sailed out of Capetown harbour, Mr. and Mrs. Gandhi stood on the last point of the breakwater to bid him farewell. As Andrews watched their lessening figures he reflected on the outstanding fact of the last few weeks—the fact that these new friends, to whom the racial churches denied an entry, had brought to him afresh the experience of the presence of Christ. He had felt that Presence in Mrs. Gandhi's motherly compassion towards him in his bereavement, and in the burning passion of Gandhi's sacrifice for the weak and the oppressed. "To be a Christian," he wrote, "means not the expression of an outward creed but the living of an inward life."* Pondering on these things, reading Tagore's *Sadhana*, recalling Munshi Rama's glowing words about the holy land of India, the very source and home of all faith, it seemed to him that it must be from India too that the beauty of Christ had sprung, and not, as he had once thought, India which had learned insight from the Nestorian missionaries of Christ. On the voyage he wrote out his thoughts :

"I am beginning to understand from history that Christianity is not an independent Semitic growth, but an outgrowth of Hindu religious thought and life besides . . . Christ appears to me like some strange, rare, beautiful flower whose seed has drifted and found a home in a partly alien land. India, in this as in so many other ways, is the great Mother in the world's history. Christ the Jewish peasant lived instinctively, as part of his own nature, this non-Jewish ideal of *ahimsa* which is so akin to Hinduism. He had the Universal Compassion, he had the Universal Charity, as marked in the agony of crucifixion as on the sunny Galilean hills.

The leading consequence of this central position would be that we might see in the world's higher religions a branching family tree . . . It will mean a lonely pilgrimage for me, for it means giving up claims for the Christian position which everyone in the West whom I know and love could not conceive of doing."†

* "Written down at the time" and quoted in *Christ and Labour*, p. 106.

† Letter to Tagore written on R.M.S. *Briton*, early in March, 1914.   Long extracts were published in *The Modern Review* in 1922, under the title *Buddhism and Christianity*. In a series called *The Quest for Truth*, in *Young Men of India*, 1928, Andrews speaks of this as a time when "strong personalities may have upset the balance of judgment."

The prophecy of loneliness was fulfilled. Andrews did not publish this document for many years, but he was too transparently honest to keep silent about his doubts, and he was at once accused of heresy. Yet as the letter itself shows, he never wavered in his personal devotion to Christ Jesus the Son of Man.

"Almost all the Indians in London," led by Sarojini Naidu, were waiting at Waterloo Station to welcome and garland him. He spent only three weeks in England, but he carried away two precious memories. One was of intimate talks in Gokhale's sick room in London, when Gokhale implored him to take his politics into his religion and make no divorce between the "being" and the "doing." The other was of his saintly father, softened by age and sorrow, no longer eager to argue his religious views, but listening to Charlie's stories of Gandhi and saying, "God *is* Love ; He accepts all those who love."

On April 17th he landed again in India, "never," so he declared, "to leave it."*

* To Mahatma Munshi Rama, 5th April, 1914.

CHAPTER VII

SANTINIKETAN AND FIJI

1914-1916

I

From the shrine of the West you have brought us living water ;
We welcome you, friend.

The East has offered you her garland of love.
Accept it and welcome, friend.

Your love has opened the door of our heart ;
Enter, and welcome, friend.

You have come to us as a gift of the Lord.
We bow to him, friend.*

SO ran the song of welcome with which Andrews was received
into his new home at Santiniketan, one morning late in April,
1914. But he was not yet free to remain ; there were Punjab
University examination papers to be valued, duties in St. Stephen's
College to be completed, and Government officials in Simla to be
interviewed about the Smuts-Gandhi agreement.

Simla was "worse than South Africa," and Andrews found
himself the centre of a storm. Lord Hardinge and a few other
officials were as friendly as ever, but some very cruel things were
being said about him in both official and Christian circles. The
outcry about his "heresy" was coupled with a demand that he
should "declare himself a Christian," and even some of the Indian
Christians whose battles for racial justice he had fought so often
joined in the reproaches. He remained silent. "If my deeds are
not Christian," he wrote, "no words will make me so."† It was
also widely rumoured that he had some sinister connection with
the "Delhi Conspiracy Case," because he had once befriended one
of the men implicated and because the C.I.D. had discovered

* Bengali original and English translation both by Rabindranath Tagore.
† To Mahatma Munshi Rama, 22nd May, 1914.

104

"seditious views" in Swami Rama Tirtha's writings, to which Andrews had written a preface. When he visited Lahore and resigned his University Fellowship, very few of his colleagues on the Syndicate expressed any gratitude for all he had done or any regret at his going ; and Lahore Hindu circles were full of the tale that he was a Government spy.

Andrews' letters to his most trusted friends alone show how deeply he suffered that month. But they also speak continually of joy, and when he came back to Delhi, Susil Rudra was deeply impressed.

> "There is a brightness and a joy of an unspeakable sort in his face," he wrote. "It is certain that he has got to things which come from felt spiritual power. He moves people wherever he goes."*

Still he was the same old impetuous Andrews. He made a fiery speech to the St. Stephen's College students about South Africa. "You were a bit unfair to the Europeans," suggested a colleague. "I didn't mean to be fair !" blazed Andrews. That was a characteristic outburst, but it was also characteristic that in his second speech he made generous amends.

It was a relief to be in Delhi again among those who loved him. The members of the Cambridge Brotherhood did not all see eye-to-eye with him, but their affection for him was unchanged by his resignation from their work, for they had long realised that he was "a prophet," and that the Brotherhood was not his real sphere. "We need bold ventures and experiments," wrote Allnutt. "It may be that some day we shall have reason to be thankful for what such men as Andrews have been able to achieve as pioneers in a new era of missionary enterprise."†

"Pioneer" was at that time almost the last word which Andrews would have applied to himself. He longed for retirement and quiet ; on June 15th, after ten restful days with Tagore at Ramgarh, he arrived at Santiniketan. Willie Pearson was already there—he had gone there direct from South Africa. They lived together in a corner room close to the poet's quarters, where he worked in a bare little "cell" on the roof. It was an interlude of idyllic peace. Willie Pearson was a genius with boys, and he and

* To J. E. Andrews, 21st May, 1914.
† Cambridge Mission to Delhi, *Report*, 1914.

Andrews coached the younger ones and acted with them by moonlight in an Irish children's play called *The King*. It seemed that Andrews had reached at last what he had so desired—a refuge from the urgent impetuosities of *doing* ; a time of silence and of growth in *being*, a home-coming after storm.

Then, in August, there came the tremendous emotional shock of the outbreak of war. The Boer war had meant little to Andrews ; this time, with his mind full of thoughts about Christ and *ahimsa*, he was compelled to face the issue as a Christian, and came to the conclusion that as a Christian he could not fight.*

This issue however was completely overshadowed by another crisis which had to be faced at the same time. When he went to Santiniketan he had volunteered to Bishop Lefroy to help the church at Burdwan, thirty-five miles away, by occasionally taking services. He liked to think that in that very church Susil Rudra had worshipped as a boy, when his father was its pastor. On his second visit, early in August, he spoke—under the shadow of war —on the Pauline Hymn of Love. But as he conducted the service, taking upon his lips the phrases about which he had so many mental reservations ("I believe in Jesus Christ . . . born of the Virgin Mary—I believe in the Resurrection of the body") the ambiguity of his position suddenly became intolerable. The long indecision was ended—he could continue no longer to trifle with the meaning of words or compromise his intellectual honesty !

Bishop Lefroy was away in England. Andrews wrote to him, saying that he could not conscientiously continue as a priest, and wished to renounce his orders. He told all his friends what he had done, and at the same time sent a statement to the press to prevent the idea going round that he had "renounced Christianity itself."

His action brought him still greater loneliness and suffering. Even Susil Rudra was troubled, though his friendship remained unbroken. The strain under which Andrews had laboured led

* He was nearly forty-four years old, and in Holy Orders. It is not therefore easy to understand how military service could have been a practical issue for him, as he says in *What I Owe to Christ* (p. 277) that it was. None of his many letters or reminiscences of the war period contain the slightest reference to it. The point must remain obscure.

to a serious physical breakdown, and he was treated in a Calcutta nursing home for "nervous dyspepsia." As soon as he could travel, he went into hospital at Simla, oppressed by a terrible sense of failure, but praying humbly that he might not "hit back, or become resentful, or play truant." When he came down again to Delhi a few weeks later, he met the Christian students of his old college. One who was present* has described the scene :

> I can never forget with what patience and humility he listened to our questions and criticisms and how lovingly he answered them. He told us with what great struggle and searchings of heart he took the step of resigning his priesthood—that Jesus shone more in his heart since then untrammelled by dogmas and doctrines . . . He begged us to love him and support him in his Christian witness.

In his extremity Andrews turned to his non-Christian friends, and they did not fail him.

> "Charlie has been writing to me," wrote Gandhi to his father. "— You are likely to be grieved over his having given up the clerical robe. I hope however that such is not the case. His action is no change ; it is, I feel convinced, expansion. He preaches through his life as very few do, and he preaches the purest love . . . Charlie has evidently a mission (of) whose extent even those who are nearest him have no conception. May I plead for your blessings to Charlie in all his work ? It will be such a comfort to him to know that nothing he has done has grieved you."†

In these months Andrews clung to Tagore with a restless devotion which expressed itself, whenever they were separated, in painful and unreasoned anxiety for the poet's health and safety. Tagore met his needs with the insight and patience of genuine friendship. Faithfully he reminded him that human love, when not disinterested, must be shunned at any cost; he saw the tendency for his friend to slip into that vagueness and laxity which two years earlier he had so strongly condemned, and he urged him to return to his God, and to cling fast to the priceless heritage of his Christian devotional life.‡

Sudhir Rudra, on his way to serve with the Y.M.C.A. in France, came to Santiniketan to say goodbye. "Don't you miss the Holy Communion, sir ?" he asked. Andrews pointed to the

---

* Fr. G. Y. Martyn.
† M. K. Gandhi to J. E. Andrews, 20th October, 1914.
‡ cf. Andrews' tribute in *The Visva-Bharati Quarterly*, October, 1925.

little boys playing nearby. "These children are my Holy Communion," he said. The words expressed a very genuine experience—the young man remembered them with gratitude many a day on the Flanders front. Yet much as the "sacrament of common life" meant to Andrews, Tagore was right in his insight, and his influence held Andrews back from any further breach with the liturgical traditions of his past.

In point of fact, Bishop Lefroy did not accept Andrews' impetuous resignation. He agreed that in view of his intellectual and moral difficulties it would be right for him to refrain for the time being from exercising his orders, but he refused to close the door against Andrews' resumption of the Christian ministry if and when he should desire it. In later years Andrews looked back with gratitude on his wise forbearance.

II

Another factor added to the loneliness which Andrews' affectionate nature found so hard to bear. He had not fully realised that the suspicion of being a spy might follow him even to Santiniketan. He and Pearson were the first non-Bengalis to join the staff, and some of their fellow-workers found it difficult at first to believe in their disinterestedness. It was only with Gandhi's help, during the latter's visit to Santiniketan in February, 1915, that Andrews finally overcame these doubts. It was Gandhi who showed him the need for even greater generosity and forbearance towards those who misunderstood him—Gandhi who assured the young Indian teachers that he was worthy of their trust. Before the end of the term his affectionate humility had captured their hearts.

With increasing friendliness life at Santiniketan held plenty of fun and laughter. The *ashram* was soon chuckling over Andrews' attitude to material possessions—his own and other people's. He needed a travelling rug for the journey to Delhi, and as he had given his own to a poor woman with fever, he borrowed one from a young teacher, Sudhakanta Roy Chowdhury.* On his return his servant appeared at Sudhakanta's house with a rug—"a much

* To whom we are indebted for the story.

superior rug, with the name S. K. Rudra on the corner." When this was pointed out to Andrews he merely said, "Well, after all, it's a rug." "Andrews is like a river," commented Rabindranath with a twinkle in his eye. "He enriches one bank at the expense of the other. If you want to lose anything, give it to Andrews."

Many evenings were spent with Dwijendranath Tagore—"Borodada"* as everyone affectionately called him. They soon became fast friends, for Andrews could enter into Borodada's enthusiasm for Sir Walter Scott, his own first literary love ; and he delighted in the old man's robust scorn of the puny present, his magnificent laughter and his sparkling fun.† Most of all he loved him for his humble wisdom and innocence of heart ; and sometimes the old philosopher would speak with him about the few great texts, in the Upanishads, the Bhagavadgita, and the Sermon on the Mount, in which he found the satisfaction of all his needs.

Each week, after his religious discourse in the Mandir, Rabindranath would talk over his teaching with Andrews, discuss the great traditions of Hindu thought and interpret the Upanishads. At other times Andrews spent many hours with Rabindranath's songs and lyrical dramas. There were times when he was intoxicated with their beauty, when his delight in them burst all bounds, and he would spring and leap and sing aloud as he walked alone under the stars in the great open spaces beyond the *ashram*. This poetry could change for him the very light and colour of the world ; yet it was not the magic of word-music that captured him so much as the soaring nobility of thought. Rabindranath's hymns and the great texts of the Upanishads blended in his thoughts with familiar phrases of Christian devotion, and on those solitary walks over the wide plains were shaped the experiences which form the basis of his later books of meditation—*Christ in the Silence, Christ and Prayer*.

With Gandhi's visit to Santiniketan their friendship entered its second phase. When Gandhi returned to India in the winter of 1914-15, he had promised Gokhale that he would take no part in

* "Eldest Brother."

† See *The Visva-Bharati Quarterly*, 1938, for some delightful reminiscences.

Indian politics for a year, and he began to build up a new *ashram* of national service at Sabarmati, near Ahmedabad, on the same lines as "Tolstoy Farm" and "Phoenix" in South Africa. When he visited Santiniketan he urged the boys and teachers there also to do without servants and do all their own cooking and cleaning. Andrews entered with enthusiasm into this experiment, but he was more sceptical of the wisdom of reinforcing it by taking a vow—and on the whole the partisans of the vow stood the test less successfully than the others.

Gandhi then sent Andrews a copy of his proposed Sabarmati Rule ; Andrews replied at length, objecting not to vows as such, but to the inclusion of a vow of celibacy. The central, catholic idea of Hinduism, he contends, is that only a man who "takes with him no empty, attenuated, emasculated life experience, can live truly the life of the Sannyasi."* The word "emasculated" came directly from Tagore, whose teaching reinforced Westcott's social ideal of a consecrated family community. When Andrews visited Sabarmati later in the year, he fell in love with it at once for its service of "the poorest, the lowliest, and the lost,"† but he argued vehemently with Gandhi about his "moral tyranny." ("I never did mind disagreeing with Mr. Gandhi," he once commented. "It only makes us love each other better!")‡

So seriously did he regard the question of the high estate of marriage that he consulted Tagore about whether he should not himself marry, as his friend Stokes had done. He had no particular lady in view, he said, and his uncertain health and fortune made him shrink from the responsibility—but what did Tagore think ? Tagore suggested, roguishly and acutely, an invalid wife !

III

Andrews went up to Calcutta for Rabindranath's birthday celebrations on May 8th, 1915, returning the same evening to Bolpur alone. Twenty-four hours later he was seized with Asiatic cholera. The boys and teachers were nearly all away for

* Letter undated, March-April, 1915.
† *Gitanjali*, No. 10.
‡ To Mahatma Munshi Rama, 16th March, 1916.

their summer holiday. His Muslim cook, Jawahri, nursed him faithfully through the first terrible night, but before a doctor could be got he was so near death that a place was actually chosen for his grave. Tagore, hearing the news, came hurrying to his side ; the knowledge that he was coming, and the sight of his face at last, brought back the flickering desire to live.

A very long convalescence in Simla followed. Rudra was with him, and marvelled at the wonderful serenity of spirit which had transformed the old restless Charlie. To Andrews himself, as he felt his vigour return "like a sudden burst of spring," it seemed that he had come through the Valley of the Shadow to a deeper love and knowledge of Christ, in which was joy and also peace. But his interpretations of Christian experience and of Christ's place in history were as deeply coloured by his intercourse with Tagore as they had been the previous year by Munshi Rama and Gandhi.

> "I must expand the truth of Incarnation," he writes, "to the whole of human life, indwelt by God—His visible Image, His Logos . . . The Atonement must be widened out far far beyond a single act of Christ, however representative . . . I am sure now that Tennyson's craving for individual contact and recognition after death is morbid and wrong. True and simple love must break these bonds, before it is wholly rid of self."*

In the last particular, however, the supreme value he placed upon individual human love was too strong for his theory, and the pendulum soon swung back :

> In the future, after death, shall not the vast Ocean itself be a sounding of even deeper depths—*no loss of consciousness*, but an even larger life ?*

Most of all he brooded on the problems of "being" and "doing" —on God's eternal changelessness and His creative, suffering love :

> Love seems to be *both* an eternal verity, independent of place and form and time, *and* dancing with motion, embodied. Is the Creative Self eternal as the Unchanging Nature ? In the West violent passion has usurped love's place, and in India calm benevolence. It all goes back to our idea of God. What is the *Sat* ? The paradox of motion and rest in one alone satisfies me.

As he grew stronger these thoughts of the eternal paradox were sharpened by new calls to action :

> Simla is the meeting-place for all the wrongs and injustices and tyrannies

---

* Various letters to Rabindranath Tagore, June-October, 1915. (Italics ours.)

of all the millions of all India.   I can find even momentary relief from the strain of cruel wrong only in action . . .   Yet it is all the while merely picking up a grain of sand here and there from the infinite seashore of misery.*

It was then that on the "infinite seashore of misery" he took up the cause of the indentured labourer.   In March, 1912, G. K. Gokhale had made a powerful and eloquent plea in the Central Legislative Assembly that the degrading system of indenture should be abolished, and Andrews had followed his work with the greatest interest.   In South Africa, however, he himself had had little opportunity for direct work of this kind, though the pitiable figure of the run-away coolie who had taken refuge at Phoenix while he was there remained in his mind as a symbol of the system.   Now in Simla there came into his hands a remarkable book called *Fiji of Today*† which drew attention, not only to the strategic importance of Fiji in the Pacific and the significance of Indian immigration there, but also to the scandalous condition of the indentured Indians.   Other evidence poured in.   Official statistics showed that the suicide rate among indentured labourers in Fiji stood at the appalling figure of 926 per million—far higher even than in Natal.   A vivid narrative in Hindi, *My Twenty-one Years in Fiji*, recounted the experiences of Totiram Sanadhya, who had been inveigled into indenture when a boy in Benares.   These, too, Andrews studied.   Meanwhile, he read in the newspapers that the Colonial Sugar Refining Company, the wealthy Australian concern which controlled almost the whole industry in Fiji, had sent a deputation to India to counteract Gokhale's anti-indenture campaign, lest it should ruin their trade.

Gokhale was dead, worn out by his unremitting labours, and Andrews took up his unfinished task.   It came to him as a commission from Christ.

> "One morning about noonday," he writes, "while I was thinking of these things, lying on a chair on the verandah, I saw in front of me the face of a man in a vision. I was not sleeping ; my eyes were quite open. It was that poor run-away coolie I had seen in Natal. As I was looking the face seemed to change in front of me and appeared as the face of Jesus

---

* To R.T., July, 1915.
† By the Rev. J. W. Burton, 1910.

Christ. He seemed to look into my face for a long long time and then the vision faded away."*

He was still very weak, but he spent himself to the uttermost. There was no one to assist him : with his own hand he wrote long, careful memoranda to the Viceroy and to every Provincial Governor he knew, and especially to his friend Sir James Meston, from whose province the majority of Fiji labourers were drawn. Lord Hardinge was not hopeful of success, but he asked Andrews to give all the help he could to the Commerce Department in preparing their despatch to the Secretary of State. This was the famous Despatch No. 41 (Emigration), and it contained the following sentence :

> It is believed in this country, and it would appear not without grave reason, that the women emigrants are too often living a life of immorality in which their persons are at the free disposal of their fellow-recruits and even of the subordinate managing staff.†

It became more and more clear to Andrews that the success of the cause depended on a new and independent investigation of indenture on the spot, and that he was called by God to undertake it. Pearson readily agreed to accompany him ; the expenses were met partly by the Anti-Indentured Labour League of Calcutta and partly by the Imperial Indian Citizenship Association of Bombay.

Before they left India, Andrews personally visited every important Emigration Depot between Allahabad and Calcutta and inquired into the methods of the *arkatis* or professional recruiters. In 1915 these were at their worst. The wages of unskilled labour in North India had risen, and men were not likely to be attracted by the promise of twelve annas‡ a day in Fiji when they could get as much by carrying earth for the foundations of New Delhi. The *arkatis* therefore resorted widely to trickery and even sometimes to hypnotism ; educated lads were promised work as clerks or teachers ; upstanding young Sikhs were attracted by tales of openings in the police ; and the fact that twelve annas in Fiji would scarcely go so far as four annas in India was never

* Unpublished reminiscences. See Appendix for the poem written at this time.

† Dated 25th October, 1915. Published as a supplement to the Government of India *Gazette*, 18th November, 1916.

‡ Roughly one shilling.

I

explained to the simple peasant recruits. Women recruits, for whom a higher rate was paid to the *arkatis*, were secured by sheer kidnapping and intimidation. Andrews estimated that deceit of some kind was practised in eighty per cent. of the cases, and the evidence given him in Fiji confirmed the estimate.

IV

Willie Pearson was an infectiously high-spirited companion, and with him by his side Andrews' own spirits recovered something of the light-hearted fun which had made him the life and soul of St. Stephen's College cricketing tours. Even sea-sickness could be treated as a joke when the pair could quote to each other Tagore's humorous lines about "taking truth simply" :

> Whatever may come, my heart, take truth simply.
> Though there be some who can love you, there must be others who never can !
> Things may or may not fit you, and events happen without asking your leave.
> So if you must have peace, my heart, take truth simply.

They enjoyed shocking their Australian fellow-passengers by their unconventional dress, and still more by their unconventional remarks :

> Willie began by suggesting that the Northern Territory should be handed over bodily to India for colonization. It was a rash and wild utterance—something like telling an Englishman it was time he cleared out of Egypt—and the remark went all round the ship.*

They enjoyed, too, the delightfully human anxiety of the Australians to convince them that Australia was the one country in the world worth living in—a *young* country, that could snap her fingers at time and change.

> " 'Istory !" said one enthusiast, "What's 'istory ? We don't care a rap for 'istory in Australia—we haven't got any. Now, that Westminster Abbey of yours in London : you think it's very fine, don't you ? But do you think I took the trouble to go inside it ? Not I ! We don't want none of your 'istory, we don't. We're a *young* country ! And that other Cathedral, near to Cook's at Ludgate Circus—do you think I went inside that ? Not I ! I did go and watch them pigeons feeding outside, but I never went inside.

* Letter to R.T., 10th October, 1915.

" . . . But I'll tell you one thing that will surprise you—you can get a better afternoon tea in Melbourne than you can get in London ; and you can get a whiskey and soda cheaper in Melbourne. It's a fine city, Melbourne. —Sydney ? Why, Sydney's a mere nothing to it. Melbourne's going to be the finest city in the world some day. I'm a Melbourne man myself and I ought to know." The sun was just setting, spreading out its wings like a golden eagle. I said, "What a wonderful sunset !" He said, "Oh, that's nothing to what you'll get in Melbourne !"

In Melbourne and Sydney they found much friendliness, and as in South Africa, the works of Tagore were an "open sesame" into cultured Australian homes. Only among the officials of the Colonial Sugar Refining Company there was racial arrogance and suspicion :

"Where are your credentials ? The Indian people ?* They are a subject people and can't act that way. You are an agitator ; the Fiji Government will soon send you about your business . . ."

After five hours of this sort of thing one day I went and sat in the City Gardens among the lilac and roses till I got back my sweetness of temper— but I lay awake most of the night afterwards.†

Very early one November morning, under a leaden sky broken with bars of golden light, the mountains of Fiji loomed along the northern horizon. As the ship drew nearer the loveliness of the land appeared—the breakers on the reefs, the green lagoon waters with their gay submarine fairylands of coral, the white ribbon of palm-fringed beach. Andrews soon found that even the wretched Indian labourers had eyes to see its beauty. "Everything God made is beautiful in Fiji," said one lad to him a few days later. "Only man (*sc.* indenture) is bad."

They were only five weeks in Fiji, and worked in different areas during part of the time so as to cover as much ground as possible. On December 7th, when the visit was almost over, Andrews met the Executive Committee of the Planters' Association and put before them the conclusions he had reached, promising to give the fullest consideration to any evidence which in their view pointed in another direction. He gave warm praise to the Company for its excellent schemes of land settlement for the freed labourers who remained in Fiji after their indenture had

* Andrews was accredited by the Indian National Congress.
† To R.T., 23rd October, 1915.

expired, and to the Government for the strictly enforced law forbidding the free sale of intoxicating liquor to the Indian community. He recognized the existence of many well-managed estates belonging to humane employers whose indentured labourers were contented and happy. But he made it plain that the *system* of indenture must go. "I am anxious that Indians should come to Fiji," he told them, "but the conditions must be consistent with India's self-respect."

The conditions he then laid down were the starting-point of all his future work for Indian labourers abroad ; in after years he insisted on the same principles in a dozen different situations. No labour contract could be contemplated which was not a free *civil* contract ; no recruiting except in *family* units. Good houses with proper privacy must replace the filthy "lines" where men and women were herded like cattle with no respect for the sanctities of family life. A good public steamer service should replace the disgraceful "coolie ships," and keep Fiji in healthy contact with India. Andrews spoke with a touch of fire about the degradation of marriage :

> You have treated their religion as though it were nothing at all. You have simply made them pay five shillings and give in their names at the Registry Office, and then they were married. *When* they were married exactly, no one could tell ; and this has gone on for thirty-two years ! I am thankful that the Colony is taking it up and recognizing the sacred side of marriage.

The evidence on which these recommendations were based was never challenged. It was not a pleasant task to lay it before the Company's unsympathetic officials in Sydney, but when Lord Hardinge saw it, he at once accepted Pandit M. M. Malaviya's motion for the abolition of indenture, and on March 20th, 1916, he announced in the Imperial Legislative Assembly :

> I have obtained from His Majesty's Government the promise of the abolition of the system in due course—that is, within such reasonable time as will allow of alternative arrangements being introduced.

"We feel today," wrote Andrews to Mr. N. B. Mitter, who had been his interpreter in Fiji, "that God has overwhelmed us with His goodness in allowing us to have our share in this great fact. It means the taking away of one more abomination from

God's earth."* "Yesterday when the news arrived," wrote Pearson, "our *ashram* had a holiday and all the boys rejoiced with us. I am so glad and want to say Joy ! Joy ! Joy ! and *Jai ! Jai ! Jai !"†*

The joint report was published on February 19th, 1916, and was dedicated to the memory of G. K. Gokhale. Its temperate but relentless pages reveal its author's anger, not only about the unspeakable moral degradation of a life in which it was the best men, not the worst, who committed murder, but also about the utter meanness of the subterfuges by which the labourer might be exploited. When the "agricultural work" specified in the contract could be made to include driving the loaded sugar-trains, the employer was getting skilled labour from his more intelligent coolies at a fraction of the market rate, and recognizing no obligation to compensate them for injury by accident. Andrews' passionate love of fair play revolted against the injustice of it, just as his passionate chivalry leaped out to save womanhood from an intolerable wrong.

But the thought of the children haunted him most of all— children doomed from babyhood to disease and vice. For there would rise up, in poignant contrast, the memory of three happy days spent on the journey out at Christchurch in New Zealand, where his younger sister Maggie had welcomed him to her colonial home. As Charlie watched her among her little ones he was deeply moved, for in every look and gesture his own dead mother seemed to live again. The children had swarmed over Uncle Charlie, and listened with shining eyes to his tales of the wonderland of India. They had their birthright of happiness and health. But the children of the coolie lines had nothing—not even the innocence of childhood. Andrews pictured the Son of Man's eyes flashing with anger, and the stern words spoken of the man who should cause the little ones to stumble rang in his ears : Better for him that a mill-stone were hanged about his neck and that he were drowned in the depth of the sea ! These were the things that in 1917 sent him back to Fiji.

* To H. B. Mitter, 24th March, 1916.
† "Victory !" In Bengali the word sounds much like the English "joy."

CHAPTER VIII

THE END OF INDENTURED LABOUR

1916-1918   AGE 45-47

I

THE year 1916 brought Andrews another interlude of silence and happy growth. He and Pearson lived together at Santiniketan, Pearson devoted to his boys, Andrews working with Tagore at his translations. Peals of laughter would ring out continually from the room where they worked. Andrews also attended Rabindranath's memorable school classes on Shelley, listening to the Bengali explanations and helping with "revision classes" and the teaching of English composition.

He had little of Willie Pearson's genius with boys. He delighted to watch their tireless energy, and he would return to the *ashram* after his absences with gifts of toys and games, but he soon grew weary of their continual company. A sick boy would call out all his devotion ; and once when some difficult boys were about to be expelled, it was Andrews who pleaded that they should be given another chance, and whose influence helped them to make good. But in general he was more at home with older students and teachers.

There was one boy however who became an unusually close companion. This was "Mulu" Prasad Chatterji, whose quick and practical sympathy with the downtrodden made Andrews feel that he could talk with him about South Africa and Fiji as freely as with many a man of twice his years. Mulu would spend his evenings in the villages, teaching the Santal and Dom children and playing games with them ; with Andrews' backing he was one of Santiniketan's pioneers in social service.

In May, 1916, Rabindranath paid a long-projected visit to Japan. Andrews, Pearson, and the artist Mukul Dey went with him. They had a wonderful welcome, and Andrews took on

himself the task of defending the poet against the hundreds of
reporters and other persistent people who swarmed round them.

"We have been trying to see the humorous side of it and 'take truth
simply'," he writes. "Willie is having the time of his life with Mukul as
a companion enjoying all the new things. I cannot enter into it all in the
way they do as I am too occupied with inner problems and thoughts."*

The problems which occupied him were concerned with the
national life of Japan—the threat of vulgar commercialism to the
ancient love of beauty, the danger that the chivalrous Samurai
ideal of purity, simplicity and truth should be degraded into an
idolatry of war. Two incidents of Tagore's tour made a profound
impression upon him. Tagore was requested to write a verse of
commemoration for two popular heroes who had fought to the
death in pursuance of a private feud. He heard the request in
silent distress ; silently, a little while later, he handed over the
lines which were his answer :

They hated and killed, and men praised them ;
But God in shame hastened to hide its memory under the green grass.

Tagore's outspoken criticism of a narrow nationalism earned him
the taunt of being "the poet of a defeated nation." His reply was
the lovely *Song of the Defeated*. The memory of how his sensitive
humanity had been wounded by this aggressive militarism
coloured all Andrews' later work for the nationalist cause in India.

The visit to Japan left another permanent impress upon
Andrews' thought. It was his first introduction to Buddhism as
a living religious force. The Buddhist traditions of Japan quickened his imagination and set him dreaming of the past. One of
his happiest memories was of how their train stopped at a little
wayside station for the poet to receive the salutations of a company
of Buddhist monks. He pictured heroic Buddhist missionaries
reaching Japan from Bengal along the very route by which he
himself had travelled. In June Pearson went on with Tagore to
the United States, but Andrews and Mukul Dey returned to India,
and on the return journey they spent a week in Java and visited
the great remains of Buddhist civilisation at Borobudur. The
moon was full, and night after night Andrews wandered alone in
the great galleries, with the calm stone figure of the Buddha

* To Gogonendranath Tagore, undated.

meeting him at every turn. In the quiet hours there flooded into his heart a fresh insight into the significance of that supreme personality of Asiatic history.

> There came to me a new vision of humanity in its suffering and sorrow, its sacrifice and love of service, intimately bound up with the supreme personality of the Buddha himself . . . preaching to the lowest of the human race—nay, preaching also as St. Francis did to the very birds and beasts and trees and flowers, the same message of universal love.*

The experience brought no dramatic outward change in the direction of his life ; but it set the seal, as it were, upon those experiences in South Africa and Santiniketan which had so profoundly modified the point of view from which he regarded the religious strivings of mankind. Once and for all the European perspective was left behind.

II

Andrews' return to India was due partly to ill-health, but partly also to disturbing reports about Fiji. There was a rumour that the Indian and Colonial Offices had made a pact that recruitment for indenture should be continued for a further period of five years. Lord Hardinge's term as Viceroy had come to an end, and Lord Chelmsford had taken his place. Andrews wrote to him for information, but up till the end of 1916 he had received no satisfaction. He therefore challenged the Government in the public press. When the existence of the pact with the Colonial Office was confirmed, a great wave of indignation swept the country, and Andrews left Santiniketan to share in the nation-wide campaign for the immediate stoppage of all recruitment.

In such a cause Gandhi was the unquestioned leader, and he brooked no half-measures. "We shall picket the coolie-ships," he declared, "if the system is not ended by the thirty-first of May." He marshalled his men ; Polak, who had done so much already to publicise the scandals of indenture, lectured from end to end of India. Andrews himself went from city to city utterly regardless of the limits of his own physical endurance. At Allahabad he was prostrated by one of the severe choleraic attacks to which after 1915 he was always liable. Weak and in pain, he continued

* *Modern Review*, 1922.

to dictate his letters and appeals from his bed in Sapru's house. As soon as loving nursing could set him on his feet he was off again, to Madras—Poona—Bombay—Delhi, where he found himself charged with "stirring up hatred in war-time."

He had his reply ready. He pointed to the damning Despatch 41*, which thanks to his exertions had been adopted as the official opinion of the Government of India, and had been published as such only a few months earlier. "The Government of India cannot write that despatch," he declared, "and then agree to send Indian women to such a life for five years more." The appeal for the honour of women had in fact been the keynote of all his speeches, and he had made the appeal *to women* even more than to men. An attempt to rally women's opinion on a matter of public policy was something new, and it succeeded beyond all expectations. Andrews' appeal to Indian women on behalf of their sisters in Fiji was printed in several Indian languages and distributed in thousands at the *Magh Mela*, the great annual fair of Allahabad. "In a few days it was the talk of all the United Provinces." A deputation of Indian ladies sought and obtained an interview with the Viceroy. Lord Chelmsford listened ; he also saw Gandhiji. On April 12th he announced the cessation of all recruitment as a special war measure under the Defence of India Act.

It was clear, however, that the whole question might be revived at the end of the war. Andrews therefore went back to Fiji to study every aspect of the case in detail, carrying with him, in lieu of Willie Pearson's laughing comradeship, the gay and gallant lyrics of Tagore's newly-published *Cycle of Spring*. On May 25th he was keeping his mother's birthday in Australia when good news came from England. Mr. Chamberlain had declared in the House of Commons that the indenture system would *not* be revived.

In spite of this auspicious coincidence, however, conditions in Fiji seemed even more desperate than before. The effects of the war were being felt. The cost of living rose steeply, and indentured labourers starved ; one man, on trial for attempted suicide, confessed that he could not bear any longer to hear his children cry for food. The obligation to provide a return passage

* See Chapter VII, p. 113.

to India for those who desired it on the expiry of their contract was being evaded "because there were no ships," while Indian leaders in Suva commented bitterly that there were always plenty of ships for the sugar cargoes. A labourer who had left his little daughter in India followed Andrews pathetically from place to place to ask the same unanswerable question—when could he get a ship ? Andrews embraced him with tears in his eyes, counselling patience, but with hot indignation in his heart.

Faced with this human misery, he set himself three immediate objectives. The first was an increase in the wages of indentured labour. By dogged persistence he got the standard daily wage increased by twenty-five per cent.—threepence a day—from August, 1917. It was far too little, but it was all he could do. His second aim was to protect the wife whose term of indenture expired at a later date than her husband's. He persuaded the "North side" planters to agree that she should be freed when her husband's term expired, instead of being compelled to complete her contract. The proposal was rejected by the Governor's Committee, which represented planters, officials and the Fiji Legislative Council ; the committee proposed instead that husband and wife might be required jointly to work off the remainder of her indenture.

> "That is," commented Andrews, "the wife's position of extreme moral danger is to be exploited to give the employer the advantage of a man's work instead of a woman's. There are certain public actions which speak volumes as to the general level of opinion reached in any small community, and this appears to be one of them."*

Thirdly, he asked for the cancellation of all remaining indentures by January 1st, 1920. Again the North Side planters agreed ; again the Governor's Committee refused, saying that a new system of "free" immigration must first be established.

Nevertheless, Andrews did not despair. There was a higher court of appeal than the Governor's Committee, and his painstaking study of every relevant "blue book" and table of statistics had given him a piece of corroborative evidence of the utmost value. When he returned to India early in March, 1918, Mr. Montagu, the Secretary of State, was with the Viceroy in Delhi.

* *Modern Review*, September, 1918.

Andrews laid before him the official Medical Report of the Government of Fiji.* "When one indentured Indian woman," ran the damning admission, "has to serve three indentured men as well as various outsiders, the result as regards syphilis and gonorrhoea cannot be in doubt."

"That settles it," said Montagu. "Ask what you like."

On January 1st, 1920, the last indentured labourer was free.

III

Many men would have been content with such an achievement. Not so Andrews. In 1917 he was in Fiji for over four months, and by far the greater part of his time was given to the building up of a free and healthy Indian community life. He made himself familiar with every situation which might hold the seeds of racial friction in a country which was still happily free from colour prejudice. One such was the Indian's position as tenant of tribal land ; another, the economic grievances of Indian "labour" against white "capital." He worked untiringly at practical plans for health and education, for the raising of the marriage age and the restoration of the shattered family life. He made long tours through the districts where Indians were settled, sleeping anywhere, sometimes with a friendly planter, more often in the tiny Indian homes. One planter who had given him a casual invitation to "drop in when he wanted a bed," arrived home late one evening to find Andrews asleep in the bed, while his Indian cook was in the seventh heaven of delight that he should have been privileged to serve him. When the host woke at dawn next day the guest was seated on a rocky ridge a quarter of a mile away, deep in meditation. The planter never saw him again—he was off to the next little Indian settlement to plead, perhaps for the hundredth time, for cleanliness, education, the care of the sick.

In dealing with the Colonial Government Andrews showed a disconcerting mastery of the facts of history. Lord Salisbury had declared in 1876, when indentured labour was first recruited : "Above all things we must confidently expect as an indispensable condition of the proposed arrangements, that the Colonial laws

* Council Paper, 54.

and their administration will be such that Indian settlers who have completed their term of service will be in all respects free men with privileges no whit inferior to those of any other class of Her Majesty's subjects resident in the Colonies." Andrews reminded Fiji of the practical implications of that pledge, not only in matters of political franchise, but in the organisation of educational and health services.

Little by little, progress was made. After wearisome negotiations the Education Department was won over to the principle that village schools working in Hindi should be eligible for grants-in-aid,* and an enlightened planter, Mr. R. A. Horricks, carried the necessary Bill through the Legislative Council. Teachers were found and a few schools were actually started. Some of the smaller sugar companies promised to employ women matrons in their district hospitals if qualified women could be found. It was hard, lonely, uphill work, difficult in itself, and made still more difficult by official coldness and the hostility of the wealthy Company whose profits Andrews had challenged. The Company report for 1917-18 accused him of being "in league with well-known leaders of sedition whose object is to overthrow the British Empire" ; even on the Indian side a fanatical Arya Samaj missionary, with whom he had done his utmost to work on friendly terms, accused him of "double-dealing." Sick at heart and sick in body he struggled on, and if sometimes he lent too credulous an ear to tales of wrong and oppression, or spoke with a bitterness which seemed unfair to those well-intentioned planters who blundered only through ignorance, these were the faults of a loving nature burdened almost beyond endurance. It was among the Indians of Fiji that he was first named, in 1917, "Deenabandhu," the Friend of the Poor.

Tendentesque manus ripae ulterioris amore†—that immortal phrase of poignant yearning came back to Andrews' mind as he watched the half-starved, homesick people who stood on the quay as his ship drew away from Suva, and heard the cry that wrung his heart with pity—"Send us ships : let us go back to India."

* Which had formerly been confined to schools working in English.

† "And stretching out their hands in sick longing for the farther shore," Virgil.

In Fiji he had associated very closely with the Fijian Christians ; when he reached Australia he once more came into touch with the religious life of his own people, after more than three years of almost complete isolation. He warned the churches of the terrible danger that the evils of the coolie lines would infect the Fijian population also. He challenged Australian Christians with Christ's stern words about those who "offend these little ones."

"May there not be something to repent of in Christian Australia," he demanded, "where the wealthiest company in the land is now grown rich and prosperous out of this very indentured labour with its terrible fruits ?"*

He challenged Australian women with his picture of the degradation of womanhood for profit. The Company fought him with all its wealth and influence.

Stage by stage Andrews travelled westward across the great continent. Worn out as he was, the burden of his self-appointed task seemed almost intolerable, and when at last he reached Fremantle he was filled with a desperate home-sickness for India. Yet on the very point of embarkation he was constrained by a strong inward constraint to remain in Australia. He travelled right through the country for a second time, and was rewarded : two ladies with experience in India volunteered for work among Indian women ; a qualified nurse offered him her services and was appointed to the District Hospital of the Melbourne Trust ; the Australian Women's Association resolved to make their own inquiry in Fiji—an inquiry whose report confirmed his at every point. The women did other things—they mended his ragged coats and shirts and replenished his stock of socks and handkerchiefs ; but so absorbed was he in his work that he never noticed the difference !

IV

The wonderful transformation of Indian life in Fiji since 1920 is due to many factors ; the greatness of Andrews' contribution is in the fact that he not only secured the abolition of a system which made all progress impossible, but also understood the positive conditions which were essential to the progress of the community,

* Speech to Australian Christian students, reported in the *Modern Review*, May, 1918.

and from the first did his utmost to secure them. The qualities of mind and character by which he succeeded are well summed up in one of the tributes paid to him after his death :

> On the surface it seemed as though the gentle sentimentalist had little chance of bargaining with hard-boiled industrialists and matter-of-fact officials, but when they met it was the prophet in homespun who was fit to get the better of the men of the world. His intellect retained the keen edge of its Cambridge days, his memory was a storehouse of facts, and he added to both an intense perception of broad moral issues. To the innocence of the dove he united the wisdom of the serpent, and the unexpected combination often produced inspiring results.*

To these qualities we may add a third—that which endeared him so greatly to so many—the limitless generosity of his friendliness to the humble and obscure. It was like him to take a long special journey across New Zealand, when he might have been resting with his sister, to give a few hours' pleasure to a tiny group of Gujerati woodsmen ; it was like him to spend his last morning in Fiji pleading for mercy for a condemned murderer who, like so many others, had been more sinned against than sinning.†

"The abolition of the indentured labour system," said a distinguished Civil Servant‡ who had known him since his Cambridge days, "was Andrews' greatest single service to the Indian people."

POSTSCRIPT

There was no indentured labour in India itself, but the men driven by grim circumstances to leave their village homes for the great city mills were only too often as badly housed, as disastrously cut off from healthy family life, as ruthlessly exploited, as those on the Fijian sugar estates. If they were not so hopelessly isolated by distance and the ocean from home ties, they were often worse off than the indentured labourers in the nature and circumstances of their work. The sugar fields were preferable to the stifling heat and filth of the factories, and the surroundings of the most disgraceful "coolie lines" were cleaner and sweeter than those of an Indian slum tenement. "There is no need to go to South

* T. G. Spear in the Andrews Memorial Number of *The Stephanian*, 1940.
† He heard in New Zealand that his plea had been successful.
‡ Sir Geoffrey de Montmorency, in a conversation.

Africa or Fiji," commented Andrews' friends. "The same evils are rampant in our own industrial cities."

Towards the end of 1918 Andrews had an opportunity to test that statement. Fiji was not the only country affected by the wartime rise in the cost of living, and Indian industrial workers were beginning to organise themselves to fight for a living wage. Gandhi had already led such a struggle in Ahmedabad, and later in the year the newly-formed Madras Labour Union became involved in a dispute with the management of the Buckingham and Carnatic Mills. The latter declared a lockout and refused to recognize the representative status of the Union or to negotiate with it. This was the essential point at issue, and Mr. B. P. Wadia, one of the organisers of the Union, asked Andrews to come to Madras and help them.

Andrews lived in the Labour Union headquarters, surrounded by the workers' own homes. His mediation ended the lockout (the management promising to recognize the Union), and after the dispute was over he remained to study the working of the mills. They were among the best in the country, yet the resemblance to Fiji at some points was all too close. Respectable labourers were living in villages five or six miles away, and walking daily to and from their work, in spite of the twelve-hour shift which was then customary, "because they didn't like the people's habits near the mill." It was not difficult to guess what that meant. The proportion of men to women in the "lines" was three to one, drunkenness and prostitution were rife, and men spoke of "mill dustoor"* as they had spoken in Fiji of "Fiji dustoor."

"What was needed," an intelligent workman said to Andrews, "was a powerful and trustful Labour Union." Andrews knew that so long as the headmen in the mills were corrupt, trustworthiness could only be secured by the help of disinterested social workers, and he appealed for young educated men to give themselves to this nation-building work. His concern for the indentured labourer thus led direct to his later work for the welfare of industrial workers in India.

* "The custom of the mill."

CHAPTER IX

THE AFTERMATH OF WAR— AMRITSAR

1918-1919   AGE 47-48

I

ON the outbreak of war in August, 1914. England had had the full moral support of India, and it was confidently expected that when the war was over Indians "would become the free and equal citizens of a great Empire."* But during the next two years much of the original goodwill was lost. Among Muslims it had always been a difficulty "that the Government of our Caliph should be at war with the Government of our King-Emperor,"† and internments on small suspicion made the administration unpopular. In 1916 the Congress and the Muslim League prepared the agreed scheme for self-government known as the Lucknow Pact; early in 1917, Mrs. Besant, B. P. Wadia, and G. S. Arundale were interned for voicing the demand for immediate Home Rule, though they were not under restriction for long.

On August 20th, 1917, Mr. Montagu, as Secretary of State for India, made in the House of Commons his historic statement of British policy—"the progressive realisation of responsible self-government in India as an integral part of the British Empire." During the following winter he visited India to confer with the Viceroy; and the Montagu-Chelmsford report on political reforms was published on July 12th, 1918.

Unfortunately the report of the Rowlatt Commission on the causes and control of revolutionary terrorism followed hard on its heels. The proposals of the Commission included certain provisions for the trial of revolutionary suspects, and restrictions on the publication of evidence which

* Sir S. P. Sinha, Congress Presidential Address, Bombay, 1915.
† Muslim League Presidential Address, 1915.

"were at once taken to imply the denial to the individual of the right to be tried openly by his peers. . . .

"Inevitably the two reports were read together, and educated Indians can hardly be blamed for the conclusions they drew . . . They had confidently expected a complete change in their status, and they now saw the Government of India taking new powers for repressive action, and the proposed reforms being whittled down by unsympathetic officials and a hostile Parliament."*

Other factors—poor harvests, high prices—increased the general discontent ; and Indian soldiers, hastily demobilised and with the promises made to them unfulfilled, drifted back to their villages disappointed and dissatisfied. But at the root of the widespread resentment which followed the Armistice was the feeling that the British were making a determined if unavowed effort to return to pre-war conditions.

The National Congress at Delhi in December, 1918, protested that the "Rowlatt Bills" interfered with the fundamental rights of the Indian people. The Bills were nevertheless published in January, 1919, and passed by the Legislative Council in the third week of March, though not a single non-official Indian member voted for them. Simultaneously, Gandhi published his "Rowlatt pledge" of civil disobedience ; those who took it pledged themselves to break any law which might be selected by the directing committee (short of infringing morals) as a protest against the new legislation. On March 30th a *hartal*† for public mourning was observed in Delhi. Hindus and Muslims were united : for the first time in the history of the great Jama Masjid mosque, a Hindu, Swami Sraddhananda,‡ was invited to speak in its precincts. On the following Sunday, April 6th, there was a *hartal* throughout India, and Gandhi and Sarojini Naidu spoke in mosques in Bombay.

So far the demonstrations had been peaceful, except for a disturbance in Delhi, where the police had opened fire. But the arrest of popular leaders in the Punjab during the following week provoked serious and widespread riots in which buildings were

---

* Thompson and Garrett : *The Rise and Fulfilment of British Rule in India*, p. 604.

† Cessation of work.

‡ i.e., Andrews' friend, Mahatma Munshi Rama.

K

burned and several Europeans killed. On April 13th, the Hindu New Year's Day and an important public holiday, a public meeting was announced in an enclosed piece of ground at Amritsar known as the Jallianwala Bagh, and large crowds gathered there. These crowds were ruthlessly fired on by troops under the command of General Dyer, and there were many casualties. Next day violent rioting broke out at Gujranwala, and was punished by bombing and machine-gunning from the air. Large areas of the Punjab were placed under martial law. Gandhi called off his campaign ; it was, he said, a "Himalayan blunder" to have called the people to non-violent revolt before they were disciplined for it.

Andrews was with Rabindranath Tagore on a tour of South India while the Rowlatt Bills were being debated. He wrote to Gandhi that he thought that only *satyagraha* (non-violent civil disobedience) would be effective against them, but he was doubtful of the ethics of submitting to a committee's judgment in the matter. He took no active part in events, however, until reports of the Punjab disturbances reached Santiniketan. Then he could no longer bear to stand aside. On April 17th he arrived in Delhi, intending to go straight to the Punjab.

Susil Rudra, Swami Sraddhananda and other friends urged him with one voice to stay in Delhi itself and do what he could to avert the threat of martial law with all its attendant miseries. Large elements of the European population were seized with a hysteria like that of 1907, and the Anglo-Indian press was doing its utmost to stampede the local authorities into repressive action—"nothing appeared too provocative for the censor to pass." Andrews knew of at least one clear case of the use of the *agent provocateur*. A man had come rushing down the Chandni Chowk in the heart of Delhi crying out that Swami Sraddhananda had been arrested. By a fortunate accident the Swami's son happened to be passing. "It's a lie," he shouted as the people ran excitedly together. "My father is safe at home." The mischief-maker fled and disappeared, and what might have been a serious riot was thus prevented.*

For days together Andrews worked late into the night, collect-

* See *To the Students*, p. 55.

ing all the available facts about the *hartal* where the trouble had started, and keeping in the closest touch with the District Commissioner and the Chief of Police. Confidence was at last restored and martial law was not declared.

Meanwhile ugly stories were reaching Delhi of the methods used to "restore order" in Amritsar. There had been public floggings ; in one street where an Englishwoman had been assaulted, all Indians were being made to "crawl," although it was the people of that same street who had rescued her from the mob. Andrews stayed only to satisfy himself that his witnesses were speaking truth, and went up to Simla, with the words of bitterly insulted men ringing in his ears : "Take away your d—d reforms ! We don't want them and we won't have them. Answer us this—are we to be treated like serfs ?"*

With difficulty he obtained a hearing, and a promise that flogging should be stopped. It had done its work, officials assured him ; it had restored the Government's "moral prestige." Andrews subdued with difficulty the white heat of his anger. He had brought no empty protest, but a solid programme of conciliation. Let there be Orders in Council, he urged, by which the consent of the provincial Legislature must be obtained before the Rowlatt Acts could be applied to any province ; let the Press Act be impartially administered, the Muslim leaders, Mohammed and Shaukat Ali, released from internment,† and Sir Edward Maclagan ("a true gentleman loved by all") installed speedily as Governor of the Punjab. The officials listened coldly ; baffled and defeated, Andrews felt he could do no more.

Meanwhile *The Tribune*, a responsible nationalist newspaper of Lahore, had been suspended for a week, and its editor, Mr. Kalinath Roy, placed on trial for sedition, on the strength of certain articles published in the first two weeks of April. The other Indian newspaper editors in the city asked Andrews for his help and mediation, and he started out for Lahore at once. When his train reached Amritsar on the morning of May 12th he found himself under military arrest. "It was not in the public interest,"

---

* Letter to Rabindranath Tagore, April, 1919.

† They were interned in January, 1915, under the Defence of India rules.

he was told, that he should enter the Punjab. In the late afternoon he was examined and sent back to Delhi. The examining Commissioner had been his contemporary at Pembroke !

The *Tribune* case wounded him deeply. It was not merely that he thought the whole prosecution unjustified ; worse than that was the action of the Punjab Government in prohibiting Mr. Eardley Norton, the Calcutta barrister whom Kalinath Roy had briefed in his defence, from entering the martial law area. This seemed to Andrews a "flagrant denial of British justice," but all his efforts to get the order rescinded failed. He went back to Tagore, and was with him at the end of May in Calcutta when the poet publicly renounced his knighthood, as the most effective protest against the course of events which it was in his power to make.

II

To Andrews the records of British international diplomacy in 1918-19 were as disturbing as the events in India. In May, 1918, Lord Chelmsford had invited Gandhi to the Imperial War Conference in Delhi, and Gandhi had asked Andrews to join him. In the train on his way there Andrews read in the English *New Statesman* an account of the predatory "secret treaties" unearthed by revolutionaries from the Russian Foreign Office ; Great Britain was a signatory of these treaties, notwithstanding her public declarations of the disinterestedness of her fight for freedom. Andrews thrust the papers before Gandhi. "How can you take part in a war-conference while this sort of double-dealing is going on ?" he demanded. Gandhi thought the case "not proven," and decided to give Britain the benefit of the doubt ; he went off on his recruiting campaign, as he had promised, and Andrews continued the argument vehemently by correspondence, changing his ground to that of pacifism and *ahimsa* :

> I do not see the analogy of the dumb man in your letter. It seems dangerously near the argument that the Indian who has forgotten altogether the blood-lust might be encouraged to learn it again first and then repudiate it afterwards of his own account . . . At the same time I do agree with you entirely that it is a free India choosing her own path which can give the world the highest example of *ahimsa*, not the present subjected

India. But even then—cannot you conceive of that very freedom being won by moral force only, not by the creation of a standing army to meet the army of occupation ?*

In December, 1918, the National Congress meeting at Delhi asked that India should *elect* her delegates to the Peace Conference. This suggestion was ignored, and the representatives of India were nominated by the Government. The history of the Peace Conference confirmed Andrews' suspicions that double-dealing had in fact taken place ; and when the Viceroy called for national thanksgiving for "the triumphant peace which under the mercy of Providence has been vouchsafed us," Andrews bluntly called the appeal blasphemous, and denounced the treaty as unjust and dishonourable.†

To his thinking there was a further ominous significance in the compromises on the principle of racial equality which had been found "necessary" in framing the constitution of the League of Nations. No sooner was the war over than the old troubles raised their heads in South Africa, and Andrews regarded the points at issue in the Transvaal and in the Punjab as essentially the same.

> The Declaration of Rights alone is vital *in India and South Africa*, and all "reforms" are absolutely useless while fundamental human rights remain insecure.‡

When the Government-nominated delegates returned from Versailles with descriptions of the equal honour they had received with other Dominion representatives, Andrews retorted with an eloquent piece of plain speaking :

> When an attempt was made to include, in the preamble of the League of Nations, a brief statement asserting the principle of racial equality, this proposal was rejected as likely to wreck the whole conference—South Africa and Canada being loudest of all in their opposition.
>
> Japan had been the first to bring forward this proposal, but her *amour propre* was satisfied in other directions. She was given the German Territorial "rights," so-called—the rights of the robber and the spoiler— in the great Shantung province of China. She was allowed to treat Korea as a conquered country whose internal affairs were no concern of the League of Nations.

* To M. K. Gandhi, 23rd June, 1918.
† Statement to the Press, 9th July, 1919. See also *Modern Review*, August, 1919.
‡ *The Bombay Chronicle*, 3rd August, 1919. (Italics ours).

China alone withdrew altogether from the treaty, refusing to be a party to her own disruption and disintegration . . . Will she be able to hold out for long ?

Where was India all this while ? Shepherded by the Secretary of State, the representatives of India raised no voice of indignant protest on behalf of the helpless Koreans or the despoiled Chinese, or on behalf of the equality of all races within the Parliament of Man. No delegate from India refused to sign the Peace Treaty.

It was a subtle irony of fate that on the very day when the Maharajah of Bikaner was making his impassioned speech about the growing recognition of India within the Empire, public meetings had to be held in different parts of India to protest against the new indignities that were being heaped upon Indians in the *Transvaal within the Empire*.*

III

During the summer of 1919 Andrews received many requests for help in various kinds of labour problems. The one that touched him most was an invitation from the planters of Malaya, where he had spent three weeks on the way back from Fiji, to make recommendations on labour conditions for their guidance. But with the thought that he might be needed in the Punjab in his mind, he could not go so far afield. He spent most of August in a labour investigation in Ceylon. When he returned the ban on his entry to the Punjab had been withdrawn and Sir Edward Maclagan had taken office as Governor. Among his first official acts was a drastic reduction of the sentences in the "Lahore Conspiracy Case," and the release of the editor of *The Tribune*, Kalinath Roy.

On September 4th the Viceroy announced the appointment of the Hunter Commission of inquiry. Pandit Madan Mohan Malaviya headed the Congress committee for the preparation of evidence, to which Andrews was at once co-opted. It was doubtful from the first whether he would be able to remain in India to give evidence in person, and his chief aim was therefore to heal the wounded self-respect of the cowed and terrified people, and "to make the path quite plain and simple for others to give evidence without any fear of the police or the C.I.D."†

* *The Bombay Chronicle*, 5th August, 1919. (Italics original.)

† To R.T., September, 1919 ; see also *The Tribune*, 7th November, 1919.

He wired first to Karachi for Gurdial Mallik. Gurdial had been one of Sir N. G. Chandarvarkar's students in Bombay when Andrews returned from Fiji in January, 1916. The lecturer had brought his guest to the class, and Gurdial had said to him, "Sir, India is grateful to you." He had been greatly struck by Andrews' reply, "My boy, it is I who should be grateful to India for being what I am." When his course was finished Gurdial had visited Santiniketan, where Andrews befriended him again. Now he came eagerly to help.

In Lahore and Amritsar Andrews was joyfully welcomed. The people thronged the house where he stayed from morning till night, coming to tell their stories. In Lahore there was much that he could do as mediator. To and fro he went between Government House and the committee's headquarters in Ferozepur Road, explaining difficulties, making suggestions, till his fellow-workers dubbed him "the Shuttlecock" ! He would ponder some plan of conciliation far into the night and then be off betimes to Government House on a bicycle, clad in some disreputable dressing-gown, and hard put to it sometimes to gain admission. He won concessions of great practical value, such as a public scrutiny of the accounts and estimates for the "punitive tax" imposed on the riot areas ; and it was his advocacy that secured the release of the Punjab patriot Bhai Parmanand from the Andamans Penal Settlement a few weeks later.

Then with Gurdial Mallik as companion he visited the villages. In Ramnagar, it was alleged, an effigy of the King-Emperor had been burned. The people were terror-stricken, and every effort to persuade them to tell the true story failed. The last night came; Andrews was sleepless and in pain with one of his recurrent attacks of choleraic dysentery. He spent the hours in prayer. Then the two men went together to the village *Gurdwara* where men and women had gathered at dawn for worship. When the singing and scriptural readings were over Andrews came forward and with clasped hands pleaded earnestly that they should speak. "And lo, the very priest, who had so long refused to open his lips, stood forward and related the whole story, from beginning to end, with childlike candour."*

* Reminiscences by Gurdial Mallik, *Visva-Bharati Quarterly*, 1940.

At Sangla a man slipped furtively into Andrews' room at midnight, handed him a roll of papers, and was gone. After Andrews returned to Lahore, he began to work on his private report for Lord Hunter, and turned these papers up. They purported to be eye-witnesses' evidence of the behaviour of the military, but he was unhappy about them—they did not ring true. As he pondered restlessly, a Moslem tailor from Sangla appeared in the doorway. "Saheb," he said, "it isn't true. We were made to write that, to throw dust in your eyes. But after you had gone I could not be easy, for there is something in your face that compels a man to speak the truth."

While they were in Gujranwala they heard of a certain *lambardar* whose village was on the railway line about twenty miles from Lahore. Telegraph wires had been cut, and the *lambardar*, a man who had served in the army with courage and distinction, had been seized on suspicion and publicly flogged. He was quite innocent, and the insult so preyed on his mind that his friends feared for his reason. Andrews sought him out.

"Go away," said the *lambardar* bluntly. "I've nothing to say. I've had enough of Englishmen."

With tears in his eyes Andrews persisted. Very gently he embraced the old soldier and begged him to say what had been done to him. Bewildered but softened, the *lambardar* stripped off his shirt. For a while, Andrews could not trust himself to speak. Then he said, "Guru Nanak, in the Granth Saheb, enjoins on us forgiveness. I want you to forgive me. The sin is mine because it is my countrymen's." He bowed down and touched the other's feet. "No, no !" cried the soldier, springing back, "you must not do that !" Then he burst into tears, great sobs of relief that went on for some time. "Saheb," he said when he could speak, "this is the first drop of comfort I have tasted for six months. Now I do not want anything else. I am happy again." "Is it all over ?" asked Andrews. "Everything is over, I am quite happy"—and indeed he looked a different man.

Gurdial Mallik, watching, had a sudden inspiration. "C—. F—. A—," he thought, "Christ's Faithful Apostle !" No one who ever knew C.F.A. thought the name ill-chosen.

Gandhi arrived in the Punjab in mid-October—"like a moral avalanche," as his friend remarked. Between his forceful personality and the tender strength of Pandit Malaviya, the contrast was extreme. Not the least of Andrews' services to the Punjab then, perhaps, was the way in which he brought them together, for he understood and loved both the moral fervour of the one and the healing sympathy of the other.

But he was urgently needed in South Africa, and on November 15th he bade farewell to the Punjab at a monster meeting in the Bradlaugh Hall, Lahore. There he condemned, without palliation or partiality, the acts of cowardly brutality which had disfigured British and Indian records alike. His words reached farther than he dreamed. Hundreds of miles from Lahore, a young man read them aloud from the newspaper to a group of listeners in a temple porch. "He is a just man," said one. "Englishmen are not all bad, after all."

In Lahore the vast non-Christian audience, with India's greatest national leaders in its ranks, listened reverently as Andrews applied the words of Christ to the needs of the Punjab.

> "While I have been in Lahore," he told them, "I have gone out each morning into the Montgomery Gardens, and looked up to the sky before dawn, with all its stars. I have watched the sun rise over the great eucalyptus trees, and in the vast silences of Nature there have come to me these words from my own scriptures—the words of Christ my Master :
>
> 'Love your enemies, bless them that curse you, that ye may be the children of your Father in Heaven ; for He makes His sun to rise on the evil and on the good. Be ye therefore perfect, as your Father in Heaven is perfect.'
>
> "I would urge you not to dwell upon vengeance but rather upon forgiveness ; not to linger in the dark night of hate but to come out into the glorious sunshine of God's love."*

Only a short while before, he had been refused entry to a Christian church not many miles away. "This House of God is not for rebels," they had told him.

* *The Tribune*, 16th November, 1919.

137

CHAPTER X

THE AFTERMATH OF WAR—
AFRICA

1919-1920   AGE 48-49

I

EVER since he returned from Fiji the "Friend of the Poor" had been called upon for help in an increasing number of situations of racial or economic friction. Of much of his self-effacing service in this and the following years scarcely a hint remains—stray glimpses show him always pleading the cause of the poor before the powerful, now here, now there. Yet he himself still looked upon such calls as interruptions—needful, even divinely appointed, but still interruptions—of the real work of his life. He would return to Santiniketan from his expeditions of mercy full of resolve. "Now," he would say, "I am going to settle down. I shall take on the history class tomorrow." Tagore knew better. "Sir Charles," he would reply solemnly, "I shall see that there is an up-to-date railway guide always on hand !" "Andrews' personal love for me," he wrote to Swami Sraddhananda, "deludes him into thinking that his work lies here, and thereby he does himself injustice. His field of action is world-wide."* This comment had been evoked by one of Andrews' letters from the Punjab.

"I *have* to go to South Africa," he wrote, "but it is as certain as the day that I shall come back to the *ashram*, disciplined in mind and spirit for the real work of my life, which lies there and nowhere else."†

The ironical Muse of History must surely have smiled. The next three or four months held little dramatic incident or achievement, but the tangled problems with which Andrews wrestled in East and South Africa were in some ways more typical of "the real work of his life" than anything that had gone before.

* 13th November, 1919.
† To R.T., 3rd November, 1919.

Andrews went to East Africa and Uganda to make an impartial investigation of grievances which, already serious in 1914, had been exacerbated by the war. The whole region had been a field of Indian commercial enterprise for centuries, and when Britain claimed imperial suzerainty at the end of the nineteenth century it was ostensibly to protect her Indian subjects there. Europeans came in any numbers only after the Uganda Railway was built, and particularly in the six years preceding the war. Unfortunately many of the most influential of them came from South Africa, and brought with them the attitude towards both Indian and African displayed by the most arrogant among the South African "whites." Then came the war. The danger of invasion from the adjacent German territory of Tanganyika led to the establishment of a military government, which imprisoned and deported Indian suspects on grounds which the community in general felt to be entirely inadequate, if not in some cases deliberately fabricated. In defence of the authorities it must be said that at least one Indian revolutionary extremist was living in Kenya during those years ; but much ill-will was caused by the deportations. The Europeans were angered in their turn by the well-intentioned but ill-timed suggestion of Sir Theodore Morison that India, not Britain, should be given the Tanganyika mandate in the peace settlement.

The main grievances of the Indians were their exclusion from the ownership of land in the fertile Kenya Highlands, the recurrent threat of restrictions on immigration and of commercial and residential segregation in the townships, and the inequitable conditions of representation in the Kenya Legislative Council. European politicians were pressing the post-war claims for "self-government" in a way which made it clear that their real aim was the local control of the affairs of the colony by a white population of less than ten thousand all told, and the permanent exclusion of its twenty-three thousand Indians and its millions of Africans from any real voice in its policy. Not long before Andrews arrived a Government Economic Commission, on which the European settlers were strongly represented, had published its findings. Without taking any Indian evidence, it laid the blame for Kenya's economic difficulties at the door of the Indian population, and asserted that "Indian competition deprives Africans of incentives to ambition and opportunities for advancement."

The effect of that sentence on Andrews was to make him study more closely than ever the condition of the African population and the relationships between Africans and Indians. The leaders of the settlers' party, knowing his South African reputation, were of course bitterly hostile, and lost no opportunity of abusing him as a "bastard Englishman" and treating him as a pariah. But— as in South Africa—there were friendly Englishmen too. Many a youngster fresh from England in Government or Railway service regarded with gratitude and respect the competent and experienced Indian who taught him his job, and was ashamed of the system which prevented the Indian from ever rising to his own position and salary. Some of these lads, no doubt, succumbed to the prevailing atmosphere ; but others to their honour never did succumb. Prominent in the "opposition" was Mr. MacGregor Ross, the Director of Public Works,* to whose home Andrews and his Indian friends were made welcome. Andrews learned much from him about the Africans—the insecurity of their tenure of their ancestral lands ; the industrial policy, savouring un- pleasantly of "indenture," which broke up the family and tribal life and was the real root of the Colony's economic difficulties ; the scandalous bullying and criminal violence which "are inevi- table whenever men are given both political control over a subject people and an opportunity to profit by their labour."†

Andrews spent several weeks travelling in Kenya and in Uganda—that land of romance and Christian heroism to which he had once longed to dedicate his life—and entered into every detail of the situation. From that time on he was master of the political and historical facts, and could marshal them when occasion demanded with unrivalled clarity and force. From every quarter he collected evidence to refute the charges of the Economic Commission, and the still more cruel charge that Indians as a class had a low standard of sexual morality. He got

* His book, *Kenya from Within*, is a racy and revealing account of the situation at the time of Andrews' visits.

† Norman Leys, *Kenya*, q.v. for the whole subject.

written statements from missionary doctors who served all communities ; he met the Baganda Native Parliament at Lukiko and obtained a letter signed by the Prime Minister and the Chief Justice. "We *do* want the Indians to remain in our country," it ran, "as we consider that their being here would improve our country. . . . We find them moral people." He watched the Africans loitering contentedly in the Indian wayside stores, the Indian artisan working alongside his African apprentices, the laughing African labourers on Indian estates. He treasured and used the many African "addresses of welcome," which assured him with obvious sincerity that "the Indians and the missionaries are our best friends."

His experience convinced him of the strength and justice of the Indian case in Kenya, but it convinced him also of the "weary futility" of an exclusive preoccupation with political "rights" or with the acquisition of material wealth. The one led too easily to faction, the other to a temptation to "play jackal to the British lion" in the exploitation of the African. "Why," wrote a friendly Englishman, "is the Indian colony so self-absorbed, so aloof from African emancipation movements ?" Andrews knew that there was truth in the criticism implied. "Have you not been tempted, my friends," he asked at one of his meetings, "to spend too much time on money-making ? The sight of this absorption in material things has been a pain, a fear, and a grief to me far more keen than any harsh outward wrong that has been done to you by men from the outside."* In the same speech he suggested that the concentration of interest on politics only, might be "as dangerous to a healthy mind as intoxication to a healthy body."

Therefore wherever he went he spoke in his broken Hindustani not about politics, but about God. The Sikh Gurdwara, the Moslem Anjuman, the Arya Samaj Mandir, the Christian church, were all open to him ; he pleaded in them all for a deeper religious life, expressed not in sterile controversy but in a life of inward peace and of service to the poor and oppressed of every race. He pictured in glowing terms the possibilities of an *ashram* in some East African forest, welcoming men of every creed to a life which

* Speech in the Arya Samaj Mandir, Zanzibar, January, 1920.

should reflect the ancient Indian ideal of retirement and meditation, of *vanaprastha* and *sannyas*. But most of all he pleaded for disinterested service of the African inspired by religion. He described many times how the Indian traders with whom he travelled in Uganda, Hindus, Moslems, and Parsees, had insisted on turning aside to visit a remote station where lived some Irish Roman Catholic missionaries. Their simplicity and devotion had made a deep impression on the Indians.

"Mr. Andrews," they said to me, "we are all of us making money here in Uganda. But what are we doing for the Africans themselves? What can we show to the credit of our nation to compare with this?"

Andrews took up and repeated that question, not only in Africa but in India also.

What spiritual benefit so far has India conferred upon East Africa? . . . Where are the spiritual adventurers of the modern age who leave the shores of India not for commercial greed but out of pure love?*

As soon as he returned to India in 1920 he put this as a practical challenge before Indian Christian students, and negotiated with the Bishop of Uganda to give them opportunities for service. That scheme fell through, but it was characteristic of Andrews that he should have made the attempt, in his own Christian community, to embody his principles in action. It was characteristic also that his conception of the Christian service needed in Africa was one that included as its chief element the fight for justice to the African—a fight in which men of goodwill of all religions must bear their part.

"Thoughtful and earnest people who take up the Indian cause," he wrote, "should throw all the moral weight they possess into the prevention of the appalling exploitation which is decimating the African population. If nothing is attempted from the Indian side to right these cruel wrongs, if no voice at all is raised against a system of forced labour which has helped to reduce the native population by 21 per cent. in ten years, there must be something radically wrong."†

In 1919, as Andrews contemplated for the first time the "appalling exploitation" and "cruel wrongs" of the Kikuyu and Masai peoples, his thoughts turned with special love and longing to the young lad at Santiniketan who had listened with such under-

* *Young Men of India*, April, 1923.
† *The Modern Review*, August, 1923.

standing and sympathy to his tales of oppression and wrong in
South Africa and Fiji. "Mulu" was dead ; he had died not long
before ; but one day, when the sorrows of the people lay heaviest
on Andrews' spirit, there came to him, intangible but very real,
an uplifting sense of comradeship, and the conviction that it was
then Mulu who stood by his side and silently bade him take
courage. That the experience of powers renewed should have
come to him in that form is itself characteristic of the whole bent
of his intensely affectionate and sensitive mind.

II

Andrews' visit to South Africa was timed to coincide with that
of the Government of India representatives who had been deputed
to watch the Indian case at the Asiatic Inquiry Commission of
1920. For one of them, Mr. G. L. Corbett, he conceived a very
warm regard, and he did much to help them to establish friendly
relations with the local Indian leaders, who were inclined at first
to be sceptical and suspicious of any co-operation whatever with
the Commission. The spirit of some of the evidence given before
it certainly foreshadowed grave troubles ahead, but the findings
of the Commissioners, though they had grave defects from the
Indian point of view, proved of real value in fighting the segregation proposals of later years, so that the policy of co-operation
was justified by the event.

Andrews' chief interest however was in social and economic
conditions, and he found the poorer section of the Indian community of Natal in a wretched condition. Ninety per cent. of
the Indian population were sugar estate labourers, and although
the last of the original indentures had expired in 1916, many of the
people were so miserably poor that they continued to "re-
indenture" themselves, often being induced to do so under the
influence of drink. Their misery had been increased after the
war by the Government of India's restrictions on the export of
rice, while wealthy Indian merchants in Durban did not scruple
to withhold their stocks in order to make still greater profits out
of the rising prices. Andrews did not expose these malpractices
publicly ; he invited the merchants individually to a private

meeting and there spoke straight from the shoulder. Next morning one of them released his whole stock of rice at "control" rates. Andrews protested to the Indian press about the carelessly selfish nationalism of an export policy which had deprived the destitute Natal labourers of their staple food.

This was an early example of the divergence of class interests within the Indian community in South Africa which was a factor in all Andrews' future work. Another thing which he felt deeply was the havoc wrought among the poor by strong drink. Not only was there no law such as existed in Fiji to control the sale of intoxicating liquor to Indians, but the Indian political leaders opposed any such proposal on the ground that they must have the same "rights" as Europeans. This too was typical of many future problems, where the claims of "self-respect" apparently conflicted with those of humanity.

Andrews was worn out and ill, and the squalor and want around him haunted him night and day. Repatriation to India seemed to him to be "the only door of escape from an intolerable wrong." A clause in the Gandhi-Smuts agreement of 1914 provided a passage to India at the cost of the Union Government for those who wished to return, at the price of forfeiting South African domicile. This clause had been in abeyance during the war, and Andrews, thinking only of the human need and not of the political repercussions, and with the encouragement of the Indian leaders whom he consulted, now persuaded the Government to operate it, and in addition to give a small money grant to each Indian repatriated, in order, as he hoped, to make the resettlement in India easier.

This action raised a veritable hornets' nest. The wretched "coolies" were at once made a pawn in the political game. The anti-Asiatic extremists pressed forward the scheme in a way that compromised its voluntary character from the start, and explained to the Europeans how it might be used to rid the country of destitute labourer and wealthy trader alike.

In the bitterness that followed, some of the South African Indians spoke contemptuously of the ease with which Andrews could be deceived ; interested persons, they said, had "put up" the coolies to complain of imaginary miseries and get him to play into the hands of their enemies. But if he was deceived, it was not in his estimate of the pitiable plight of the coolies ; his diagnosis of their misery was only too accurate. His error lay in the remedy which he proposed. Human communities cannot be transplanted and re-transplanted at will. Once transplanted into Natal, their one hope of making good was to take root and grow there, to learn, as Miss Molteno had told them long ago, to call Africa their Motherland. To uproot them from their precarious hold upon the new soil was to court disaster.

Andrews, under Miss Molteno's influence, had seen this ; his policy in Kenya, where he had insisted that every problem should be regarded from the African point of view, was in harmony with it. But his pity for the "coolies" of Natal disturbed his judgment, and his knowledge of India was incomplete at a vital point. He knew the great cultural traditions ; he knew also the city slums ; but he did not know the rigid village society of the Tamil Nad or the United Provinces, and he had little conception of the diffi-culties of a man who should return with a wife of an unacceptable caste to a circle where the gap left by his departure had long been closed. The idealistic picture of the motherland of India which he had once painted was very different from the reality which the returned emigrant might experience when he reached home.

Actually no harm was done politically. Only a very small proportion of the labourers took advantage of the offer, and the Government of India's vigorous protests against unfair induce-ments, coupled with the less disinterested indignation of the Natal sugar-planters who feared for their labour-supply, soon put an end to the movement. Andrews did all in his power to retrieve his error, and humbly took all the blame upon himself, only pleading that he had had no thought beyond the relief of human suffering. In the burden of care which he assumed for the welfare of the returned emigrants in India, and which was to come upon him before another year had passed, he atoned abundantly for a false step for which his South African advisers must share the responsi-bility with him.

L

PART FOUR

THE FRIEND OF THE POOR

CHAPTER XI

VISVA-BHARATI

I

IN December, 1919, the Government of India Act embodying the Montagu-Chelmsford proposals had become law. After the events in the Punjab it was received with coldness, yet such was Gandhi's influence that he was able to persuade the Amritsar Congress to agree to work the reformed constitution.

New difficulties at once arose. Indian Muslims had been induced to support the war on the strength of an official statement by Mr. Lloyd George in January, 1918, which they regarded as a promise that in the post-war settlement the spiritual and temporal authority of the Sultan of Turkey, who held the sacred office of Khalif, should not be impaired. By the end of 1919 there was a growing suspicion that this "promise" would not be kept, and the peace terms with Turkey, which were published in May, 1920, confirmed these fears. Mahomed and Shaukat Ali, who had been released from internment by the Royal Amnesty of 1919, led a widespread agitation to which Gandhi gave his support. The Treaty of Sèvres was signed by Turkey, under compulsion, in July, 1920 ; August 31st was observed in India as "Khilafat Day," and early in September a special session of the Indian National Congress resolved on a seven-point programme of non-co-operation with Government. Gandhi and the Ali brothers toured the country amid scenes of wild enthusiasm. Great mass meetings, student strikes, the establishment of "national" schools and colleges, followed in breath-taking succession. The regular session of the Congress at Nagpur in December, 1920, restated its object as "the attainment of *Swaraj* by all legitimate and peaceful means" (omitting the word "constitutional," which it had

hitherto employed), and hand-spinning and the uplift of the
"untouchables" became prominent in its programme.

From May, 1920, to July, 1921, Tagore was absent in Europe and
America. The narrow and militant nationalism which was
rampant during the war had revolted him, and he had conceived
a great longing that scholars and thinkers of all countries should
unite to combat it. He planned to extend the scope of his own
educational work, and to create at Santiniketan itself an international cultural centre which he called Visva-Bharati.* The
chief purpose of his protracted visit to the West was to seek
for support and co-operation in this new enterprise.

During Tagore's absence one must picture Andrews established
in his simple room at Santiniketan, watching over every detail of
the welfare of the school, while an ever-increasing stream of
visitors claimed the aid of his unrivalled experience in problems
at home and overseas. The amount of work he got through was
amazing. From early in the morning often till close on midnight
he would be at his desk, answering letters, writing articles, drafting
memoranda. There were no "office facilities." Over and over
again he copied out important articles, six or eight times, with his
own hand, and himself hurried with them to the post office in the
blazing midday sun. ("Mad dogs and Englishmen go out in the
midday sun" was a popular song in which he took a special
delight.)

He had, however, two young and enthusiastic assistants.
Gurdial Mallik had now joined the Santiniketan staff. Benarsidas
Chaturvedi had been corresponding with him for five years
about Indians overseas, and in 1918, and again in June, 1920,
had visited him at Santiniketan. "Tell your father I want you,"
Andrews said to him on the second occasion, and in July he left
his post in the Chiefs' College at Indore and came. Even so
Andrews' own burden was great. In January, 1921, he returned to
the *ashram* with a severe attack of influenza. After his first visit to
returned Fiji emigrants stranded at Matiaburz near the Calcutta
docks, he kept his bed—but dictated thirty-five letters, telegrams
and articles, some of them long and important ones, in one day !

* A bald literal translation is "World-Culture."

In rare hours of leisure, Benarsidas persuaded Andrews to dictate informal reminiscences of his life, and to allow them to be used in a Hindi biography.* Andrews was reluctant, but yielded to the plea that the story of his life would help to combat the growth of popular hatred for all Englishmen as such, and contribute in some degree to better understanding between the two countries.

II

The best reflection of Andrews' personality and work during that dramatic year is to be found in his surviving letters and speeches. They give, first, a vivid picture of the Santiniketan school itself.

To Rabindranath Tagore   *August 11th, 1920*

Here in Santiniketan we are building up ourselves in our own strength and not relying on any outside help at all. There is freedom and independence here such as there is nowhere else in India. We have had some visitors who noticed this the very first thing. I only wish they could have seen the Literary Sabha meeting last night. You would have thought yesterday in this corner of the *ashram* that the whole world depended on getting this evening's meeting arranged ! Everything was done by the boys themselves. They were up before four in the morning to get lotuses and plantains and flowers and decorations. Such enthusiasm ! Such splendid fury of energy ! Such marvellous results—all in a few hours ! A stage erected ; the room draped and lighted with Japanese lanterns ; a portico erected ; the floor in front of the stage covered with beautiful chalk designs ; the musicians seated under the strong electric light and seen through muslin drapery—all created out of nothing like Aladdin's wonderful palace and vanishing into nothing next morning . . .

While I am writing it is the Wednesday holiday. The *ashram* is humming all day long like a busy hive and these little boys are scampering about round my verandah and inside and outside of my room, and out into the football field. We live our life at a splendid white heat of enthusiasm. Such energy is not really dissipated but becomes the true energy of growth. It differs utterly from the drug-like excitement of the jaded political life outside.

To Rabindranath Tagore   *August 31st, 1920*

I wish so much that you could have been with us last night, to have enjoyed the acting and music of *Valmiki Pratibha.*† We chose the occasion

* These are the "unpublished reminiscences" quoted in this book. The Hindi biography, *Andrews the Friend of India*, was published in 1921.

† One of Tagore's own musical plays.

of Swami Sraddhananda's visit to the *ashram* to perform it, and the boys quite excelled themselves and the girls also . . . Swamiji was immensely impressed and he was also very deeply struck by the Art and Music Room. The whole *ashram* was at its very best. We had a beautiful sunrise and sunset and it was not excessively hot. After the whole play was over the crowd broke up singing *Santiniketan*. It was Purnima* and it all looked so beautiful. When Swamiji spoke to me about it, he said that what struck him most was the freedom of everything and the happiness of the children.

Other letters are full of practical concerns—the finances of the *ashram*, the cleanliness of the kitchens, the struggle against caste and provincial prejudices in matters of food.

To RABINDRANATH TAGORE   *August 6th,* 1920

I was in some difficulty about making two ends meet for a short time, but now I have money to meet all emergencies. The East African merchants in Bombay have been very good and they have given liberally.

We have a Mahommedan Visva-Bharati student from East Africa and he is very happy here. The boys have been eager to have him with them in the kitchen. It has been so good to witness and is worth a good deal of the *talk* about Hindu-Musalman unity that is common everywhere. There is no difficulty at all in the *general* kitchen. The real trouble is going to be in the Gujerati kitchen and I am doing everything very quietly to break it down. I want to get the doors opened between the two kitchens and have them as one room . . . All will come right in time. But at present it is all wrong. They would even dislike my dining with them and they are sitting in little groups according to their special caste. This must silently be broken down and with tact and patience we shall do it.

To RABINDRANATH TAGORE   *September 6th and* 11*th*

We had great trouble for a time with some parents who came up and interfered with all arrangements and made the children keep caste distinctions and separate lines and gave orders to the cooks, etc. We treated them with the utmost courtesy and everything possible was done to conciliate them, but in the end it was quite impossible and some of the children were withdrawn. I cannot tell you what a relief it has been now that it is all over.

To RABINDRANATH TAGORE   *September* 1*st*

Since the narrowly orthodox guardians have taken their boys away we have been happier still ; for we have realised more clearly together what the *ashram* stands for and what we must on no account abandon ! The

* Full moon.

best thing of all is that those who are naturally very orthodox among us have been entirely on our side. There is much more freedom of access now between the two sides of the school—the Gujerati and the Bengali.

Reports from the travellers that they were being encouraged in America to expect donations totalling five million dollars, and that the poet was thinking of adopting the phrase *Five Million Dollars* as his *mantram* or holy incantation, drew from the harassed Andrews, who was again almost at his wits' end for money, the comment that "five thousand rupees in the bank is worth five million dollars in the bush !" A little later he returns to the subject.

To RABINDRANATH TAGORE *October 3rd and 5th*

We are obliged to give a fortnight (holiday) at Pujah time and I am going to take the opportunity and go round to Delhi and Hyderabad (Sind) and Karachi and Ahmedabad and Bombay trying to obtain funds to meet these very heavy charges.

. . . The Co-operative Stores is creditor to the school and workshop to the amount of 5,000 rupees which has to be paid off immediately ; so just as the pangs of hunger drive the forest animals afield so the pangs of the Co-operative Stores are sending me out on a thrice-hateful and thrice-hated task. Meanwhile every step of the way I shall be repeating my own modest *mantram*, "5,000 rupees" !

The accounts of such anxieties are mingled with pen-pictures of more domestic concerns, such as this one of his own devoted servant Jawahri* and the poet's servant, Sadhu.

To RABINDRANATH TAGORE *November 22nd*

Sadhu is having the time of his life. When any guest comes he mono-polises him at once and does his work splendidly. When no guest is here he dusts your rooms from morning to night. He never comes near me at all and it is better so. Because he and Jawahri don't get on and if Sadhu *doesn't* come Jawahri can grumble that he has to do all the work himself, and that grumble keeps Jawahri in a good temper and so everyone is pleased. I cannot tell you what a relief it is that Sadhu had ceased coming to dust my room in the mornings ! Jawahri manages the whole business in five minutes while Sadhu would go on for hours and hours . . . Jawahri is absurdly fond of me and treats me like a spoiled child. If ever I don't take proper food he scolds me like anything.

* This is Andrews' spelling. A more usual one would be Jauhari.

III

Throughout the year the letters reflect the impact which the political tension in all its aspects made upon Andrews himself and upon Santiniketan. At first they are full of the critical situation in East Africa.

To Benarsidas Chaturvedi   *July 1st, 1920*

I have been overwhelmed with work. I did want so much to send you a telegram in reply to your own which gave me such great delight, but I have now to save every pice and could not afford it. I have been ill again since you left and all the heavy work has told upon me. I cannot tell you what a relief it will be when you are able to come !

The enclosed disgraceful calumny* has come from East Africa by this mail, and I cannot tell you how much it has pained me ... Not only have I never taken a single pice, but I have ruined myself completely in sending money to keep up the schools and nurses in Fiji when I could not get help for them. I have had to spend every pice I ever had ... It is the most deadly calumny, for it ruins all work if once it sticks. I think you should at once state in the Hindi papers how cruel the accusation has been and what the true facts are. It was the same in Fiji and now it has begun in East Africa.

To Rabindranath Tagore   *August 11th*

All the work I tried to do in East Africa has been destroyed by Lord Milner's latest announcement, which gives way in every single particular to the bitter anti-Indian clamour ... I can only say this, that the case was put as clearly before him as any man could place it. I gave Polak† all the documents and facts, which were quite overwhelming, showing that Indians had done all the pioneer work, had opened up the country, had made the Uganda Railway, etc., etc. Polak marshalled them with the utmost skill. Nothing was left undone and nothing more could have been done if I had gone to England myself ... Montagu saw all my papers and was entirely and enthusiastically on our side. I was so feared and hated for doing all this that the press in East Africa started the slander about me that I was being handsomely paid by Indian money. But really there was no need for this added slander ; Lord Milner himself was on their side all along. His final pronouncement means nothing else than serfdom.

To Rabindranath Tagore   *September 6th*

Where I feel that Mr. Gandhi has failed is in the relative importance he attaches to things. He has become so wholly absorbed in Khilafat, this

* A newspaper cutting referring to him as "an Indian-paid propagandist."

† H. S. L. Polak, his collaborator in S. Africa up to 1914, had afterwards settled in London.

East African question has hardly interested him, and yet it is here on a question like this that India stands side by side with the whole of Asia. East Africa is really what one may call a "test case" for Great Britain. If Indians cannot be treated as equals in a vacant or almost vacant part of the world where they did all the pioneering and where they were the first in occupation—*a part of the world which is on the equator*—it means that the so-called freedom of the British Empire is a sham and a delusion. This is what I mean by a test case ; and the British Commonwealth will not stand that test . . . This is what makes me feel that Mr. Gandhi is *right* in his non-cooperation, far more than the Khilafat question. But probably he is politically wise in this way, that only a religious question will as yet move the masses in India.

The question of the "Khilafat" is discussed in many vehement letters to Gandhi himself.

To M. K. Gandhi   *September 23rd*
I hate the Khilafat doctrine of a Turkish Empire which was too sacred to be touched and which involved the refusal of independence to another race. My objection to that still holds, and until you can get Mahomed and Shaukat Ali to be absolutely frank on that question and not to equivocate, you cannot expect to have my wholehearted support. You have *not* made your meaning clear, and there is no trap in my question. It is as simple as A.B.C. Will you or will you not accept Arab and Armenian and Syrian independence in lands which are obviously theirs and not the Turks' ?

At the same time Andrews could not take a merely critical or negative attitude. After long thought he sent a brief letter to the press.

To The Editor, "Indian Daily News"   *September 19th*
Sir,—Having witnessed with my own eyes the humiliation of Indians, I can see no possible recovery of self-respect except by claiming an independence from British domination not less than that of Egypt. This requires absolute unity of moral purpose for its fulfilment, not compromise or concession. I deeply regret that at such a critical time I personally should have added one pang to Indian humiliation by weakly countenancing repatriation in South Africa.

The claim of independence had been publicly made at last. This letter, and Andrews' articles on the subject which were reprinted in pamphlet form as *Independence : the Immediate Need*, made a tremendous impression in India, not least on such alert young minds as that of Jawaharlal Nehru.* Andrews himself explained his motives more fully to Rabindranath.

* See his *Autobiography*, p. 66.

To RABINDRANATH TAGORE   *September 22nd and 28th*

I felt strongly that I could not actively join in Mr. Gandhi's Khilafat movement as such.   I am out against "Empire" altogether, and to agree to the Khilafat demand (for an Ottoman Empire) would surely cut the ground under the Indian demand for independence . . .   But I felt it was impossible to remain silent when feelings were so deeply stirred.   And if I were to speak out at all I could not say anything less than what I have put down . . . .

I do not think it will be taken up at present.   It is in a sense before the time.   But it is so hopeless to have the *aim* wrong, and I wished to say with all my heart that independence alone could bring recovery of respect.

Other letters are equally impatient and outspoken about the "racial imperialism" involved in untouchability and the connected evils of capitalist exploitation.

To M. K. GANDHI   *September 9th*

How far can we accept the Bolshevik idea of a struggle against *all* forms of capitalism ?   Are *we* out and out against capitalism in India ?   Or are we only out and out against imperialism ?   Personally I am coming more and more to see that the two are one and the same thing—that capitalism is the alternative driving force of all this imperialist aggression . . .

We *must* honestly and fairly and squarely face the non-Brahman movement and all that it implies.   I have just come across this passage in the Chhandogya Upanishad : "Those whose conduct has been pleasing will quickly attain a pleasing birth, of a Brahmin or a Kshatriya or a Vaisya ; but those whose conduct has been abominable will quickly attain an abominable birth, of a dog, or a hog, or an *outcaste*."   This kind of thing appears to me every whit as bad as the religion of the "white race" which is being proclaimed in Africa today.   Congress, so far as I am aware, is still in the hands of the high castes.   It is not possible to bring this isolationism to an end ?

Gandhi's visit to Santiniketan after the Special Congress at Calcutta, and Andrews' visit to Gujerat during the October "Pujah" holiday, gave the two friends opportunities for arguing in person.   One of Gandhi's characteristically crisp letters summarises the results of the arguments.

M. K. GANDHI TO C. F. ANDREWS   *November 23rd*

In its present condition the English connection is hateful.   But I am not as yet sure that it must be ended at any cost . . .   The connection must end on the clearest possible proof that the English have hopelessly failed to realise the first principle of religion, namely brotherhood of men.

. . . I don't want Swaraj at the cost of the depressed classes or of any other classes for that matter. This threat of being boycotted is giving me the keenest pleasure. In fighting the Government the motives of co-workers can be mixed. In fighting the devil of untouchability I have absolutely select company.

I V

After the Calcutta Special Congress there appears a theme which is recurrent throughout the cooler season.

To RABINDRANATH TAGORE   *September 27th and November 28th*
    I have another *mantram* more potent even than "Goat's Milk"* or "Five Million Dollars," but not less impossible of fulfilment. It is "No More Visitors." Now I understand what you meant when you said you had cursed me up and down for being away at Christmas-time last year ! This last fortnight the cup of suffering and forbearance has been running over the brim, and "curses not loud but deep" have been in my mind and on my lips most of the day and night ! Ever since the Congress we have had an average of some dozen to sixteen every day . . . I have told Dinu's tea-party that I am going on strike—Non-cooperation, Satyagraha and Passive Resistance all at once—and that I will *not* look after any more Bengali ladies !
    . . . Guests, guests, guests, guests and still more guests ! I am obliged to spend all my time in seeing that the *goru gari*† goes down to the station and in arranging that meals shall be reserved for four or five or six, and keeping Jawahri in a good temper and finding out conveniently early trains for departure. If therefore I do not curse you as you cursed me it is simply in order that the chain of causation may not remain unbroken and the wheel of cause and effect may cease to revolve.

Among these visitors were some from Rajputana whom Andrews interviewed in order to save Gandhi from additional burdens. They told him of the scandals of "forced labour" in the Rajputana States. "I listened to their story far into the night," he wrote to Tagore. "Afterwards I could not sleep, but lay awake picturing the scenes they had described." A short time afterwards came a letter from Stokes describing how the Government of India was implicated in similar practices in the Simla Hills. During the Pujah holidays Andrews therefore added to his self-imposed tasks the investigation of this form of oppression also.

* A reference to Mr. Gandhi's practice of drinking goat's milk instead of cow's milk in conformity with a long-standing vow.
  † Bullock cart.

The next group of letters record some of his experiences on his travels.

To Jagadananda Roy*   *October 16th*

I know how glad you will all be to hear that everything passed off extremely well at the Bihar Students' Conference at Daltonganj. . . . I put on my Swadeshi *dhoti* and *kurta* and I remained wearing them during the whole of my stay at Daltonganj and on the return journey. The students appreciated this very much and many of them spoke to me about it. Also I had to make three whole speeches in Hindustani, and if the students appreciated that also I am sure I did *not*, for I was trembling with fear the whole time and felt like the little boys who stood up on the platform afterwards trying to speak in English in a competition. Two of them stopped altogether in their confusion and I was nearly as bad !

All down the railway line from Sone East Bank we were welcomed at every station. People came in from the whole countryside. It is the most wonderful thing in the world to see how the *whole* country is awakening. Most of the stations were so small that they had no platform. Yet there was a crowd waiting and the Station Master and staff lined up to welcome the train. I tell you, Jagadananda Babu, it is a wholly *new* India today. Remember that these were not townspeople but villagers living in the depth of the country, and they had come away from their fields simply out of love for their Motherland.

To Narsinghbhai Patel†   *Matiana, Simla Hills, November 3rd*

I want to tell you and Kikubhai and others about my time in Gujerat . . . I was at Dakkur on the *mela*‡ day of the moon eclipse. There was an immense gathering of village people. It is estimated that over one and a half *lakhs*§ were present. The evening meeting was like a great sea. The moon was in eclipse when the meeting began, with a yellowish light showing round the edge. The flaring gas-lamps showed a silent audience scattered over hundreds of yards of ground and a small platform in the middle. We had to walk nearly a hundred yards through the dense masses of people before we reached the platform. There was perfect order. No one moved as Mahatma Gandhi went forward, and a cry went up from thousands and thousands of throats—*Bharat Mata ki jai ! Hindu Musalman ki jai !* It was like a great tidal wave coming in upon the beach and bursting into foam. Behind the platform on one side was a dense mass of women in rows upon rows. I have rarely seen so many at a meeting in India before.

* The Headmaster of the Santiniketan school.
† A Gujerati member of the Santiniketan staff.
‡ Festival.
§ i.e., 150,000.

I watched the faces of the crowd and it seemed as though no one was observing the eclipse, which was going on all the while. All were intent upon the meeting itself and upon the speakers. None looked towards the moon. When Mahatma Gandhi got up to speak the shouts of *Mahatma Gandhi ki jai!* were like great crashes of thunder. For some minutes it continued and it was so spontaneous and heart-given . . . .

I must close this letter now. The morning sky is just breaking with the early light of dawn and we are starting at the first possible moment as we have thirty miles before us before sunset in order to reach Kotgarh.

To Rabindranath Tagore   *Kotgarh (undated)*

I leave Kotgarh in two days' time to go on as quickly as I can to Santiniketan. I am very thankful indeed that I have come up here. The conditions of forced labour or *begar* are such that the villagers are sinking under them into a hopeless slavery. I have seen things now with my own eyes and I have had the details fully explained to me by Stokes on the spot . . . The time has come to strike at its very root and release these poor people from their cruel bondage. They have flocked around, telling me what it has meant to them, and they have new courage and will act together.

To W.W. Pearson   *November 12th*

Stokes and I went out together and got through to Kotgarh in two days and had about five hours' talk there with the District Commissioner (who had come out to see things for himself). He took a reasonable view of the matter and I pressed upon him the need for immediate action. The peasants themselves were prepared to refuse all forced labour or *begar* in the future. He was considerably impressed by the fact that I had come out all that way for this purpose and was eager to make terms. In the end he agreed that forced labour for the *Dak** should cease immediately. This was the vital point to start with, because in past years these villagers have *actually died in the snow* while doing *begar* and they dread the *dak begar* more than anything else. Then we agreed that up to March 1st the Forest and P.W.D. officers might take *begar* labour for their own personal use, pending a complete change of system. This will amount to practically nothing as these officials travel very little in the winter. The D.C. has promised to have the whole system changed by March 1st. If not he quite agrees to Passive Resistance being offered. Then the pleasure hunters from Simla will immediately be prevented from taking any *begar* labour at all. The consequence will be that the price of *free* labour will rise and the villagers will get a living wage by carrying loads when they wish to do so and when their work allows it.† I have often been told, "Why go out to Fiji to stop indentured labour when there is practically slavery going on in India

* Postal service.
† This anticipation was fulfilled to the letter.

itself ?" I had not realised the truth of this till I went fully into this accursed *begar* system in the hills.

When Andrews returned to Santiniketan he found letters awaiting him from Rabindranath, who was anxious lest his absorption in the political excitement of the times should be detrimental to the quiet constructive work of the *ashram*.

To RABINDRANATH TAGORE   *November 15th*

As ever happens, you have found out what was wrong in me and have set it right. I have been too carried away by the exciting atmosphere of the times in which we live and it had obscured the spiritual vision. Not that—while I was away even—I entered at all deeply into the political current. Everywhere I spoke against it in its merely emotional phases and in its appeals to anger and passion. But I have had ever in mind the words about Christ : "The smoking flax shall he not quench," and I have dreaded to be cold and indifferent in such an atmosphere as we have at present . . . But while I say this in partial excuse, I know full well the justice of the rebuke from you which I needed, and I have taken it to heart. May God grant that the ashram itself may never suffer from these impulses of mine.

Although Andrews agreed that Santiniketan should develop undistracted by the day-to-day political strife, he also felt that the longing for "independence" which he had voiced had an educational significance that should not be missed, and many of the letters he wrote during the cold weather of 1920-21 describe the working out of these ideas in school practice. The immediate practical issue was that of the Calcutta University matriculation examination, for which Santiniketan boys had been appearing as "private candidates."

To RABINDRANATH TAGORE   *September 22nd*

We all of us feel the equivocation of having to sign a declaration that the boys have "not read in any school" for twelve months before the examination, when they have been reading all the while in our own school. We may explain these words away, but we feel that now the whole country is moving forward to independence we should be independent too.

To RABINDRANATH TAGORE   *December 8th*

There was universal acclamation at your decision to abandon the matriculation. So now, in the kitchen we have no Brahmins' lines, for no one cares a pin about it, at last ; and in the school we have no matriculation, for none of our teachers cares a pin about it.

To Rabindranath Tagore   *December 8th*

We are all so thankful that the matriculation can now be finally abandoned. Now the Preparatory will have to decide for themselves with their parents. I think that some are certain to join Visva-Bharati. We shall certainly get all the children we need. I trust that they will come more from other provinces. My idea is that we should not aim at taking more than about a hundred in all. These would be as it were the background, and then there would be our teachers who themselves were research students and learners and we should be one family together. The idea of All Souls', Oxford, has always deeply interested me, which is almost purely a college for research and where the conventional student who wishes to take "degrees," etc., is not encouraged. But perhaps I am thinking on too far—only, to live with Gurudev and in his work is productive of looking ahead, and I find myself always doing so.

Of one thing I am becoming more and more certain—that is, we must keep simplicity and poverty which do not mean shoddiness and meanness. I get a little anxious when I hear of the possibility of large sums from America. God knows we want them : but I would rather be stinted than be extravagant.

To Rabindranath Tagore   *Poona, December 28th*

Before I started for Poona we had to decide about the matriculation and here I have to tell you about our weakness. I read out your letter in which you gave us all permission to abolish it, but when it came to the actual test, there were many who were for delay till you returned . . . The result was that when the vote was taken the proposal for immediate abolition was only carried by the chairman's casting vote. I felt very strongly that this was not sufficient and that such an important change should not take place without a two-thirds majority . . . It is most disappointing but I am sure you will agree that it is better to confess our weakness than go forward with a divided house and a pretended strength. One very touching thing was the manner in which the boys were anxious *not* to abolish it ; for, they said to me, their parents might take them away and there was no place on earth like the *ashram*.

Then, in January, Calcutta students "struck," demanding the nationalisation of their Colleges.

To Rabindranath Tagore   *January 15th, 1921*

After what has happened in Calcutta all are saying "we must not for very shame have the matriculation now !" Sastri Mahasay feels it a disgrace that we should be held back by timid fears of consequences. I have had the greatest difficulty in advising patience. I have gone on the one principle throughout that we must act together as one family and not

161

M

let bitterness spring up in our hearts. It has been a difficult time because feelings have been intense ; but not one word has been said to give pain and we have all agreed that we must act in unison.

To RABINDRANATH TAGORE   *January 31st*
    Everything has been settled amicably and unanimously at last, and we have agreed completely to abandon the matriculation immediately and work out our own curriculum. It is not a day too soon. Now the highest class in the school will be called the Visva-Bharati class and it will lead on direct to Visva-Bharati . . .

The development of the literary and artistic work of Visva-Bharati gave Andrews special delight. The same letter goes on to describe the work of a party which was commissioned to copy cave paintings in Gwalior State.

    Our artists are sending home to us water-colour brush sketches of the frescoes from Gwalior which have filled us with delight. Their enthusiasm and joy in their work is glorious. Here are things which Mr. Gandhi finds it difficult to understand, and he would suspend them all while we got Swaraj—but not I, not I !
    Khitimohan Babu is going to Kathiawar soon to collect the folk-songs and traditions before it is too late.
    The students have come out (*sc.* on strike). Now they are saying to the leaders, "Give us work to do : we want to help our own countrymen in the villages." I know how you would wish that we should take our part. We have fully agreed that Surul should be used for the purposes of a training centre.
    . . . This evening a little thing has happened which has given me great joy. I think you know that I have as yet not set foot in the Gujerati kitchen because I do not want in any way to hurt anyone's feelings. But tonight the Gujerati boys have come themselves and asked me to take my meal with them. This is a great advance and it is worth all the trouble we have been through to have made it.

The village training centre was started and twenty students began work at Surul with Nepal Chandra Roy ; but the doubts which Andrews felt about the weakness of the student movement as a whole he repeated in a letter to Gandhi.

To M. K. GANDHI   *February 19th*
    I am afraid we shall see an immense number of students going back and no college nationalised at all. Very few indeed have taken up village work actively and thoroughly. I am almost at sea . . . I still cling to the thought of purification. But the purification I am chiefly thinking of

is what these few students are doing with Nepal Babu, living on their own cooked food in the villages, sleeping often on the bare ground, taking the children of untouchables along with others into their village schools and (among other things) teaching the spinning wheel. But in Calcutta are hundreds, if not thousands, "slacking" most of the time through our fault . . A boy from a Dacca school, whose older brother was my student, came to see me, saying, "Sir, I wish to serve the poor." But somehow I cannot for the life of me feel that the whole movement is directed to that deepest of all ends yet, and I am impatient.

Andrews went to Poona in December, 1920, for an all-India meeting of Christian students. It meant much to him to be welcomed once more into Christian circles in India, though a few of the students present were still inclined to be suspicious of his "credentials." "Are you a Christian ?" they asked doubtfully. "If these boys cannot see in my face that I am a Christian," commented Andrews sadly, "what is the use of *telling* them that I am a Christian ?" But those were a minority ; the greater number heard him with deep respect "because we knew he lived the life before he talked of sacrifice."*

One of the joys of Poona was to hear of plans to found two Christian *ashrams*, the Christu-kula Ashram at Tirupattur and the Christa Prema Seva Sangh at Poona. The seed-thoughts of the Brotherhood of the Imitation of Jesus were bearing fruit. It is significant that Andrews urged the young pioneers to work in the fullest possible way *within* the Christian fellowship of the Church. There was no longer any need, he felt, for the lonely and costly step that he himself had taken in 1914. At the same time he took every opportunity of bringing Indian Christians into closer touch with the great national heritage of culture as represented by Santiniketan.

To RABINDRANATH TAGORE   *January* 15th

On the human side, if I may so call it, I do not think the *ashram* has ever been stronger. There are deep human affections growing up like tender plants, and these are the true foundations, not bricks and mortar . . . We have had two further developments of very great interest. The Parsee community of Bombay has now become acquainted with us, and we have started very well . . . Secondly, we have at last broken down the barrier of the Indian Christian community, and we have now the son of the most intellectual and influential of Madras Christians studying with

* Fr. G. Y. Martyn in a letter to the authors.

us. This is one of the immediate results of my visit to Poona to the Indian Christian conference.

To RABINDRANATH TAGORE   *March 13th*, 1921

One thing which has been very near my heart has been to try to bring Indian Christians back into the rich and full current of Indian life. It has been wonderful the change that has been effected lately. Now, instead of regarding me as *haram*, I find them coming to me from every side and actually welcoming with joy and thankfulness the letters I send them in answer to their own. And above all they have been coming in great numbers for a short stay at Santiniketan.

He fostered with scarcely less enthusiasm the growing interest of the Parsee community in the *ashram*. Some of its members shortly afterwards suggested the foundation of a Zoroastrian Institute in the Visva-Bharati. Andrews' comment shows his care for the larger issues involved.

To RABINDRANATH TAGORE

With regard to the building of a Zoroastrian Institute I am perfectly happy in my mind—just as I should welcome with all my heart an Islamic Institute. But I feel that our simple central place of worship, with its white marble pavement and its absence of all imagery and symbol—except the pure white flowers the children bring at the time of religious service—is the best expression both of our individual freedom of belief and our common worship of the One Supreme. Each of us may add what colour he likes to that pure whiteness. But if we build our separate mosques and chapels and fire-temples we stand in danger of repeating over again the religious divisions of the world.

This section may fitly close with the beautiful testimony which Andrews wrote to Tagore on his fiftieth birthday.

To RABINDRANATH TAGORE   *February 12th*, 1921

Today I am fifty years old according to our Western reckoning, and fifty-one according to the more accurate Eastern calculation. How the years have flown by ! It has been a crowded life full of incident and change ; and yet all the while the inner peace at the centre of my life has been deepening and the storms of religious doubts and questionings have ceased to rage, as they did in the earlier days when I first knew you. There is a very beautiful Psalm of Deliverance in the Old Testament, and it has been much in my mind this morning. There is this passage in it, which can be taken in another than the literal sense :

"They that go down to the sea in ships, that do business in great waters, these men see the works of the Lord and His wonders in the deep.

For He commandeth and at His voice the stormy winds arise.

They mount up to heaven and go down again to the depths : their soul is melted because of trouble.

Then they cry unto the Lord and He bringeth them out of their distress.

He maketh the storm a calm.

Then are they glad because they are at rest ; so He bringeth them to the haven where they would be.

O that men would therefore praise the Lord for His goodness."

In Santiniketan I have found "the haven where I would be," and out of the storm a calm . . . I have been thinking of all these things this morning, as I have bowed my head in worship to the *Santam, Sivam, Advaitam.** The friendship of these little boys, who are always in my room, all day long, and playing in my verandah, has kept me from feeling that I am growing older year by year ; and the *ashram* itself, like your dream of *Phalguni*, is a Cycle of Spring that never grows old. And when one gets a magician, a snake-charmer, and a circus, all in a single week, with the boys rushing into my room to tell me how the man stood on the back of the white horse as it galloped and jumped through fiery hoops, and how the horse stood up on its hind legs and put its forelegs round the circus manager's neck, and a thousand other things—when one gets all this on one's fifty-first birthday the cloak of winter slips off very rapidly indeed and he is discovered as spring !†

* "the Peace, the Life, the One."

† The reference is to Tagore's play *Phalguni*, or *The Cycle of Spring.*

CHAPTER XII

THE OPPRESSION OF THE POOR

1921-1922   AGE 50-51

AT the eclipse meeting in Gujarat in October, 1920, Andrews had witnessed "the personal devotion of multitudes to the *guru* who sacrifices himself for the idea"*—the national awakening, not confined to the towns or the educated classes, of which he had dreamed fifteen years before. Gandhi was proclaiming everywhere his fivefold programme of national regeneration— the redemption of the outcaste, the brotherhood of Hindu and Muslim, the honouring of women, freedom from drink and drugs, the practice of *swadeshi*.† As the five fingers spring from one wrist, he would say, holding up his hand, so these five aims must be controlled by the unifying spirit of *ahimsa*.

Andrews threw himself heart and soul into this programme, not as a politician but as a man of religion, believing that vital religious principles were at stake in it. "Independence, complete and perfect independence for India, is a religious principle with me because I am a Christian," he declared. "But independence can never be won if the millions of the untouchables remain still in subjection. England cannot be England to me, the England I love, if she holds down Ireland and India by military force. And India cannot be India to you, the India of your dreams, and of my dreams also, if she does not give *swaraj* to her own depressed classes."‡ Against the exploiters, whoever they might be, he stood up for the exploited poor ; against every kind of bullying and oppression, he upheld before the nation the ideals of non-violence and truth.

* See Chapter IV, p. 45
† "One's own country"—the principle of the local provision of essential goods.
‡ Speech to Calcutta students, 19th January, 1921, reported in *To the Students*, p. 46.

I

In March, 1921, there occurred serious and widespread railway strikes, which affected a large number of men in the great workshops at Howrah, Lillooah and Kanchrapara in the environs of Calcutta, as well as at Lucknow and elsewhere. There was a tendency in some quarters to dismiss all industrial discontent, both on the railways and in other industries, as the work of political agitators. The truth was that the cost of living had enormously increased, a general rise in wages was long overdue, and workmen were often scandalously badly housed, in spite of the enormous war profits which had been made by many of the firms. Early in 1920 the railway employees had been promised a Committee of Enquiry into their grievances ; when they finally struck in March, 1921, they had waited over a year for the promise to be fulfilled.

Andrews went to meet these men, saw their living conditions with his own eyes, and by dint of long and patient discussions sifted their demands and complaints. In the end he was able to persuade them to withdraw such claims as seemed to him unreasonable and exaggerated, while he himself undertook to place before the agents of the railway companies in Calcutta and the Railway Board at Delhi the solid need of reform.

This result was not achieved without some exciting incidents.

One Sunday evening at Howrah, after darkness fell, I was gathering together the chief *mistris* and others to hold an important meeting about the strike. We walked about half a mile to a small *maidan.** As we were going down a lane, I saw that a very large gathering had collected. Everyone was armed with *lathis*,† some were very big. There were at least five hundred present. A man came running to me and said that this crowd was just starting to attack the Gurkhas who had done *zulum*‡ in the bazaar that afternoon.

I went into the middle of the crowd at once and there was loud shouting and for a moment I did not know what was going to happen. This crowd had never seen me before and did not know who I was. I got up on a small chair and for some minutes I could hardly get silence at all. They were waving their sticks and saying that the Gurkhas had insulted them and they were going to take revenge. I was not quite certain for a

* Open space.
† Heavy sticks.
‡ Acts of bullying violence.

few moments whether they could be restrained at all, and those with me were alarmed also. At last when I got a hearing I told them who I was and they very quickly got quiet. Then I spoke about Mr. Gandhi and how I was with him in South Africa, and said then that they must put down their *lathis*, and then one by one, somewhat unwillingly, they put them down.

After this I told them that if the Gurkhas had done *zulum* I would report it ; but they must themselves remember how they were to blame for going down this very Sunday morning to the station yard, and committing all kinds of acts of violence. I told them I had been myself three whole hours up and down the line trying to find the crowds who had done damage to property and nearly killed two persons. I said to them that they must not forget this and they must not do it again. If they did it again I would absolutely refuse to help them.

They listened to this very quietly indeed and then I said to them, "Will you promise to do no violence ?" and they all shouted "Yes, we promise." Then I called out "Mahatma Gandhi ki jai !" and they shouted "Mahatma Gandhi ki jai !" and the meeting broke up without any more speeches. They were all laughing and quite willing to come back with me. By the time we got there we were an extraordinarily happy crowd. It is a vivid example of how like children these poor people in India are.

I heard afterwards from the highest authority that if they had gone that night to attack the Gurkhas the order had been given that they were to be fired on immediately, because they had actually overpowered a Gurkha guard that very morning.*

These things were accomplished in the midst of constantly recurring illness :

At Lillooah I was brought from hospital to attend a meeting of strikers. They agreed to return to work in consideration of the concessions made in Calcutta, while I acted as deputation to the Railway Board on the points which the Calcutta authorities could not deal with. The meeting was unanimous and they all shouted "Andrews saheb ki jai !"†

Andrews' aim was a speedy and honourable settlement for the sake of the men themselves, who had no strike funds to fall back on. His work was made more difficult by agitators, who were often quite ignorant of labour questions, and were sometimes unscrupulous, but who had great influence over simple and superstitious workmen because they wore the ochre robe of the religious devotee.

* Unpublished reminiscences.

† Unpublished reminiscences.

At Kanchrapara I was attacked in a very violent speech by a *swami* who said in Hindi, "You are one of those English sahebs who live in luxury and fill their stomachs out of the sufferings of the poor of India." Is not that an amusing description of me ?*

But it could not have been easy always to be amused.

Andrews drew up for the Railway Board a masterly memorandum on the causes and cure of strikes.† Its analysis and exposition of the just and reasonable demands of the workmen is a witness to his practical business ability. But the principle on which he laid most stress was the need for direct human contact and personal friendliness between managers and men, and as a corollary the end of the invidious racial discriminations which disfigured the railway service. He pleaded for a change of atmosphere, a change of attitude on the part of the management which would make it possible for the men to regard themselves as fellow-workers in a great co-operative enterprise. The railway workman might be in the wrong, often was in the wrong, in his immediate pretext for a strike ; but until reasonable security of employment and the benefits of a provident fund were open to him, until decent family life was possible in his quarters, above all until the galling distinction between Indian and "Anglo-Indian" had been brought to an end, the sense of injustice which made him a victim of irresponsible agitators would not be removed. Surely, Andrews argued, a contented labour force is as important to the railway as the stability of the permanent way ! Why not pay as much attention to the former as to the latter ? He knew well, nevertheless, that there was a political as well as a humanitarian factor to be taken into account, and that so long as political distrust of Indians remained they were not likely to be given a real share in the control of such a vital undertaking as the East India Railway.

II

While Andrews was at Kanchrapara news of other distresses began to reach him. In 1919, when there was much hardship in the United Provinces, a larger number of people than usual had

* To B.D.C., 17th May, 1921.
† Published in *Young Men of India*, August, 1921.

found employment in the Assam tea-gardens, where the demand for labour was brisk. Then came the slump, severe unemployment followed, and the starving labourers left the gardens and started homewards. By road and rail they poured into Chandpur, a small town in East Bengal ; from that to Goalundo, the railhead for Calcutta and the west, was a ninety-mile journey by river steamer.

The Chandpur officials, alive to the danger of an epidemic in the town, acted promptly, and sent the refugees forward to Goalundo with all speed. The tea-planters however took alarm at the disappearance of their labour supply, and their representatives brought pressure to bear both at Chandpur and in Darjeeling to check the exodus. The Bengal Government announced that free passages to Goalundo would be discontinued. When this was known, three hundred desperate people "rushed" a steamer, and the officials had not the heart to turn them off again. Those who had failed to board the ship took refuge in the railway station near the quay. It was then that serious trouble began ; the planters' representative had been somewhat roughly handled in the scramble for the steamer, and a party of Gurkha soldiers was sent down at night, and drove the wretched refugees out of the railway premises on to a shelterless football field. They had neither the strength nor the will to resist, and the brutality with which they were treated raised a storm of public indignation.

This happened on the night of May 19th ; on the evening of the 21st Andrews landed at Chandpur. Next morning with the first light he was out to see things for himself, and to talk to the labourers, the townsfolk and the officials. Within the day he had persuaded them to recommend unanimously to the Bengal Government a grant of five thousand rupees towards the cost of the steamer fares for the stranded people, private charity providing the rest. By the third day after his arrival, without waiting for the Government's reply, enough money had been raised to send nearly five hundred healthy people on to Goalundo at full rates. Four thousand however still remained, no word came from the Government, and the dreaded epidemic of cholera had begun. Andrews started himself for Darjeeling to see what could be done, leaving a vigorous local committee to organise relief for the sick and hungry in Chandpur.

He returned a few days later sick at heart. The situation seemed to him obviously one for the Ministry of Health to deal with ; instead, the Home Department was handling it, auto-cratically. He had gained one point ; there had been no intention, he was assured, to forbid travel at the usual cheap "concession" rates, although the Order was so peremptorily worded that steam-ship officials had interpreted it in that sense. At concession rates, the relief fund would meet the need.

When Andrews reached Calcutta on his return journey he found that the assurance came too late. Popular indignation against the Gurkha outrage had expressed itself naturally in *hartal*. Strong extremist elements in Bengal, blind to all other considerations, then persuaded the railway and steamship employees to embark on a prolonged strike, for which there was no industrial justifica-tion and which was frankly political in intention. The disastrous effect of the strike upon the stranded coolies was considered as of no importance. Andrews was present at a meeting in Calcutta when it was argued seriously that "a few thousand coolies in a cholera camp might be sacrificed if India's three hundred and twenty millions could obtain Swaraj."* When his turn came to speak he urged every argument he could muster against this exploitation of the weak and ignorant—coolies and railwaymen alike—for a so-called national cause.

> I have never said and never could say that all strikes are "wrong." To my thinking Non-cooperation itself is simply a National Strike against injustice. But I have seen with my own eyes the violence of labourers under bitter pangs of hunger. The non-violent character of the national movement was every hour in danger so long as the Howrah-Lillooah strike continued. These futile outbreaks ought not to be repeated. *It is we, the educated, who ought to suffer. We ought not to make the poor the sufferers.*†

He pleaded in vain. By the time he reached Chandpur the strike was "on." Hundreds of people, certified free from in-fection, waited eagerly to embark for home. Andrews and his "volunteers" had the heart-breaking task of sending them back,

* Account in *The Indian Problem*, p. 79 ff.

† *Ibid.* (italics ours).

weeping with disappointment, to their stricken camp. A few days later they did sail—but it was a European crew that coaled and manned the vessel. The cup of humiliation seemed full.

Back in East Bengal, Andrews was too fully occupied with his own peculiar work—the work of mediation and publicity that he did so supremely well—to give much personal assistance in the cholera camp itself. But his overflowing friendliness was an inestimable contribution ; the warmth of his trust and appreciation and the sparkle of his gentle humour kept the most diverse elements working together in a splendidly generous service to the needy. One day the Bishop of Assam, the Rt. Rev. H. Pakenham Walsh, with his wife, arrived at Chandpur and asked to be allowed to help. It was not an auspicious moment ; the attempt to co-operate in relief work with Government agencies had broken down in spite of all Andrews could do, and the nationalist volunteers looked with disfavour upon a couple of strange Europeans who did not wear the orthodox homespun garments. The distinction between an official and a bishop was too fine for them to draw ! Andrews' resourcefulness was equal to the occasion. "You see," he explained shamelessly, "they aren't English ; they are Irish Free Staters ! Just give them a trial." The trial was agreed to ; Andrews tactfully withdrew and left the new recruits to find their own feet. When he returned they were well established—the tireless cheerfulness with which the bishop carried the cholera buckets to the latrine, and his wife's skill with orphan babies, had earned the respect of all. One is reminded of the remark made by a witty Irish churchman who had once visited St. Stephen's : "I find it difficult to believe that Rudra is not an Englishman and Andrews an Irishman !"

But the most abiding impression made by Andrews on his fellow-workers was not that of his wonderful friendliness and utterly reckless self-devotion, great as these were—it was that of a great calm amid the storm. "He was the very embodiment of peace and quietness ; his very presence was like balm in that excited and turbulent atmosphere . . . He was the calm happy spirit that lifted one above the turmoil into peace."* He moved

* Bishop and Mrs. Pakenham Walsh, to the authors.

in a region holy, withdrawn, invisible—and he fought all the better because his spirit was "above the battle."

Something of the warmth and radiance of his own personality is reflected in his description of the little lad, convalescent after cholera, who lay on deck as the last ship-load of refugees, and Andrews with them, drew away from ill-fated Chandpur :

> The steamer came round a bend of the river quite close to the shore. Bright healthy children on the bank were running along and shouting "*Gandhi Maharaj ki jai ! Gandhi Maharaj ki jai !*"
>
> I looked at the invalid child on deck. His face shone with excitement and he raised his head with great difficulty. Then he waved his hand to the children running along the bank, and cried in a voice that was pitifully weak, "*Gandhi Maharaj ki jai !*" As I stood watching him, lying there on the deck and waving his hand, the tears came streaming from my eyes. The thought came like a flash to me that here in this child's faith God Himself was being revealed. Through all this suffering and pain, *God manifests Himself in forms of deathless joy.**

There were two more tasks to be done. The first was to see that labourers returning to the Gorakhpur district from distant Assam were not boycotted in their own villages, as some of those returning from Fiji the previous year had been boycotted. He went from village to village, "pleading with the people to take them to their hearts even as the Chandpur people took them to their hearts."† In this work he had considerable success, though his footsteps were dogged and his spirit wounded by a *sadhu*, who had himself been deported from Fiji as a mischief-maker, and who abused and cursed Andrews publicly because he had not prevented the wretched Fiji-born Indians who were stranded by the Calcutta docks from returning to their native land.

The second task was to warn both the opposed political forces, British and Indian, of the danger of the situation in East Bengal. He wrote to Gandhi to ask him to go there in person.

> East Bengal is on the very border line of violence . . . it is highly emotional, quick tempered, hot and passionate. These strikes in such inflammable material are like straw to a fire, and I have been greatly anxious about an explosion. What I felt was that only *you* could really preach *ahimsa*. I have done my very best and they have given me such

---

* *The Modern Review*, August, 1921. The quotation is from the Upanishads.
† To M. K. Gandhi, 21st June, 1921.

treasures of love. Time after time the passion has died down as I have spoken about you. They do really understand that in my presence no word even of violence must be uttered. But when I am not at their meetings or leave after speaking I have constantly heard that the old passion flames up.

The terms offered by both steamship and railway companies are honourable terms. But ... there is a strike mania. At a meeting I held about Chandpur (in Calcutta) the whole meeting was against me except three or four, who were such co-operators as Krishna Kumar Mitter and one or two Marwaris. The Marwaris say they will give any money I wish for the distressed labourers into my hands, but they will not trust anyone else because it will go to the "strikes."*

Andrews was as outspoken in his condemnation of the official attitude to the events at Chandpur as he was in his criticisms of the "nationalist" exploitation of the situation :

The Government by its action has come more and more to side with the vested interests, with the capitalists, with the rich, with the powerful, against the poor and the oppressed. That is the terrible indictment. That is why the poor, in their misery, have flocked to Mahatma Gandhi, who understands his own people.

... The year 1921 in no way differs essentially from the year 1919. The so-called Dyarchy has been proved up to the hilt to be the old autocracy over again. I am taking the test which the new Viceroy has laid down and I am judging by actions rather than by professions. In Darjeeling I was not introduced to a single Indian member for the purpose of consultation. I do not charge Sir Henry Wheeler and Lord Ronaldshay with consciously or deliberately slighting their Indian colleagues, but I do say that the mentality of autocracy at Darjeeling is still unchanged, and that the Responsible Government promised by the Reforms Act, by which ought to be meant respect for Indian opinion and Indian initiative, is still entirely absent.†

This speech caused a Member to demand in the House of Commons‡ that "this so-called gentleman" should be sent to England to be tried for sedition. The local officials in Bengal knew better than to take any such disastrous course. "You

---

* To M. K. Gandhi, 21st June, 1921. The "distressed labourers" whom Andrews worked almost single-handed to relieve included not only the tea-garden coolies but also the rank and file of railway employees. When the strike failed as a political weapon, the extremists who had fomented it left the men they had used to make what terms they could. Andrews alone, who had opposed the strike from the beginning, stood by them and pleaded their case.

† Speech reported in the *Annual Register* (India), 1921.

‡ 15th June, 1921.

know," said one of them, "we don't know what to do with a man like that. If we put him in prison *he* wouldn't mind, and there'd be the hell of a row ! If today the Viceroy were to say *Do this*, and Andrews were to say *No*, ninety-nine per cent. of Indians would obey Andrews rather than the Viceroy."* Montagu too had seen something of Andrews' influence, and the phrase in which he is said to have described him, "God's own fool," shows some insight into the nature of the man he was dealing with.

But "fool" Andrews was not, except perhaps in the same sense as those shrewd and outspoken "fools" in Shakespeare's plays. The Royal Commission on Indian Labour endorsed at every point his estimate of the root causes of the 1921 unrest. They remarked, as he did, on the gulf between owners and men ; they declared that "causes unconnected with industry play a much smaller part in strikes than is generally supposed," and that the exodus from the Assam tea-gardens was due not to political agitation but to a wage level totally insufficient to meet the cost of living.

The epilogue to the drama of Chandpur was played at Simla in June, in the house of Andrews' old friend Sir Tej Bahadur Sapru.

I was living at Simla as Law Member of the Government of India (he relates) when Charlie walked in one day, unheralded as always, and invited himself to stay with me. When we were alone at dinner that evening he "went for me" vigorously because I had consented to serve in what he called "this Satanic Government." I gave as good as I got. "*You* ought to go and see the Viceroy," I said. "See the Viceroy ? Never !" "You shall and will go," I persisted. "No !" I wrote to Lord Reading nevertheless, and next morning there came a note from the Viceroy asking Charlie to come and take tea with him. Charlie rushed into my room waving the note. "You really *are* Satanic !" he cried between provocation and amusement. "Well ?" I said, "Are you going ?" "No, of course not, I won't go." "Indeed and you will," I retorted, picked up the telephone, and told the Private Secretary that he would come. Then, still protesting, he had to be dressed and sent (he had hardly a change of shirt). He came back subdued and pleased. "Yes," he said, "You were right and I was wrong. He is a good man ; I am glad I went ; he is not like an ordinary Viceroy !"‡

* The anecdote is related by the Rev. E. C. Dewick, to whom the comment was made.

† *Report*, 1930. The figures show that in 1928 average earnings in the tea-gardens were 50 per cent. higher than in 1921.

‡ Story related in conversation with the author.

III

In July, 1921, Rabindranath Tagore returned from Europe. For many months the non-co-operation movement, with Gandhi's great personality at its centre, had been one of the subjects most often discussed in his correspondence with Andrews. Tagore disliked the negative flavour of the word "non-cooperation" itself; his whole nature, as artist and prophet, aspired to the vision of a co-operative world, enriched by the pooling of all its resources of the beautiful and the good. The artist in Andrews shared Tagore's doubts, while at the same time the crusader in him responded to Gandhi's heroic singleness of purpose.

"I enclose Mahatma Gandhi's speech in Calcutta," he wrote to Tagore in January. "It is a great speech as he delivered it. It has all the call back to simplicity and frugality and sacrifice which makes his high appeal so powerful. But somehow it is, like war itself, a thrusting back into the bare primitive, not a grasping of the richness of the future which awaits mankind. It seems to miss all that art means and music means, and song. I know that Mahatmaji would say "Quite so : but are we not at war ?" I know there is a truth there, and we must be ready to strip life bare, at times. But *quite* bare ? No !"*

During the months that followed Tagore's return, Andrews' mind was almost wholly absorbed in the divergence of temperament and attitude between his two great friends. The profound reverence in which he held Tagore as his *guru* prevented him from debating with him the points at issue with the same vehemence and freedom as he did with Gandhi, whose arguments he would bring to Tagore to be discussed and re-discussed. So eagerly did he seek for common ground between them that Borodada, whose own opinions were strongly pro-Gandhi, nicknamed him "The Hyphen" !

Gandhi visited East Bengal and Assam, as Andrews had asked him to do, and when he passed through Calcutta there were very long conversations between him and Tagore at which Andrews was present. Tagore found much that was disturbing to him in the trend of nationalist sentiment. Even some of the youths whom Andrews had accepted for village training at Surul preferred the

* To R.T., 26th January, 1921.

excitement of political agitation to the hard work of daily teaching in a "national" school.

> Rabindranath Tagore felt that the popular attitude had become one of wild excitement rather than deep moral conviction. As he expressed it in a remarkable phrase, it shouted to him, it did not sing. It was an outburst of pent-up feelings leading to violence of speech and action, rather than the sustained power of patient soul-force . . . A further divergence was the poet's inability to take any part in the *khaddar** movement, because it appeared to be put forward as a universal panacea for India's poverty, while he regarded it only as an accessory method of rendering help.†

Gandhi accepted Tagore's warnings against a bigoted or parochial nationalism, and called him in a noble phrase "The Great Sentinel." But he reiterated his conviction that to place the manufacture and use of homespun cloth in the forefront of his programme was a practical and immediate method of relieving the stark poverty of India.

> Our non-cooperation is neither with the English nor with the West —it is with material civilization and its attendant greed and exploitation of the weak . . . The hungry millions ask for one poem, invigorating food.‡

Andrews' whole sympathy, and Tagore's also, was with that cry of an anguished heart. But when Gandhi went on to drive home the lesson of *swadeshi* by a dramatic bonfire of foreign cloth, Andrews deluged him with letters of distress.

> I know that your burning of foreign cloth is with the idea of helping the poor, but I feel that you have gone wrong. There is a subtle appeal to racial feeling in that word foreign, which day by day appears to need checking and not fomenting. The picture of your lighting that great pile of beautiful and delicate fabrics shocked me intensely. We seem to be losing sight of the great outside world to which we belong and concentrating selfishly on India ; and this must, I fear, lead back to the old, bad, selfish nationalism.
>
> . . . I was supremely happy when you were dealing giant blows at the fundamental moral evils—drunkenness, drug-taking, untouchability, race arrogance, etc.—and when you were, with such wonderful and beautiful tenderness, dealing with the hideous vice of prostitution. But . . . . destroying in the fire the noble handiwork of one's own fellow men and

---

* Spinning and wearing homespun cloth.
† *Mahatma Gandhi's Ideas.*
‡ Ibid.

N

women, of one's brothers and sisters abroad, saying it would be "defiling" to use it—I cannot tell you how different all this appears to me ! Do you know I almost fear now to wear the *khaddar* that you have given me, lest I should appear to be judging other people, as a Pharisee would, saying "I am holier than thou." I never felt like this before.

You know how when anything you do hurts me I must cry out to you, and this has hurt me.*

The fact that the burning coincided with a famine in the Khulna district of Bengal, the picture of whose shivering naked villagers was always in his mind's eye, made it appear all the more intolerable. Gandhi answered him affectionately and in detail : †

To me it seems utterly degrading to throw foreign cloth in the face of the poor because we have no longer any use for it . . . If the emphasis were on all foreign *things* it would be racial, parochial, and wicked. The emphasis is on all foreign *cloth*. India is racial today ; the people are filled with illwill. I am transferring the illwill from men to things.

. . . Of course with me the burning is not so vital to the movement. One may be in it although one may not like burning. From Mahadev's‡ talk I gathered that you had begun to doubt the truth of the whole movement. I therefore wrote to you that even if you did my affection for you would remain unaffected. But naturally it consoles me to find that you believe in the movement as much as ever.

From the midst of these painful heart-searchings Andrews was once more called away to Kenya.§ Even before he left the "Moplah Rising" had occurred in the South. When he returned to India in December, 1921, the long-dreaded outbreak of violence had come. In November the visit of the Prince of Wales had been the signal for an outbreak of violence in Bombay which for five days Gandhi and his co-workers were powerless to control. Gandhi did not call off the non-cooperation movement, but he imposed on himself a five-day fast of penance. He also asked Andrews to give a religious message at the annual meeting of the Congress at Ahmedabad. Andrews consented, but with conflicting emotions :

Here is Christmas Day (he wrote to Tagore) and I am on my way to the Congress, and the noise of battle and strife is already meeting me all along the way. Civil disobedience treads upon the very brink of violence the

* Quoted in *Mahatma Gandhi's Ideas*, p. 279. Written August, 1921.
† Letters dated August 13th, September 14th and September 25th, 1921.
‡ The late Mahadev Desai, Gandhi's secretary.
§ See next Chapter.

178

whole time ; and yet there *are* things which are truly heroic—a new spirit infinitely beyond the servile spirit of the past.

My own mind is torn. I *have* to speak out at Ahmedabad, but it is very difficult indeed to know what to say. I *must* speak against these veiled violences—these intimidations, social boycotts, burnings . . .

I think of Aurobindo Ghose saying : "It is useless to speak : the people have gone mad." Is silence best when one is tired out and one's faith dim ?

On the first day of the Congress Andrews stood before the immense concourse at Ahmedabad wearing a European suit of "foreign cloth," and explained frankly why he was not in his usual homespun Indian dress. The audience listened with unabated affection and respect. One nationalist newspaper* had in fact strongly supported the nomination of Andrews as President of the Congress itself, declaring that his objection to the burning of foreign cloth was no bar to his election, and that he was the high priest of the movement for "self-purification." This proposal was not adopted, but the influence of Andrews' thought was plain when a resolution advocating complete independence for India was brought before the meeting. "This is your *shararat*,† Charlie," said Gandhi with a twinkle as he listened to the speech.

IV

Andrews had played his part, as in duty bound, in the dusty political arena of 1921. But in the latter months of the year he grew very weary of the strident controversies and the strife of tongues. He grew more keenly aware of what he had long known—that no relative or temporal good, not even the noblest struggle for justice and righteousness, can by itself fully satisfy the human spirit.

All the Utopias must have some place in them for the *Sannyasin*. The Kingdom of God upon earth must ever have its highways and avenues open towards the unexplored. Otherwise human life, however perfect, must feel its finitude.‡

In the first months of 1922 he found the rest of heart which he needed, not in the retirement of the *sannyasin*, but in the fellow-

* The *Janma Bhumi*.
† "mischief."
‡ *Modern Review*, October, 1921. The whole article is very revealing.

ship of the weak and needy, where controversy was silenced and love was the only language needed. For six weeks he was in South India, in the Moplah areas of Malabar, Cochin and Travancore, where he found "Hindu-Muslim unity shattered and untouchability blighting the country."* His articles on the situation gave offence to certain sections of Hindus because he did not throw all the blame for the previous year's outbreak on the despised and exploited Muslim Moplahs. The real root of the trouble, he was convinced, was the wrong of untouchability which lay heavy on low-caste Hindus and Moplahs alike. One terrible scene was branded on his memory for ever afterwards. Among the wretched hovels of some Cherumas in Malabar he saw a poor woman with her baby and two young children, and stepped forward to caress the little ones and show his friendship. The mother uttered a dreadful cry and shrank away, while children clung to her wailing. "She actually thought I had advanced to strike her. What centuries of human misery lay behind *that* !"†

Among the lowest of the untouchables, the Cherumas, Pulayas and Nayadis, news spread of the coming of "Gandhi's brother." Great meetings of them assembled, and Andrews moved gently among them with his enthusiastic interpreters, the young nationalist Hindus and Christians. So accustomed were they to contumely that it took some time even for Andrews to overcome their cringing fear and win their confidence. Most grievous of all was the discovery that his own fellow-Christians in the Syrian Church of Travancore were in effect a "superior caste" practising untouchability, though some of the young men were fighting it.‡ Mr. K. K. Kuruvila, his host at Kottayam, was one of these. Together they arranged for a common meal in the "untouchable" quarters. Very few Christians came, alas, but those who did so remembered how Andrews had trudged barefoot to and from the gathering, bruising his feet on the rough road, in his eagerness to be at one with the lowliest of his fellow-men.

* To R.T., 27th January, 1922.
† Sermon in Madras, February, 1922, often repeated.
‡ Much progress has been made in recent years.

The lonely struggle continued. In Madras the Sheriff convened a public meeting to support the Legislative Council's protest against the anti-Asiatic policy in Kenya. Here was a cause in which all India might have stood united. Yet the "non-co-operators" wrecked the meeting, howling down the "moderates" on the platform. Andrews, the chief speaker, faced the ill-mannered crowd. "I am going to say only five words," he declared, "I—am—ashamed—of—you !"

Ten days later he was two thousand miles away, living in one cramped, bare little room in the Indian railwaymen's "lines" at Tundla, in the midst of a strike whose sheer pathos called out all the tenderness of which he was capable. The underlying cause of it was the intolerable bullying practised by privileged "Euro-pean" employees towards their Indian subordinates. The insults rankled, and at last the men struck work, impulsively and without notice. By a tragic irony the case upon which they had acted was a very weak one, grossly exaggerated by the victim. Andrews took the unpopular side, and set himself to persuade the men to return to work, disregarding the sneers that "he must have been bribed." By days of quiet, patient, friendly argument he won them over : a private meeting of railwaymen voted unanimously for the resumption of work. Then everything was undone by a public meeting. Outsiders mingled with the crowd ; an un-known mob orator intoxicated his hearers by an entirely irrelevant speech—and the strike was on once more. All Andrews' work had to be done over again from the beginning ; it took more than three weeks, and in all that time, though Delhi was only a few hours' journey away, his was the only personal inquiry made. The indifference of the general public hurt him deeply. "We *deserve* to suffer inconvenience," he wrote scathingly to the news-papers. "If these poor men are ignorant and gullible, it is the fault of our own negligence."*

"I am tired almost to death," he wrote to Tagore.† "There can of course be no rest, no convenience or comfort or retirement in such a life as this. But I am among the poor and understanding something of their

* See articles in the *Modern Review* for March and May, 1922.

† 26th February, 1922.

burden. Always it is the poor grass—these illiterate men—that gets trodden under foot."

Meantime civil disobedience had come to a tragic end. After twenty-one policemen had been lynched by an infuriated mob at Chauri-Chaura, Gandhi called off the campaign. He himself was arrested and imprisoned, but the nobility of his demeanour at his trial went far to heal the general bitterness. As for Andrews, the terrible occurrence at Chauri-Chaura only increased his conviction that political and social liberties were inseparable.

"When I think (an Indian student had said) of the oppressions and exactions which my family and others like them, the landowners, visit on the poor in our part of India, I'm surprised they don't all rise up and murder us all in our beds." "What part is that ?" someone asked casually. "Chauri-Chaura in the United Provinces," he replied.

"The greatest problem of India today," wrote Andrews, "is the oppression of the poor—and there is no tyrant so relentless towards the poor as the man who is abject and servile to those who are above him."*

* The *Modern Review*, March, 1922.

CHAPTER XIII

"COMPASSION ON THE MULTITUDE"

THE intense emotional conflicts of the non-cooperation days were now laid to rest. During the two years of Gandhi's imprisonment Andrews made his headquarters at Santiniketan, but travelled very widely in India on missions of humanitarian service, and in 1923 visited England again for the first time since his three weeks' visit in March, 1914.

The most intransigent of his problems was that of the returned emigrants, chiefly from Fiji and British Guiana, to whose plight passing reference has already been made.* The year 1920, with its high post-war cost of living and the inevitable unrest incidental to the transition from "indentured" to "free" labour, had been a very difficult one in Fiji, and large numbers of ex-indentured labourers, together with some who had been born in the colony, had availed themselves of the first opportunity to return to India. A high percentage of them could not be reabsorbed into the economy of the districts from which they had originally emigrated ; fleeced and robbed in Calcutta, stigmatised as outcastes in their own villages, they drifted back disillusioned to Matiaburz, in the malaria-ridden mud flats beyond the Calcutta docks, in the hope that they would be able from there to get a passage back to Fiji. They turned naturally to Andrews, the only friend they knew in India, for help in their misery.

Andrews paid his first visit to Matiaburz in January, 1921. He realised from the first that the returned emigrants were "chiefly the worst characters, but with some good people settled among them," and that the most urgent problem was that of the Fiji-born. "I feel quite clear," he wrote to the Government of India officer

* See Chapter XI, p. 150.

responsible, "that if the Government of Fiji wishes to give free passage to these it should be allowed to do so."* The remainder, unsatisfactory as most of them were, were human beings in distress, and Andrews spared no pains to get them resettled in India. The problem reached even greater dimensions in 1922. In February of that year the Colonial Sugar Refining Company, whose enormous dividends during the preceding financial year were described by the *Sydney Bulletin* as "an incredible performance," reduced the wages of its Indian labourers by more than one-third, to a level which Fiji Government officials declared to be less than a living wage.† No wonder the "coolie ships" returned crowded to Calcutta.

Little by little Andrews got together a small but hard-working committee—the Indian Emigrants' Friendly Service Committee—with representatives of the Government of Bengal, the Port Health authorities, and the public. Mr. F. E. James and Mr. H. K. Mookerjee were its energetic secretaries. They met the incoming ships ; they protected the labourers from dishonest money-changers and thieves ; they gave shelter to the homeless. Andrews' persistence secured them some Government aid. It was heart-breaking work ; so few of those to whom Andrews appealed for help to resettle the repatriated families responded to his careful, personal letters ; so few of the Fiji Indians were able to use the opportunities that offered. They had been transplanted too often ; they could not take root again. "Shoot us or send us back," they would cry to Andrews when he visited them, and as the months went by the danger of violence increased. "There will be a riot if nothing is done," wrote Andrews on September 1st. Group after group sought him out at Santiniketan, travelling ticketless to Bolpur. He would listen over and over again, with tears in his eyes, to the same pitiful, insoluble problem, and then take out his last handful of coins to pay their fares back to Calcutta. They would return to sordid Matiaburz a little comforted with the memory of a warm and brotherly embrace and the knowledge

---

* Letter to Sir George Barnes, 24th January, 1921. This decision brought him abuse from those who wished to exploit the labour unrest in Fiji for political ends.

† *The Indian Review*, July, 1922.

that there was someone who cared for their fate ; and Andrews would turn with a sigh to his desk, wondering if there was any letter still unwritten, any plan still untried, which might help them in their misery.

No one will ever know exactly how Andrews himself lived during those years in India. Bodies such as the Marwari Association and the Imperial Indian Citizenship Association gave him financial backing for his work among the distressed, and enabled him to pay for some secretarial help in the cause of Indians overseas. Wealthy friends sometimes helped. Everywhere hospitable doors were open to him : hostesses, Indian and English, darned his socks, sewed on his buttons, or replenished his supply of shirts. Railway tickets were gladly bought, postage stamps provided, taxis paid for. It was not always easy to be Andrews' host. "The most unselfish of men may be unconsciously the most exacting," said one friend* very truly in speaking of him. By temperament an artist, he was wholly absorbed in the experience and need of the moment, and wholly oblivious of time. "He would want tea at five in the morning, then order lunch at one o'clock and come at four, with all kinds of people following in his train. 'Don't be flurried, my dear,' he would say to the worried hostess. 'Anything in the house will do' !"†

He was often penniless. "I wanted to wire, but had no money, so am writing instead," is a sentence not uncommon in his correspondence. When he had money, he kept the rule he had made long before in Walworth—better be deceived by the unworthy than run the risk of refusing the needy. He was deceived, of course ; a beggar to whom he had given his fare to Madras was seen, three days later, still slouching round Calcutta ; a "needy student" took an advance from him for typing a manuscript, and he never saw man or manuscript again. Andrews would hear no word against them. "Who are we to judge ?" he would say. A Marwari friend gave him a pair of gold cuff-links ; they were gone when Andrews paid him his next visit. Again and again some ragged hill-man, shivering on the Simla roads,

* Mr. T. D. Santwan.
† Mrs. G. C. Chatterji (Ila Rudra).

had his overcoat, and he returned home drenched to the skin in the monsoon rain, to be scolded lovingly and anxiously by his hosts.

Other people's property was no safer in his hands than his own, but however annoying its disappearance might be at the time, it was hard to be angry with him for long. On one occasion he had been staying at Susil Rudra's home in Delhi, and was off on one of his long exacting journeys. The old man was concerned that Charlie should get his early morning tea. "What about letting him have the thermos, Sudhir?" he asked. This was a particularly good thermos, a gift which Sudhir had brought from England for his father. "But I bought it for *you*," he expostulated. "It's no good giving Mr. Andrews anything—he never brings it back." At this point Andrews appeared. "Sudhir says he will let you have the thermos, Charlie," said Susil, "if you will bring it back." (Sudhir, *sotto voce* : "I didn't say anything of the kind !") Andrews presently returns—no thermos is in sight. "Where is the thermos, Mr. Andrews?" asked Sudhir as they sat down to a meal. "Thermos? Did I have a thermos? Oh, yes, thermos. Well, you see it was like this—there was an Anglo-Indian woman in the train and her baby was howling and yelling and she wanted a hot drink for it. So . . ."

I I

September, 1922, found Andrews in Amritsar, where the Akalis, a Puritan group of Sikhs bent on reforming abuses in the management of their holy places, were challenging the right of the *mahant* to prevent them from cutting firewood in Guru-ka-Bagh,* a short distance outside the city. The *mahant* called on the police to prevent trespass ; and as the number of challengers ran into hundreds, the police were directed to do this not by arrest, but by "using the minimum of force." The Akalis adopted the method of non-violent *satyagraha*, one little party after another going up to the guarded gateway and standing quietly before it until felled or driven back by blows, while a great crowd of their supporters looked on in silent sympathy. Andrews went

* Literally, the Garden of the Guru. *Mahant*, the chief priest of a shrine.

to see the drama for himself, and was greatly impressed by the discipline and religious fervour of this martial people.

"There has been something far greater in this event," he wrote, "than a mere dispute about land and property. It has gone far beyond the technical questions of legal possession and distraint. A new heroism learned through suffering, has arisen in the land. A new lesson in moral warfare has been taught to the world. This fact in the ultimate issue is independent of the mere legal question of trespass decided for or against the Akali Sikhs. They believe intensely that their right to cut wood in the garden of the Guru was an immemorial religious right, and this faith of theirs is surely to be counted for righteousness, whatever a defective and obsolete law may determine regarding legality.

" . . . I saw no act, no look of defiance. It was a true martyrdom to them as they went forward, a true act of faith, a true deed of devotion to God. They remembered their gurus how they had suffered, and they rejoiced to add their own sufferings to the treasury of their wonderful faith.

" . . . Many of them, old soldiers who had fought in France, said to me afterwards in the hospital : This was a new kind of battle ; we have never fought like this before. This is Mahatma Gandhi's battle."*

At the Golden Temple in Amritsar, where the Akalis assembled in multitudes to their war-cry of *Sat Sri Akal*,† Andrews' loved and trusted figure—for memories of 1919 were fresh and strong—played no small part in keeping them true to the strange discipline of this "new kind of battle."

Day after day he spent in incessant writing, striving by means of articles such as the one quoted above to uphold Gandhi's ideals during his imprisonment. Then, at the end of September, he joined Tagore for his tour in South India and Ceylon. In his loving anxiety to ease the strain on his friend he took upon himself a heavy burden of secretarial responsibility ; though at the same time, in his eagerness that Tagore's ideals should be known, he tended to arrange for him impossibly crowded programmes. But throughout the tour he devoted himself first and foremost to the "untouchables." On October 8th he preached a sermon in Madras which he repeated all over the South, taking as his text the words of Christ, "I have compassion on the multitude."

I saw only three days ago a sight which filled my heart with sadness. We went out to a village in the Madras Presidency and there was to be a

* From *The Tribune*, Lahore, 22nd September, 1922.
† "True is the Deathless One."

welcome to the great poet and I went a little before the poet and there in
the village there were villagers and others with all preparations to meet the
poet, and then in another place away from them were some wretched
poverty-stricken half-naked men, women, and little children, and I said,
"Who are these ?" They said, "These are Panchamas." I went to love
them and they ran away. They actually began to run away in fear of me,
and it broke my heart to see the fear towards me. And then I told one of
them to tell them not to run away but to come nearer, and I went to them
with love and embraced them, and though I could not speak to them in
words they knew I loved them in heart. They were kept away in the
background. They had no place in the welcome of the poet. And then
someone at a distance asked them by a sign to prostrate themselves, and
they fell down and rubbed their foreheads in the dust. That was the sight
that filled my heart with pity.

. . . There is only one thing I want to say and that is this—"I have
compassion on the multitude." That is what Christ said. That is what
Buddha said before. It is a very simple word. It needs a tender heart.
Is there not someone in this church who could take this up, live among
them, live the whole of their lives among them ? Be a Panchama, feel
their sufferings and touch them . . . If I could see my way to give up
other duties, how I wish I could do it. Why cannot some of you do that ?
I ask you as human beings, not as Hindus, not as Christians, not as Mahom-
medans, but as men who are human beings, cannot you remove the
burden ?*

From Madras he went north again among his old friends the
railwaymen. At a conference in Bombay and again at the North-
Western Railwaymen's conference at Lahore, where he presided,
he worked to establish an All-India Railwaymen's Federation
which should have a central Standing Committee at Delhi to
represent its interests before the Railway Board. Delegates met
at Allahabad, and the Federation came into being.

A typical anecdote is told of those long December journeys.
One cold morning his train had reached a big city station in
North India, and Andrews and his companion were making their
way towards the exit, woollen shawls round their shoulders.
They noticed a crowd in front of the Station Master's office ; in
its centre stood an angry Station Master, abusing a shrinking,
crouching, shivering figure—a woman. "She was warming
herself at the fire in his room, and he turned her out," said the

* Printed in *The Indian Problem*, Madras, 1923. The style is characteristic of
Andrews' spoken word.

crowd. Andrews confronted him. "I am absolutely ashamed of you," he said quietly. "You—a Christian ! You might at least be courteous." Turning gently to the woman he put his own shawl round her thin shoulders.*

In Bengal, famine threatened the villages which had been devastated by flood during the previous year. Some of the Tagore family estates lay within the affected area, and Rabindranath was much concerned about the condition of the people. Andrews went to Potisar in his name, taking letters from the Governor, Lord Lytton, to the two Collectors concerned.

"We are going down the Nagar river in a small boat," he reported, "in order to visit the villages on the bank. From morning till night the poor people sit on the bank above the houseboat and come with their petitions. I asked that no one should be kept away from me. When I go along the shore they come and follow me and it is the same wherever I go.

" . . . The most vitally immediate question is that of seed and cattle. There is one sowing due in a little less than a month's time. But how is the ploughing to be done and where is the seed to come from ?"†

Sleepless on his bed, he found an answer to his question. At seven o'clock next morning he trudged into the relief workers' camp at Atrai, seven miles away. Would they approve of approaching Government for a loan for the purchase of seed grain and for a tractor to do the work of the cattle and get the land ploughed in time ? They would ? Good ! No, thanks, he wouldn't sit down or wait for refreshments—he must be off at once to Calcutta to report to Lord Lytton.

The loan was granted ; the tractor was promised. Five weeks later Andrews wrote again from Potisar :

"It is a very good thing I came back. It has distinctly hurried up things all round, and Government are now at the present moment distributing fifty thousand rupees in Kaligram alone for seed and cattle, which was what I demanded. As Nogen Babu‡ has just said, it could not have come to the people if I had not been on the spot to press for it . . . The tractor is at work at last and the people are pleased with it. The riot which I told you about with the fishermen has been a great trouble, and I have been very glad to be down here to help to put things straight. I have done all I could and I think it is now all finished and done with."§

* We are indebted for this story to the Rev. S. N. Talib-ud-Din of Saharanpur.
† To Rabindranath Tagore, 8th January, 1923.
‡ Sri N. N. Ganguly, the poet's son-in-law.
§ To Rabindranath Tagore, 15th February, 1923.

Care for the multitude never excluded care for the individual. Between the two visits to Potisar, Andrews went back to Santiniketan. A Tamil lad from the far south had come to join the Art School, choosing Santiniketan for his work because of Andrews' presence. There within a few days he was taken ill and died. The stricken father took comfort in the knowledge that Andrews had been by his side. "He ministered like an angel, believe me, like a God-sent angel. Blessed my son was by being enveloped by this Christian love."*

Time after time Andrews would tramp into Bolpur under the stars and take the early morning train for Calcutta. Picking his way through the crowds he would walk across the city to the office of the *Modern Review* or *Vishal Bharat*, or in these days, often, to the Science College to Acharya P. C. Ray, who was organizing the students for flood relief work. "Why do you walk ? Why don't you take a bus ?" his friends would expostulate. Then they would find a fiery letter from him in their morning newspaper, asking, for example, how the citizens of Calcutta could tolerate shuddering little boys of ten years old being sent down manholes in the roadway to clean the city sewers. "You see," said the gentle voice, "I wouldn't know about these things if I didn't walk." And some at least of his hearers reflected that they themselves had walked countless times down the Harrison Road, and "having eyes, had seen not" the things which he had seen.

On one such morning, so the story goes, he called a newsboy and asked him for a paper, and then, putting his hand into his pocket to pay for it, found that the street beggars had already claimed all his change. The boy's eyes watched him closely. "You are Andrews Saheb," he said suddenly, "I shan't take any money from you." And he darted off into the crowd, leaving the paper in Andrews' hand.

Other young Bengalis, however, were decidedly critical.

"I was staying with Acharya P. C. Ray at the Science College, Calcutta," relates one of them.† "One day he told me that a great man was coming to breakfast. I felt much excited, but only a very shabbily-dressed European, who looked no better than a missionary, came in carrying a big

* Mr. P. R. Pillai to Dr. L. P. Larsen, 12th February, 1923.
† Sri Gopal Basak. Letter to the authors.

bag. After breakfast they had some serious discussions. I could hardly believe that this was the great man, but wondered whether I could get any help from him about the correspondence which was coming from Germany proposing a Students' International. Acharyaji then asked me to take Mr. Andrews (whose name I thus discovered) to the Raja Ram Mohun Library. On the way I broached the subject that was on my mind, but I had the impression that he was not so much listening as watching me—outwardly 100 per cent. a Gandhi-ite, inwardly a terrorist. Suddenly he put his bag on my head and asked me to carry it, and began to question me. Did I really know our poor? Had my organisation done any relief work? I decided that he was some sort of humanitarian and reformist, and that young Bengal revolutionaries could have no truck with him—nevertheless, that conversation played its part in drawing me into the mass movement."

III

From March 1923 onwards, Andrews' attention was once more absorbed by the affairs of Kenya Indians. In the autumn of 1921 he had paid a second short visit to the colony at their urgent request, to help them to contest the statutory discrimination against Indians as a race which had been foreshadowed in Lord Milner's proposals the previous year. The Indians had wanted to make him president of the East Africa Indian Congress, but Andrews had refused to accept the honour, saying that his desire was to serve and not to lead.

During this visit the fury of the settler extremists against this "traitor" to their cause had reached such a pitch that on at least one occasion Andrews was in imminent danger of being lynched. The enthusiasm with which he was welcomed by Indian and African alike was acidly commented upon in the press, and he was charged with betraying Christianity by his friendliness towards Hindus and Muslims. "When I think," wrote one self-righteous correspondent, "of the harm done by this person and his propaganda, I can only exclaim with the evangelist, 'Jesus wept'." A few days later Andrews left Nairobi for a second visit to Uganda. When the train stopped at Nakoro station at midnight, a party of settlers entered his compartment, seized him by the beard, and endeavoured to drag him out on to the platform, while the ringleader stood over him repeating, in tones of utter loathing and contempt, "Jesus wept ! Jesus wept !" It seems very possible that Andrews owed his life to the fact that he did not travel on the day he had originally planned, but was obliged by illness to postpone his journey for twenty-four hours ; the long wait and the uncertainty had by that time somewhat cooled his assailants' heads. A sick man already, he was very badly shaken, and was nursed back to health by his friend Dr. Cook of the mission hospital at Kampala, in Uganda. He reported the incident to the Governor, Lord Northey, who mentioned it in his despatch to London. Mr. Winston Churchill in his reply expressed his regret that Andrews should have forborne to report the names of the men concerned. "It would have been a matter of satisfaction to me," he wrote, "and doubtless to all right-thinking people in the Colony, if the miscreants had been brought to justice."

Churchill was right ; the majority of Kenya Europeans viewed such proceedings with disgust ; but they were politically passive, and the hotheads were very vocal. The lengths to which their unreasoning hatred might carry them were seen again as Andrews returned from Uganda on the lake steamer. He had been talking to a Sikh lady and gentleman and playing with their baby. A short time afterwards one of the settler passengers came up to him, trembling with almost uncontrollable anger. "Do you know," he burst out, "when I saw you with that black child in your arms I could have *murdered* you ! I could have caught you by the scruff of the neck and pitched you into the sea !"

Such was the atmosphere of Kenya in November, 1921. By March, 1923, tension had reached the danger point. The previous September the India and Colonial Offices had agreed on a series of proposals which, while never officially published, were known to include the abandonment of the policy of racial segregation and a franchise on a common educational or property test with a common electoral roll. These proposals were far from satisfying the Indian community, for they left the Highlands grievance untouched ; but they were accepted by Indians as a solid advance towards equal citizenship. The European settlers not only refused to discuss them, but threatened armed rebellion if any attempt was made to put them into effect. The Governor went to London for consultation ; so did deputations from both European and Indian groups. The latter begged Andrews to go with them as their adviser ; and he left India in April with the Rt. Hon. V. Srinivasa Sastri. "If Kenya is lost, all is lost," said Sastri.

Without Sastri's companionship the voyage would have been a very lonely one for Andrews.

> "An atmosphere of veiled hostility pervades the ship," he wrote.* "I have been a marked man and an object of intense dislike . . . I have done whatever could reasonably be done to overcome it by conforming to Western etiquette in everything and by being friendly and sociable on all occasions, but once or twice it has led to something very unpleasant being said or done which I try to forget as soon as possible. It is the penalty that has to be paid and I must not grumble—a sense of humour can accomplish wonders."

One cannot help wondering whether his efforts to "conform" were as successful as he thought they were, or whether in fact he looked much as he did a couple of years later on another voyage :

> The dear man was then wearing rather down-and-out European clothes plus *bare* feet—and the comments of his fellow-passengers were rather lurid!†

However that might be, he confessed to nostalgic dreams :

> I picture myself spending the whole of the delightful summer vacation in our College garden at Cambridge. There is a table under a tree (which I know well) where I could sit and write a book. There is solitude and peace, and no sound of motor-cars and no smoke or dust or noise. But when my day-dream is getting serenely happy comes the annoying little God called Conscience, and says in a harsh voice, "What do you mean by it ? Why are you shirking, when there are hundreds still in prison all through this hot weather in India ? Why are you not bearing the burden and heat of the day, instead of making yourself comfortable and lazy in a Cambridge College garden ?" The Kenya issue *must* be fought, even to certain defeat, rather than India and Christ betrayed.‡

The issue was fought faithfully. A pocket diary for 1923 shows May and early June crowded with appointments ; it is clear that Andrews set himself to win every man and woman who by knowledge of African affairs, by liberal and vigorous journalism, or by Christian leadership, might educate public opinion and influence

---

* To Rabindranath Tagore, undated, April, 1923.

† The Rev. E. C. Dewick, to the authors.

‡ To Rabindranath Tagore, *loc. cit.*

o

the course of events. The Secretaries and Under-Secretaries for India and the Colonies would not see him, but he spoke at the Liberal Club, dined at the House of Commons, visited such Colonial officials, educationists, and missionaries as he could reach, and went down repeatedly to Canterbury to see the Archbishop. When the peace of the summer vacation settled over the Pembroke garden, he was on his way back to India.

On one occasion during this publicity campaign Sastri and Andrews were both present at a crowded meeting at the Indian Student Hostel in London. Sastri had made a temperately worded and eloquent appeal, but he was followed by a speaker who delivered a heated attack upon the British, declaring that if they wanted violence they should have it to the full. The scene that followed is thus described by one who was present.*

> The place echoed with cheers from the students assembled in hundreds. Then C.F.A. spoke. "After the speech to which we have just listened," he began, "I cannot say to you what I had intended to say tonight" ; and he then went on to administer a loving but outspoken rebuke of the spirit which answered hate with hate, reminding them of how the Buddha, five hundred years before Christ, had taught men that
>
> > Never by hate can hatreds cease ;
> > Love only ends them evermore ;
> > Love only brings all strife to peace ;
> > That is the true, the ancient law.
>
> "Karma is true !" he exclaimed, "Karma is true ! 'What a man sows that shall he also reap.' We in India have for centuries permitted sixty million so-called untouchables to remain in our midst in conditions utterly degrading to the children of the one Father. Can we complain if others now treat us in the same way ?" It was a most moving moment, and I hardly knew whether to admire more the courage of the man, or the silence in which the students received his rebuke—a silence so eloquent of the respect and love in which they held him—and then at the close burst into applause.

The Colonial Office memorandum on Kenya was published in July, when Andrews was back in India. The proposal for a common electoral roll was replaced by one for a communal franchise ; the question of immigration was to be decided in Kenya. This was defeat. Almost simultaneously,† General

* Father J. C. Winslow, in a letter to the authors.
† 24th July, 1923.

Smuts outlined proposals for racial segregation in Natal, to be embodied in a Bill in January, 1924. Andrews shared the indignation of India to the full. But there was one passage in the Kenya memorandum which nevertheless seemed to him to mark a real advance. It ran as follows :

> His Majesty's Government think it necessary to record their considered opinion that the interests of the African natives must be paramount and that if and when these interests and the interests of the immigrant races should conflict, the former should prevail . . . His Majesty's Government regard themselves as exercising a trust for the protection and advancement of the native races which they are unable to delegate or share.

Andrews had everywhere advocated a return to strict Crown Colony Government, with no franchise at all, as far better for both African and Indian than any form of communal franchise ; he now welcomed this public snub to the advocates of "white" responsible Government. Most of his Indian collaborators however were too bitterly angry at the racial insults they had endured either to believe in the good faith of the British Government's declaration for the African, or to listen to Andrews' advocacy of the "no franchise" solution. After his dogged and lonely endurance of coldness and hostility in England, it was almost too much even for his courage to find himself isolated in India also. More keenly than ever he longed for the comradeship and enlightened counsel of the imprisoned Gandhi. A letter which he wrote in August to one of his closest co-workers, Mr. J. B. Petit, reflects his pain :

> We knew for certain we should not get *common* franchise. It was a choice between *communal* franchise or *no* franchise at all. Communal franchise means the destruction of the native ; it also means death to the Indian . . . I tell you I could have come back and convinced Mahatma Gandhi in two minutes because he understands the situation.
>
> But the Bombay committee listened to all I had to say and sent a cable about which I was not consulted both to England and to Kenya warning against the "no franchise" solution. It is desperately hard for me to have spent months and months on a problem and gone long journeys to East Africa and England and to have collected all the facts and then to have a hasty decision made against me.

There was worse to come. Sections of Indian opinion in Kenya regarded Andrews' care for African interests as a betrayal of their own cause, and a campaign of abuse was directed against him there. When the East African mail came in during the latter part of August he found a virulent letter in *The Democrat*, a Nairobi Indian paper, which wounded all the more deeply because it was signed by one who in Kenya had treated him as a friend.

"We have another kind of enemy," ran the accusation, "the insidious, bowing, cringing, khaddar-wearing, barefooted white *sadhus*, who take our side to help us lose the game . . . A careful perusal of the White Paper will show that for the purpose of defeating the Indian claims the interests of the natives are brought forward. It was Mr. C. F. Andrews who introduced this native affairs stunt into local politics."*

The writer went on to suggest that Andrews had deliberately suggested the "native affairs stunt" to the British authorities as a manoeuvre to discomfit the Indians.

Rarely, if ever, had Andrews been so cruelly hurt. He was physically ill, and for three weeks he was tormented by fever and by the apparent defeat of everything he had fought for. At last he wrote to Mr. C. Rajagopalachari, who was then editing *Young India*, sending extracts from *The Democrat* and a covering letter from himself. "The attack," he said,

"makes me at once wish to retire into obscurity and find shelter with my God, who knows how false such things are. I cannot be the same as before after such a thing has happened."

He then went on to raise the whole subject above the personal plane, and to treat it as a symptom of an insidious disease which India must recognise and combat. Distrust and suspicion, he pointed out, were always apt to run like an epidemic through a subject people, as through all peoples in times of war—witness the "spy mania" in England and Ireland as well as in India. He ended with an appeal, writing as an Indian to Indians :

"I have decided to publish this directly under my own name for one single reason. Is it not time that we determined faithfully and truly to refrain from personal attacks and ascribing personal motives ? The habit is so deadly when once it is formed !"†

The warmth of affection with which Rajagopalachari and the whole of the Indian press rallied to Andrews' support, and the indignation with which they repudiated the suggestions of *The*

* *The Democrat*, 11th August, 1923.
† *Young India*, 13th September, 1923.

Democrat, showed clearly where India's real sympathies lay. Nor was the work in Kenya and London entirely fruitless. The continual pressure that was brought to bear in religious and political circles in England by men who offered evidence to prove the need of an impartial inquiry into East African affairs, did result in 1924 in the appointment of a Committee of Investigation. In that pressure C. F. Andrews had played an honourable part.

IV

During the autumn of 1923 Andrews pondered much over what his next task should be. He continued extremely unwell, but such matters he was accustomed to ignore.* It seemed as though he might be needed in South Africa to fight the threatened segregation legislation. Then in October a visit to a students' conference in Assam brought him face to face with the evils of the opium traffic, and he wondered whether he should not remain there instead to share in the Congress campaign against it. The dilemma was tragically solved. News reached Andrews in Assam that the beloved Willie Pearson, on his way back to India after years of absence, had been killed in a railway accident in Italy. It was the final blow. Andrews' health gave way completely, and by the end of November he was on his way back to England again for medical treatment.

At first the atmosphere of Europe brought little relief. As Andrews listened to the church bells ringing out under the stars on a clear and frosty Christmas Eve, he thought of the violence, hatred, and suspicion which everywhere mocked their message of peace and goodwill. In England, Gandhi was accused of fomenting the riots which had led to his imprisonment, and abjuring *ahimsa*.

Nevertheless, the two short visits to England in 1923 mark the end of the extreme isolation and loneliness of which this chapter has told. In Andrews' old Cambridge friend, G. P. Gooch, now editor of the *Contemporary Review*, in C. P. Scott, of the *Manchester Guardian*, and in the circles to which they introduced him,

---

* "I always think of you as spent and tired and refusing to take notice of it. You give others courage, Mr. Andrews!" So wrote an Afrikaander friend a few years later. (M. E. Rothmann to C.F.A., 10th February, 1928.)

he found an England responsive to Visva-Bharati ideals, alert, eager to understand the Indian point of view. In such men as the Quaker Stephen Hobhouse and his fellow-members of the Society of Friends he found in addition a Christian pacifism attuned to the Indian ideal of *ahimsa*, and intelligent support for prison reform and the anti-opium campaign. He paid his first visit to the Quaker Settlement of Woodbrooke in the southern suburbs of Birmingham, staying with J. S. Hoyland, with whom he had been friendly since his later years at St. Stephen's College. Though several years were to pass before the time came to make England his headquarters, he worked from the beginning of 1924 in the closest collaboration with English sympathisers, and the articles on Indian affairs which he contributed to the *Manchester Guardian* date from this period.

For him the greatest joy of the whole visit was to meet Albert Schweitzer, whose book, *The Quest of the Historical Jesus*, had meant so much to him, at the home of their mutual friends, Mr. and Mrs. J. H. Oldham. As they walked together to the station at the end of the visit an incident happened which Andrews delighted to recount in India as a perfect example of the spirit of *ahimsa* at work in the Christian spirit of Europe :

. We were carrying between us on a walking-stick Albert Schweitzer's heavy German rucksack. It was a slippery morning of partially thawed snow. Schweitzer suddenly exclaimed, "Ach so !" and stopped dead, nearly upsetting me. Stooping, he tenderly took a half-thawed worm out of a rut in the road and put it carefully in the hedgerow. "There it will be quite safe," he said. "Here in the road it would be killed."*

The needful medical treatment had been secured just in time, and Andrews' health rapidly improved. Then, early in 1924, news came which sent him hurrying back to India. Gandhi had been taken suddenly and seriously ill with appendicitis in Yeravada Jail. His life was saved by an emergency operation at dead of night ; he was unconditionally released, and nursed back to health in the Sassoon Hospital at Poona.

* *Current Thought*, Madras, April, 1925, and in many other articles.

CHAPTER XIV
THE OPIUM TRAFFIC
1924-25   AGE 53-54

WITH Gandhi's release from jail, Andrews' friendship with him entered its third and most intimate phase. Springing from a common concern for the oppressed and down-trodden and a common faith in the ultimate power and reality of love, it had stood the test of much vehement disagreement over particular methods and policies, and the long separation had only drawn closer the bonds of confidence and trust.

I

"Why don't you go to Mahatmaji ?" asked Tagore when Andrews reappeared at Santiniketan in January, 1924. "That is your real work." Andrews needed no urging. During a brief visit to Poona immediately after he landed in India, he had seen enough to know how much he was needed. During the next two months he lived with Gandhi, shared in the many consultations with leaders from every quarter which took place during his convalescence, and edited *Young India*, the weekly paper which Gandhi made the vehicle of his political, social and religious thinking.

Two major decisions taken during those months had a special bearing on Andrews' life. He was present when Gandhi and George Joseph, the Indian Christian nationalist, planned a *satyagraha* campaign under the latter's leadership at Vykom in North Travancore, in order to vindicate the right of the "untouchables" to use the public road that skirted the village temple. Recalling what he had seen and heard in Assam three months before, he pressed the All India Congress Committee to make a full enquiry into the use of opium there, and took a leading part in its organisation. Tagore meanwhile was visiting China. Andrews met him at Hongkong on his return journey, and spent June, July and most of August in Malaya and Burma, combining work for Visva-Bharati with an extension of his inquiry into the use of opium in the Far East.

Meanwhile ominous political developments were taking place in India. Under the Act of 1919 the Indian Legislatures were elected on a system of "communal" franchise analogous to that which Andrews had fought against in Kenya ; the divisive tendencies inherent in the system were accentuated by the organisation of the "depressed classes" or "untouchables" for political power, and by the decision of the Swarajist Party (the political wing of the Congress) to enter the Legislatures. In August there was an ugly outbreak of communal rioting, especially in the Frontier Province. Gandhi, who was at Delhi, suffered an agony of shame ; after a night and a day of watching and prayer he entered on a twenty-one-day fast of atonement. This he did at Delhi, from September 17th to October 8th. During the fast, four hundred prominent men representing every religion and province of India met in Delhi at a "Unity Conference" and pledged themselves to the healing of communal divisions. Andrews was with Gandhi again ; once more he edited *Young India* ; once more, during Gandhi's fast and convalescence, he fulfilled the offices of friendship.

The labourer and the untouchable continued to claim their share of Andrews' attention. In 1918, on his way back from Fiji, he had spent three weeks in Malaya studying the welfare of Indian plantation labourers, and had travelled on from Singapore to Madras on the *Tara,* one of the regular "coolie ships." It was with very keen regret that he had felt obliged, the following summer, to decline an invitation from the Planters' Association itself to revisit the country and advise its members on labour policy. Conditions in Malaya were comparatively good, and Malaya was one of the only two countries to which emigration for the purpose of unskilled labour was permitted by the India Emigration Act of 1922, which had been drafted in close consultation with Andrews himself.* In 1924 he met the Planters'

* "Emigration for the purpose of unskilled labour," ran the Act, "shall not be lawful except to such countries and on such terms as the Governor-General-in-Council by notification in the *Gazette of India* may specify in this behalf." The other "specified" country besides Malaya was Ceylon.

IN SINGAPORE, 1924

WITH MRS. VIVIAN BOSE AND HER BABY DAUGHTER

Association at last, and in a speech full of appreciation of what had already been achieved, pointed to the inhuman conditions on the coolie ships as the real cause of the moral evils which were still rampant on the plantations. Men would *not* bring wives and families, he insisted, on such ships as the *Tara* ; there could be no healthy community life on the plantations until drastic reforms in the travelling arrangements had been made.

Early in 1925 he was in Travancore watching the Vykom *satyagraha*, which continued with dogged patience day after day and month after month through every kind of weather. The pluck and idealism of the young volunteers moved him deeply ; his own presence brought them new encouragement and cheer.

His next step was to throw in his lot with the All India Trade Union Congress, which had been founded in 1920. Four years of intimate experience of Indian labour problems, and a visit to the International Labour Office at Geneva in 1923, had convinced him that some central Trade Union authority was necessary and desirable. He therefore attended the annual conference of the Congress at Nagpur in February, 1925, and was at once elected President for 1925-26. This meant that he was frequently called upon during the year to advise or mediate in industrial disputes. He made a journey to Assam to complete the Opium Inquiry work, another to the flood-devastated areas of Orissa ; and he paid countless visits to Matiaburz. Yet he still planned and hoped to be a Santiniketan teacher, and when the new school year began in July, 1925, he volunteered enthusiastically to take charge of some of the classes. The offer was accepted, but a few weeks later the Rector, who himself had the deepest sympathy with Andrews' outside interests, felt obliged to point out that a school time-table could not depend upon the convenience of the teachers, and to suggest that Andrews should reckon up the number of days on which he had been away from the *ashram* during the short period that had elapsed. It was his last attempt to do regular class teaching. By November of the same year South Africa had claimed him once more.

II

To this bare outline must be added the story of the opium campaign. Andrews' breadth and clarity of vision and his power of selfless perseverance are nowhere more strikingly illustrated.

The sale of Indian opium for both the home and the foreign markets was under the control of the Government of India. Andrews' interest in the traffic had been quickened by his reading of Miss La Motte's book *The Opium Monopoly*, of whose revelations he wrote scathingly in the *Modern Review* for December 1920. The export of opium to China was illegal, but there was something very sinister about the enormous quantities of the drug, scores and even hundreds of times in excess of any possible local requirements, which were being shipped from India to Hongkong, Singapore, Bangkok and other ports fringing China on the south, and from which the authorities of these ports were deriving a huge proportion of their revenue. Andrews kept in touch with Miss La Motte, and made a careful study of all the available literature on the subject, with reference both to the export and to the home consumption of opium. Early in 1921 Doctor Manilal, who had been his host in Suva, wrote to him from Mauritius, where opium addiction was one of the problems of the domiciled Indian community, inviting him to investigate. Andrews could not go, but the invitation increased his personal interest in the traffic. Later in the same year Gandhi had visited Assam and carried on an intensive campaign against the prevalent abuse of the drug. Official quarters belittled the results. The Government Excise Report for 1921-22 declared that "the object of the non-cooperators was not temperance reform but to embarrass Government," and that by March, 1922, "conditions were more or less normal again." When Andrews visited Assam in October, 1923, however, a Government Excise officer told him that the fall in opium consumption had been even greater than the 40 per cent. which the Congress workers claimed. He urged on the local leaders the importance of collecting reliable statistics, in view of the approaching international opium conference at Geneva. His expert knowledge of the wider aspects of the subject was of the utmost value to the Congress Inquiry Committee that was appointed the following summer. This knowledge was increased by his visit to Hongkong and the Federated Malay States in 1924 ; he missed no opportunity for personal investigation. When he got back to India the preliminary report from Assam was put into his hands, and during the Delhi Fast he gave all the time he could spare to marshal and analyse the evidence. Clearly, simply, forcefully, he set out his case, and despatched letters full of careful detail to Miss La Motte and to the English Quaker, Horace Alexander, both of whom were to be present at the Geneva conferences.

Nor was he content merely to provide his fellow-workers with the ammunition of facts they needed. As in Fiji, he displayed the "wisdom of the serpent," and planned the strategy of the campaign with canny shrewdness.

Long before the Geneva conferences he had found means to establish the young Indian journalist, Tarini Sinha, in a post in England, in order that he might work with Horace Alexander on the opium question. Later on he got him a job in the League of Nations Secretariat at Geneva so that he could watch over developments there. Before the Conference he got a strong group of distinguished Indians, Tagore, Gandhi, K. T. Paul, Ramananda Chatterji and others, to sign with him a petition asking for total extirpation of the opium poppy except as found needful for medicine and science. Horace Alexander cabled to him from the conference for a special message from Gandhi ; Andrews obtained and despatched it, neatly timed to arrive at the crucial moment. Miss La Motte wrote to him describing the scene which then took place :

> Well, the petition has been presented and a fine stir it made too ! That and a telegram from M. K. Gandhi were the hits of the afternoon. When the Indian petition was read out and Campbell rose to protest it was pretty thrilling.*

It must have been an awkward moment for Mr. Campbell, the Government of India delegate, who had just made to the conference the startling statement that "not even the Government of India's most ardent opponents, including Mr. Gandhi, have ever made any reproach in respect of its opium policy."

* Letter to C.F.A., 23rd November, 1924.

Andrews disposed of this "outrageous libel" by quotations from the published speeches of Dadabhai Naoroji and G. K. Gokhale. He fed the Indian press assiduously with every item of information from any part of the world which could help to educate public opinion on the matter. He disinterred a review of the opium traffic published by Tagore in 1881 and had it translated and used. He discovered a speech made by Lord Chesterfield in the House of Lords in 1743 in opposition to a British Excise and Licence Bill, and drew the parallel with telling effect :

> Luxury, my lords, is to be taxed, but vice must be prohibited, let the difficulties in executing the law be what they will. This Bill contains the conditions on which the people are to be allowed henceforth to riot in debauchery, licensed by law and countenanced by magistrates. For there is no doubt but those in authority will be directed by their masters to encourage the consumption of that liquor, from which such large revenues are expected.*

When it came to excise, Andrews suggested with a gleam of mischief, even Lord Chesterfield was on the side of the angels !

Next, he prepared a masterly summary of the salient facts, including the proceedings of the Geneva conferences, for the use of the members of the Indian Council of State and Legislative Assembly during the Opium Debates in the spring of 1925.† Statistics and an exposition of the history of opium control lead up to an appeal to moral principle :

> In the long run, the moral credit that India will obtain in the world by taking up a truly humanitarian attitude on this question is of far more material and spiritual importance to India than a certain number of rupees which are obtained by offering to other people what is recognized as a poison.

In the Council of State the opium resolution was not passed, but in the Legislative Assembly the Government was defeated by 60 votes to 52. A magnificent speech by Andrews' old friend, Dr. S. K. Datta of Lahore, was the turning-point of the debate. Sir Basil Blackett promised an inquiry—although barely six months earlier he had declared, to the same Assembly, that "the statements made *ex parte* by Miss La Motte and Mr. Andrews do

---

* Quoted by Andrews in *The Indian Problem*, p. 117.
† Printed as Opium Supplement iii in *Young India*, 23rd April, 1925.

not appear to afford strong ground for the revision of the opium policy of the Government of India."*

Andrews was not one to let slip the fruits of victory by neglect. He visited Assam and put the Congress Inquiry Report into its final form.   He watched lynx-eyed over the work of the Inquiry Committees set up in the "black areas" : most of them indeed were eager for his help.   If they were dilatory, he paid them a personal visit ; if he found, as in one province he did find, that evidence was being suppressed because a committee member was himself involved in the traffic, he tackled the authorities. Through Horace Alexander he kept the question before Parliament, and fought to get opium returns for the Indian States as well as for British India reported to the League of Nations.†   He peppered the press with pertinent questions addressed to the Central and Provincial Governments—why not guarantee your sincerity by ear-marking opium revenue for educational and anti-smuggling measures only ?—or by continuing to increase the price of opium, as the Central Provinces have done, even when increased price means falling revenue ?—How was it that opium licences could still be bought in Assam at a price which made a lawful profit impossible ?   His gadfly pertinacity was rewarded. Slowly but perceptibly conditions improved ; Bengal and several other provinces passed useful legislation to check the abuse of the drug.   Andrews continued watchful.

III

The opium campaign reveals the hidden strength of the man's nature, a texture superficially yielding, inwardly impregnable as linked steel.   Interwoven with that strength into the very heart of the fabric is the warmth of many friendships, a warmth that glows with a many-coloured radiance as the sensitive spirit responds now to one personality, now to another.

Rabindranath Tagore he loved with a deep reverence, as a disciple loves his master.   His intellectual powers and his physical endurance were always at the service of the poet's ideals, and not

* Statement in answer to a question, 8th September, 1924.
† Certain Rajputana States are the chief sources of raw opium.

once but many times he took up the "thrice-hateful task" of collecting funds in order to spare his friend the burden. Even in November, 1923, when he was waiting in Bombay, almost a physical wreck, for his ship to England, he had spent hour after hour in helping a Santiniketan colleague, Gour Gopal Ghosh, to obtain subscriptions for the work of the ashram among his own merchant friends in the city.

In 1924, at the close of Tagore's visit to China, Andrews reached Hongkong several days before him, got into touch with all the Indian merchants, discussed the Visva-Bharati with every section of the community, wrote for the press, spoke at meetings, and arranged in detail for the presentation of a purse at the celebrations when the poet arrived. A few days later Tagore left Singapore for home, but Andrews remained behind, consolidating the results of his visit, and carrying out a similar campaign of publicity at every important town in the Malay States. He emphasized especially the international aspect of Tagore's work, and took special pains to make friends for it among the Chinese of Malaya no less than among the Indians. Among the Indians, he particularly welcomed the interest shown by those who might enrich the ashram with varied religious and provincial cultures.

"A young Malabar Hindu and a Moplah were at the meeting," runs a typical letter from Singapore, "and came afterwards to ask about being students of Visva-Bharati ; also an electrical engineer named Naidu whose grandmother had become a devotee of Maharsi* in Bangalore. He is to reach Calcutta on August 8th ; I have given him all my remaining money —Rupees 185—for passage and equipment."†

This strenuous programme was carried through, along with a multitude of other concerns, in the oppressive moist heat of the tropical monsoon, which tried Andrews' physique more than any other sort of weather. It took heavy toll of his bodily strength.

Between Andrews and Gandhi, equals in age, tried partners in service, the relationship was one of frank and outspoken affection. This is how Gandhi writes to an over-wearied Andrews driven by

* Literally "the great saint" ; the title given by popular consent to the poet's father, Devendranath Tagore.

† To Rabindranath Tagore, undated (July, 1924).

a sleepless sense of duty to record his impressions of Burma for *Young India*.

(*25th August, 1924*)

I have read your article on Burma. The thing is shocking. You have seen too much to enable you to analyse properly and trace causes. Moreover you have not had enough time to study each problem. Will you not rest and be thankful for a while ? Work is prayer but it can also be madness . . . I am printing it nevertheless because it comes from the utmost purity of your heart.

With love deeper than even you can fathom,

Yours, Mohan.

It was a joy to Andrews to know, as he could not but know, that his presence during the fast of September, 1924 shielded Gandhi from much fatigue and strain. Innumerable visitors, members of the Unity Conference and others, sought interviews with the leader, and the task of the doorkeeper was an exacting one.

Everyone tries to get me to make an exception in his case. I have to be very firm indeed and at the same time the utmost tact is needed to avoid giving offence . . . It means incessant watchfulness, but everyone knows that it is out of pure love that I am taking up this responsibility, and they obey me very easily, while it is probable that they would not obey others.*

There were some anxious days, but Andrews had no torturing fears for his friend. His own multifarious work was completed with quiet mastery, and in the still glow of sunset, or the dark hush before the dawn, he found the serenity of spirit which breathes through all the accounts of those days which he wrote for *Young India*. When the last day came, Gandhi asked him to sing at the breaking of the fast his favourite Christian hymn, *When I survey the wondrous Cross*. Andrews did so with a rapture of feeling that sank deep into the hearts of his hearers ; Gandhi's bearing of the sins of his people had given him, he felt, a deeper understanding of the meaning of the suffering of Christ.

As for Gandhi, a letter written to Charlie on 20th October, after they had parted again, affords a glimpse of the depth of feeling with which he treasured their friendship. "I have missed you every moment today," he confesses. "Oh, your love !"

Another typical letter of mingled scolding and praise refers to the morbidly tormenting anxieties to which Andrews had been

* To Dwijendranath Tagore, 1st October and 3rd October, 1924.

subject with regard to Tagore's bad health, and also to his work in the labour dispute in the Tata Iron and Steel Works at Jamshedpur.

(*Undated, September or October*, 1925)

My Dearest Charlie,

Though you do not want me to write to you I cannot help (it).

What can be the cause of Gurudev* wanting you ? God who has kept you from harm so long will keep you as long as He needs your service. But you sometimes will not help Him even when you can and must. And for you to have nervousness about anything or anybody is bad. When I see you anxious about anything I ask myself what is the meaning of "Be careful for nothing."

Your Jamshedpur report is wonderful. Only you could have written it. No beating about the bush.

I am all with you in keeping up the *langoti* for the Bhil children.

With deepest love,

Yours, Mohan.

Never again eating rich foods even to please the host. I should like that definite promise.

Other glimpses of Andrews in these years are full of that warmth and radiance which was the irresistible charm of his personality. An old Delhi colleague who went to meet him at Singapore station in 1924† found a crowd of poor Indian people waiting to welcome him. He never forgot the "look of absolute reverence" which he saw in their eyes as they watched their friend. J. S. Hoyland describes him as President of the All India Trade Union Congress, "chairing" its meetings with patient, courteous resourcefulness, humorous and self-effacing. At Dibrugarh in Assam he "rubs shoulders with sweepers and coolies, spreads his shawl for their children to sit on, and after the meeting is over locks his arms in fond embrace with each and every one of them."‡ It was the double claim of personal friendship and human misery that took him to flood-stricken Orissa in the autumn of 1925. Pandit Gopabandhu Das, whom he had met at the Daltonganj

* The name by which Rabindranath Tagore is commonly known among his admirers in India.

† Bishop Ferguson-Davie, who as a young missionary in the Punjab had greatly valued Andrews' counsel.

‡ *The Times of Assam*, 4th May, 1925, article by Padmadhar Chaliha. Andrews was often scolded by his friends for the readiness with which he would embrace even the dirtiest and most degraded of men, especially when his ignorance of the language precluded him from expressing his goodwill in other ways.

Conference in 1920, travelled to Santiniketan to beg him to come. Andrews had loved him from the first. "Orthodox in prayer and worship, yet the closest friend of the untouchables, to share his companionship was to feel oneself near to God." Out they went together along the swollen Mahanadi River in the monsoon storms, in a country boat laden with stores, bringing what comfort they could to shivering refugees marooned on the broken embankments. As in the railway dispute at Tundla, so here, Andrews was grieved by the gulf which separated the responsible officials from the poor, and by the seemingly callous lack of personal concern for their troubles. In the Puri district the waters had covered the land for four months ; day after day, with nothing to cultivate, nothing to occupy their time, the peasants watched famine draw nearer and nearer. Yet no responsible official had come to see with his own eyes the condition of the people, and when Andrews did so officialdom, in the shape of the C.I.D., shadowed him suspiciously wherever he went.*

IV

These were the last and richest years of Andrews' friendship with "Borodada" Dwijendranath Tagore. He understood with a womanly tenderness the loneliness of the old man in his increasing infirmity, and on his frequent absences from Santiniketan he would write to him almost daily letters of affection in order that Borodada might derive a few minutes' entertainment from the reading of them. "The Hyphen is veritably indomitable," Borodada would say. "Not content with joining Gurudev and Gandhiji, he is now making a grander effort to join lonely Borodada and the scholars, professors and students between Cape Comorin and the Himalayas in one bond of brotherly love." Or again, "I have made a new discovery in the science of arithmetic as follows :

Hymen : conjugal love : : Hyphen : brotherly love."†
Whenever Andrews was at home in the ashram they renewed

* The *Amrita Bazaar Patrika*, Calcutta, printed Andrews' descriptive articles on 16th October, 1925, and the following days.

† Letters to C.F.A., 26th September, 1925, 21st October, 1925.

P

their long, intimate evening talks, and many a time during the day the old man would send for him, with the innocent impatience of a child, to share a joke or a new thought, or to be assured that the English he wrote with diffidence was correct and idiomatic. Andrews would hurry to his side, and Borodada rested in his company as in that of a beloved son. When Andrews was away, "love letters," written on minute scraps of paper, often in rhyme, would follow him. For example :

DEAREST CHARLIE,
As I've no other,
O Charlie brother—
Friend in need
In will and deed—
Send I to thee
Sweet *Amritee*,*
A timely token
Of friendship unbroken.
Do not refuse
To make good use
Of this eleventh-*Magh* cake
For Borodada's sake.
Your own
BORODADA.

Another, written in March, 1924, when Andrews was with Gandhi after his operation, ends with an unwonted burst of feeling :

Give my heartfelt gratitude, love, and reverence to Mahatmaji, and no less love and respect to the only person who is to me more than all the friends I ever had or am likely to have put together, and whom I have the happy privilege to call my dearest Charlie.

In November, 1925, on the eve of Andrews' departure for South Africa, they sat long together in what they well knew might be their last talk. Next morning as Andrews started for the station he turned aside to Borodada's verandah and received in silence the old man's silent blessing. It was their final meeting.†

One of those present at the Unity Conference was Basil Westcott's elder brother, Dr. Foss Westcott, who in 1919 had

* A Bengali sweetmeat.

† Delightful reminiscences of Borodada, containing some of Andrews' most vivid descriptive writing, are to be found in *Young India*, January-March, 1927, and in *The Visva-Bharati Quarterly*, 1928.

succeeded Dr. Lefroy as Metropolitan Bishop of Calcutta. At the conference, or shortly afterwards, Andrews spoke to him of his longing for a renewal of the Christian religious fellowship from which he had been so largely cut off. Christian youth movements in India such as the Y.M.C.A. and the Student Christian Association, had welcomed him eagerly, at least since 1920 ; at Christmas, 1924, his evening talks to the Student Christian Conference in Madras, on "Christ and the Sinner," in which he told the story of his own conversion, so moved many of his audience that they desired only to seek the quiet of the dark garden outside and spend the night in prayer. His own Indian Christian friends and students had never lost their faith in him, and his brief visit to England at Christmas, 1923, had been full of the joy of new Christian friendships. But in his own church in India, and among his own people, there was painful hostility still. "I wouldn't *touch* that man's hand ; he's a traitor !" remarked a prominent member of the Calcutta Cathedral congregation very audibly, turning pointedly on his heel as Bishop Westcott approached to introduce Andrews to him. "I welcome you with all my heart to the Cathedral services, Charlie," said the Bishop. "But if you come on Sundays, with these people present, there may be painful scenes. Come on weekdays, whenever you can and will."

Andrews never ceased to be grateful for the Metropolitan's faith in him during those years of hostility. His need of it was all the greater for the closing of another great chapter of friendship. On June 29th, 1925, Susil Rudra died at Solon in the Simla Hills. Andrews was with him as he sank at last into unconsciousness, murmuring "Oh my country, my dear country," and then, distinctly, "How wonderful is God ! How wonderful is God !" "I cannot yet feel," wrote Andrews the following day, "all that his death will mean to me. My spirit is so tired and worn as well as my body."* In all the brilliant galaxy of his Indian friends it is doubtful whether there was any who had exercised so formative an influence upon his whole outlook as that gentle, wise, and humble man.

* To B. D. C., 30th June, 1925.

CHAPTER XV

SOUTH AFRICA

1925-27   AGE 54-56

I

THE Asiatic Inquiry (Lange) Commission set up by the South African Union Government in 1920-21 had reported that "the indiscriminate segregation of Asiatics in locations, apart from its injustice and inhumanity, would degrade the Asiatic and react upon the European," but suggested that a scheme of "voluntary segregation" might be found practicable. This was the signal for a renewed anti-Asiatic campaign, influenced by the parallel agitation in Kenya, of which the "Class Areas Bill" announced by General Smuts in July, 1923, was the result.

The Bill was introduced in the Union Parliament in January, 1924, but lapsed when the Parliament was dissolved. At the elections which followed, Smuts was defeated and General Hertzog's Nationalist Party came into power. In June, 1925, the "South African Mines and Works Amendment Bill," which provided that certificates of competency to be in charge of machines should not be granted to natives or Asiatics, passed its third reading in the House of Assembly. This Bill (popularly known as the Colour Bar Bill) was however rejected by the Senate. In July, 1925, Smuts' Class Areas Bill was revived in a much more drastic form as the Areas Reservation and Immigration Restriction Bill. The Government claimed that it was based upon the recommendations of the Lange Report. It proposed to forbid "Asiatics" to acquire property in Natal outside a specified coastal belt, to restrict their freedom of movement between the provinces of the Union, and to place under hampering regulations the entry even of the wives and children of domiciled immigrants. The Cape Coloured, Malay, and Mauritian Creole populations were all exempted from its operation, and Dr. Malan, the Home Minister, introduced it to the House of Assembly in a brutally outspoken speech.

> The Bill (he stated) frankly starts from the general supposition that the Indian is an alien element in the population and that no solution will be acceptable unless it results in a very considerable reduction of the Indian population in this country.

While this legislation was before the Union Parliament, provincial ordinances were promulgated in both Natal and the Transvaal, controlling the use of land and the issue of trading licences, and obviously directed against the Indian community.

Throughout 1925 a great deal of Andrews' time had been given to newspaper publicity, with the object of forming an enlightened Indian public opinion on the developments in both South Africa and Kenya. The affairs of the two countries must be looked at together, he insisted, and the same essential moral principles must be applied to both :

> The Indian, both in Kenya and South Africa, is asserting his own right of racial equality, not selfishly, but in order to obtain the same right for the African himself. It is impossible to struggle for the freedom of one's own soil while at the same time usurping the soil of another race. In Kenya the Indian is being bribed to desert the African ; in South Africa he is classed with the "native" . . .

This "bribery" to which Andrews refers took the form of a suggestion that "a suitable lowland area" might be set aside for Indian colonisation in Kenya, if India would on her part forgo the claim that all races should have an equal right to hold land in the Highlands. Andrews drew up a memorandum for the Government of India's Standing Committee on Emigration, another for the Imperial Indian Citizenship Association, and pleaded by every means at his disposal that Indians must never consent to this further expropriation of the African from the scanty cultivable land which was his by right, and that both for their own sake and his they must uphold their claim to the ordinary rights of citizenship which were at stake in the Highlands issue. His perseverance was rewarded : India officially rejected the offer.

"It has been my one constant ideal," he wrote to Tagore a few months later* in reviewing his work, "that the sympathy of India

* 28th May, 1926.

with the downtrodden and the oppressed was strong enough and pure enough to take part in this world-wide struggle for the African."

By similar hard work and perseverance Andrews and his collaborators brought such pressure to bear on the Government of India, and the Government of India in its turn exerted such pressure on the Government of South Africa, that a valuable respite was won with regard to the threatened racial legislation there. The Areas Reservation Bill was referred to a Select Committee *before*, instead of after, its second reading ; and a Government of India "fact-finding" commission, led by Mr. G. F. Paddison, sailed for South Africa on November 25th, 1925. Andrews himself, at Gandhi's request, had preceded the Commission by a few days, and as in 1920 he did everything possible to help the official delegates in their work.

I I

After Andrews' experience in Kenya in 1921, the Government of India was somewhat nervous about the possible repercussions of his presence in South Africa, and he had had an anxious wait in Calcutta before the passport was finally issued. It came at last ; Andrews booked his passage from Bombay to Beira, and then travelled by train from Beira to Durban as he had done once before in 1920. It was a tedious, weary journey ; but the happiness which isolated Indian families derived from the brief interviews they were able to snatch at wayside stations was for Andrews a full recompense for the discomforts of seven days of railway travel.

His mission took him to many parts of the Union, and at every turn he was faced with the human suffering for which racial arrogance was responsible. He talked during one railway journey to a Zulu chief (having first told the guard of the train that if he insisted on transferring him to a "European" compartment he would have to do so by force) and the conversation showed him how the iron of humiliation could enter into the soul of the educated African. At Pretoria he heard of an Indian barber who by his cleanliness and industry had built up a good custom among Europeans, and who had suddenly been ordered to put a sign over his shop, *Coloured People Only*. Andrews immediately went to him for a hair-cut, though his hair was short already ; the shop was spotless. "These are wicked times," lamented the old Muslim, seeing his modest livelihood ruined. "God will surely send a flood upon such unrighteousness, as in the days of Noah." Andrews himself did not escape the penalties of his "treachery" to the white race, and there was a clamour for his deportation. His only reference to his own humiliations, however, is in one sentence of a private letter to Tagore : "In European circles I sometimes have to bear things that are unbearable," and in the wry comment that "when they laugh at one it is better than lynching."*

The situation seemed almost desperate, but Andrews would not despair, though night after night he lay awake praying for aid. He approached everybody, and those who knew South Africa best were most amazed at the number of men and the variety of social circles with which he succeeded in making contact. Among professing Christians he made his appeal to Christian principle, and here he found courageous backing among English Christian leaders, especially in Pretoria and Johannesburg. The Bishop of Pretoria declared publicly that the Areas Reservation Bill was "a measure which treats solemn engagements as a scrap of paper."† In Johannesburg "it was a joy of joys to him to see men of all nationalities worshipping in the Cathedral, that once had been almost the storm-centre of racial prejudice,"‡ and to know that bit by bit the spirit of Christian brotherhood for which he had been pleading since 1914 was permeating the churches in the larger centres of South Africa. Among the members of such churches it was possible to get a fair and patient hearing for the Indian case, and that in itself was an achievement of inestimable value in the prevailing atmosphere of the country.

Among his fellow-Britishers, whether or not they were Christian, Andrews made his appeal to the sense of honour and "fair play." He argued that the Areas Reservation Bill was a

* To Rabindranath Tagore, 14th March, 1926.
† Reported in *The Times of India*, 18th January, 1926.
‡ Dean Palmer of Johannesburg, to the authors.

direct contravention of the Gandhi-Smuts Agreement of 1914, and was therefore a breach of treaty and a breach of faith. In a letter to the *Cape Times* he further pointed out the glaring inconsistency between the compulsory racial segregation contemplated in the Bill and the recommendations of the Lange Report on which it was said to be based, and challenged Dr. Malan either to explain the discrepancy or to allow discussion of the Bill in principle as well as in detail. From many British colonials he won a half-unwilling admiration and respect.

> "Here was a man in their midst whose convictions they did not share ; but the costliness of those convictions could not be hidden notwithstanding the modesty and deep humility with which they were held. They saw a life drenched with *duty*—a word which has not lost its appeal, even in the material atmosphere of the Rand."*

Andrews made a special effort to win the confidence and friendship of the Afrikaans-speaking population, believing that it was they rather than the British who held the key to the race relationships of the future. Miss Hobhouse had first opened his eyes to their sterling qualities, their deep godliness and the simple purity of their home life. True, their theology and ethics were largely derived from the Old Testament, with its conception of the "chosen people," and racial prejudice died slowly among them. They were at a loss to understand Andrews' attitude to races other than the white, and his eagerness to live with Indians whenever he could ; but the appeal of his sheer goodness did not fail, and he made many friends—enough to cause Dr. Malan's paper, *The Burgher*, to exhort him to cease to "dabble in politics," and to confine himself to "the pure Gospel" !

By February, 1926, the political situation still seemed hopeless, but Andrews reminded himself that there was publicity even in opposition. He had gained an entry into many newspapers, and his public lectures on Tagore were drawing crowded and enthusiastic audiences, among Afrikaander as well as English groups. He had made friends with officials and cabinet ministers, social workers and philanthropists, irreconcilables and die-hards, and had found time nevertheless to spend more than one afternoon in

* Dean Palmer, *Ibid.*

reading his favourite passages of Tagore to a blind and half-paralysed old lady of eighty.

Andrews' evidence before the Select Committee to which the Areas Reservation Bill had been referred, took the form of a memorandum. In this he explained once more why Indians felt the way of compulsion to be an insult and a humiliation. He suggested instead the way of consultation, "which is still open." As "an independent humanitarian" he put forward a definite proposal which he asked should be considered on its merits :

> That the Select Committee should ask the Government to postpone consideration of the Bill.
>
> That when tempers on both sides had cooled, a South African deputation should visit India, perhaps in October, 1926.
>
> That when a more friendly atmosphere had thus been created, there should be a Round Table Conference to discuss commercial, educational, and all other matters in which friction between the two countries might be replaced by an *entente cordiale*.

It says much for the position which Andrews had won in South Africa that these proposals were in fact accepted and carried out in their entirety. The date of the Round Table Conference was fixed for December, 1926.

III

Andrews returned to India in April, 1926. During his absence Lord Irwin had become Viceroy. Andrews had several long talks with him about South Africa, and Irwin, who was himself a keen practising Christian, was quick to recognize his integrity and selflessness. He suggested that Andrews should be a member of the official Indian delegation to the Round Table Conference ; Andrews preferred to retain his entirely independent position, but he agreed to return to South Africa in September and help to prepare the way for it.

In the summer of 1926 Tagore was once more absent in Europe, and Andrews therefore spent all the time he could in Santiniketan. But instead of taking the rest which he so badly needed before the new term's work began in July, he drove his tired hand and brain to write article after article for the Indian press about the South African situation, until a small insect-bite brought on fever and blood-poisoning. Once more it was Gandhi who called a halt, with one of his affectionate letters of mingled chaffing and scolding :

> The article you sent me was not well considered. It is not true that colour prejudice is the *sole* cause of the South African troubles. The article on Opium is too scrappy. They both show extreme mental fatigue.
>
> . . . Do you think it is God's call that your pen must be ever running ? The world will not go to pieces for the suspension of your writings. Gregg remarked that your insect-bite poisoning was a God-send, because it had stopped the flow . . . Is it not a matter of joy that you should have friends who will not always be serious with you ?*

At Santiniketan it was not Andrews' writing that counted, but his genius for personal friendship. Dr. J. H. Cousins was visiting lecturer that term, and Andrews cared for every detail which might ensure his personal comfort and add to the value of his work. He inspired a fresh zeal for manual labour, and set the boys to filling a disused well and building roads. He tackled the discipline of the school, which various factors had impaired :

> The tone is much better now. A boy called N. had to leave to bring up the standard. This was done in a way which carried the students with us, and he went quietly and I believe with a real love for the ashram still . . . Though personally I wished to give N. another chance I can well see the great importance of such an act of discipline carried through without any breach of friendship whatever.†

The greatest demands on his friendliness, however, arose out of Tagore's relations with the Fascist régime in Italy. When he reached Switzerland after the conclusion of his Italian visit, Tagore had discovered that certain Fascist newspapers had twisted his carefully-guarded public statements into an approbation of the "new order." At the same time he had been given evidence of the questionable methods used by the Party to silence its opponents. Indignant at the attempt to exploit him, he published a letter of protest and explanation in *The Manchester Guardian*. This provoked a storm in Italy, and placed Professor Tucci, an Italian scholar on the Visva-Bharati staff, in a very difficult position, which was rendered even more painful because full accounts of what had really happened did not reach Santiniketan for several

---

* To C.F.A., 24th June, 1926.
† To Rabindranath Tagore, 31st August, 1926.

weeks. Andrews gave up hours every day to befriend the lonely and isolated Italian, who, he says, was "almost frantic with grief."

"How glad I am," he writes, "to have been with Tucci when the news was coming in about Gurudev in Italy. He trusts me and relies on my friendship. He will probably leave, but will leave happily."*

Another letter written three weeks later shows the wisdom and success of his service of reconciliation :

"The Italian Consul was terribly upset, and so was Tucci, but my action in keeping back the letter† from *The Modern Review* has avoided an open rupture. Tucci has recovered from the first shock and would now gladly stay on if his Government would allow him. He has done splendid work."

There was another act of friendship which Andrews would never have suffered to be published in his lifetime. Finding that the ashram was still in financial difficulties, he not only spent himself in the distasteful role of beggar on its behalf, but also made over the whole of his own tiny capital, including the legacy which Rudra had left him, as security against the accumulated overdraft. He would have regarded it as the least and lightest of his gifts.

I V

On September 29th, 1926, Andrews sailed once more for South Africa, followed by the hopes and prayers of an increasing number of men of goodwill. Gandhi spoke for India :

I had a few happy days with Charlie before he sailed. The conference can do nothing if South African opinion is intensely hostile to Indians. He can to some extent mould that opinion. His very presence disarms criticism and silences opposition. He is the only living link between the whites and the Indians.‡

Norman Leys spoke for Kenya :

It is worth every conceivable effort if only segregation in South Africa can be delayed. The reactions would be felt right up to Kenya and Uganda.§

C. P. Scott, editor of *The Manchester Guardian*, spoke for England :

May I say how greatly I value your friendship ? It is only through

* To Rabindranath Tagore, 17th August, 1926.

† "The letter" was one from the poet explaining his action. It was published in *The Visva-Bharati Quarterly*, October, 1926.

‡ To the Misses Andrews, 1st October, 1926.

§ Letter to C.F.A., October, 1926.

men like you and the spirit which you embody that we shall ever do our duty in India.*

The healing influence of Andrews' spirit was felt all down the coast. At Mombasa a party dispute of two years' standing was ended ; at Dar-es-Salaam two newspapers, whose rivalry threatened to split the Indian community into "Hindu" and "Moslem" factions, were happily amalgamated, and Andrews backed with all his might the project for a good Indian school.

On October 20th he landed in Durban, and was faced with an unforeseen crisis. A virulent epidemic of smallpox was raging in the crowded Indian quarter, with a death rate of over 25 per cent., and the city was on the verge of panic. For the next month Andrews gave himself up wholly to the needs of the sufferers in the slums. Every day, sometimes two or three times in a day, he visited the quarantine areas. In the notorious Power House Station "barracks," where the municipality's poorest Indian employees were housed, and which was the chief centre of infection, whole families were living in single rooms, with leaky corrugated roofs and damp worm-eaten floors, amid a sea of sewage-impregnated mud. Andrews worked there single-handed, hampered by language barriers, for the authorities would not grant a second pass into the infected area, even for a Tamil interpreter. There had been an outcry in the press about the concealment of new cases ; some of this was deliberate, but much was due to misunderstanding by the frightened, harassed people of sanitary instructions issued in a language not their own. Resentment was growing, and Andrews often felt that month as if he were living on a powder-mine, so great was the tension. His own gentle but practical sympathy restored confidence as nothing else could do. "There would have been riots in the barracks," he wrote, "if I had not been there."†

Day by day throughout the crisis Andrews kept in touch with the Mayor and City Councillors, and with the Borough Health and Housing Committees. He got space in the newspapers, and kept the principles of public health in the foreground of discussion.

* Letter to C.F.A., 16th October, 1926.
† Letter to Fernand Benoit (Santiniketan), 4th November, 1926.

He urged on the City Council the necessity for a bold and thorough rehousing scheme for its employees. He organised a strong Relief Committee among the well-to-do Indians, who gave the sufferers what help they could from outside. The European community was impressed and increasingly disposed to friendliness. "Why don't you make your Congress Committee your governing body ?" said one of them to him, "and allow us to deal with that governing body as one free people deals with another ?" "Even without claiming political franchise," Andrews commented, "Indians can get this practical franchise at any time, provided only they work together."*

He himself nevertheless knew only too well how difficult it was for a community containing such diverse elements to work together under normal conditions. The rich "Arabs" (as the Indian merchants were commonly called) were "almost entirely unpatriotic," and were themselves the worst slum landlords in Durban. Andrews could get little co-operation from them. Then there were the educated middle-class leaders of the South African Indian Congress, whom the atmosphere of Durban had made so hyper-sensitive to "racial" discrimination that they were prone to see it even where none was intended. Their interests also were apt to conflict with those of the submerged mass of the Indian poor. Andrews sympathised greatly with their point of view, but it added to his perplexity about the urgently-needed municipal housing scheme :

> "If the Corporation is induced to undertake it Indians will at once say 'segregation' . . . There is far too great a tendency to judge the whole thing in the abstract and not also from the poor man's point of view. It is so very easy for people who are themselves comfortable and secure in their own property to decide that this or that scheme of housing the poor must not be adopted, because their own self-respect will be wounded. We have to consider this self-respect at its very highest value. It is a vital asset today in the life of educated Indians. But at the same time God Himself will not allow us to . . . sacrifice our own poor people, forcing them still to live in horrible slums with no conceivable possibility of decency or cleanliness, simply to satisfy something which may not after all be truly our national honour."†

* Letter to Sir J. W. Bhore, 26th November, 1926.

† Letter to Mr. J. B. Petit, 20th November, 1926. The Durban Municipality demolished the Power House Station barracks and spent £30,000 on new quarters.

A new political party, the Colonial-Born Association, had been formed side by side with the Indian Congress, and claimed to represent the interests of the poor. The Congress itself was weakened by rivalries between the Natal and Transvaal groups. Andrews, knowing how utterly ruinous such divisions could be, did his utmost to reconcile them.

> "I spend hours," he wrote,* "in trying to patch up quarrels without taking sides and without publicity. Only my personal presence has prevented an open split. Government officials despise and take advantage of our divisions. They laugh and say, 'Oh, we know how to manage the Indians !' For me, the need of weighing every spoken or written word, lest it give a handle to one against the other, is a constant mental strain."

Nevertheless, thanks largely to Andrews' own work in the early part of the year, the attitude of responsible Europeans was very much more friendly than it had been twelve months earlier. The press was open to him in a way it had never been before. In August, 1926, even before his return, a group of South African papers had of their own initiative cabled to him for articles on India, and he took full advantage of the new opportunities which came to him to spread the knowledge of India as a country to be respected for its ancient civilisation and modern achievements. He initiated the idea that December 19th, the Sunday after the Government of India's representatives arrived, should be observed throughout India and South Africa as a national Day of Prayer for the forthcoming conference. The proposal was welcomed everywhere ; in India Gandhi and Dr. Westcott the Metropolitan commended it to their people ; in South Africa, under the leadership of the Deans of Capetown and Johannesburg, English Christians joined with Indians in prayer, and Dr. du Plessis of Stellenbosch issued a similar call to the Afrikaander people. When the conference opened at Capetown the omens were better than Andrews had dared to hope :

> The Deputation has been received socially with open arms—far better than the Paddison deputation last year. General Hertzog has met Mr. Srinivasa Sastri and Mr. Habibullah face to face and *liked* them. His perfect courtesy and care has caused hotels to be thrown open, both to them and to the local Indian leaders, in this height of the Christmas season.

* To J. B. Petit, 26th November, 1926.

The press has helped to spread the realisation of India's dignity and greatness.*

Within a fortnight the scales were turned. The Areas Reservation Bill was withdrawn ; the entry of wives and minor children of domiciled Indians was permitted ; it was agreed that Indians in South Africa should be expected to conform to "western standards of life,"† and that the Government of India should appoint an Agent in South Africa. A scheme of "assisted re-emigration" under careful safeguards was also agreed on. The provisional agreement, as ratified by both governments, was read by Dr. Malan in the House of Assembly on February 21st, 1927.

The relief to Andrews was tremendous. The ill-health which had dogged his footsteps ever since the previous June had made every. day's work during those critical ten weeks a well-nigh intolerable burden.

> I was near a breakdown with anxiety (he wrote), but the joy of His presence was everything. Sastri has been magnificent. The South African delegates listened to him untiringly, and at the end Dr. Malan made a most moving tribute. Sastri said to me, "Charlie, if you yourself had dictated Dr. Malan's speech, it could not have been better done !"‡

V

No one knew better than Andrews, however, that his own work in South Africa was not yet over. The Capetown Agreement went far beyond popular European opinion in Natal, and there was an immediate anti-Indian reaction. On the Indian side, the Colonial-Born Association was bitterly opposed to any re-emigration clause whatever, no matter how well safeguarded ; one of its leaders even went so far as openly to invite the European reactionaries to join forces to wreck the Agreement. The Transvaal Indians were panic-stricken because of the clause which provided for the cancellation of fraudulent "registration certificates." A more reasonable criticism was of the absence from the Agreement

* Letter to M. K. Gandhi, 1st January, 1927.

† Andrews was aware of the ambiguity of this phrase. "My interpretation," he stated, "coincides with Gandhi's which safeguards Indian simplicity, viz.: the reasonable sanitary and economic laws of common applicability, ensuring on the part of all a standard of life in keeping with hygienic and sanitary requirements, and the regulation of all business in conformity with the European standard." (Speech at Bombay, April, 1926.)

‡ To M. K. Gandhi, 13th January, 1927.

of any reference to the Colour Bar legislation or the ordinances regarding trade licences and property. It was, as Andrews himself described it, a "brilliant improvisation" rather than a finally satisfying settlement. But in spite of everything his draft resolution endorsing the Agreement as a whole was carried unanimously and cordially at a meeting of the Indian Congress at Johannesburg on March 13th. An editorial in the Johannesburg *Star* commented in friendly fashion on the reasonableness of the Congress attitude, and gave credit where credit was due :

> The Rev. C. F. Andrews has played a notable part in making a settlement possible ; his transparent honesty of purpose, wide outlook and real sense of statesmanship have been recognized in all quarters both in South Africa and India. His influence has always been on the side of conciliation and moderation.*

There were still many difficulties to be overcome. The necessary legislation to implement the Agreement had to be steered through a Parliament where opposition was potentially strong, and where every hint of Indian dissatisfaction with its provisions might be seized upon and exploited. One Durban newspaper even stooped to print a "rumour" that "£100,000 was brought over from India to create an artificial satisfaction with the Agreement." Andrews treated that with the silent contempt it deserved, but he did everything in his power to meet the criticisms of the settlement voiced by the Transvaal Indians and the Colonial-Born Association. He persuaded Dr. Malan to make the clause about the Transvaal registration certificates non-retrospective ; he got him to agree that the three years' absence from South Africa which was to be permitted without loss of domicile, should be reckoned only from the date of the passing of the Bill, and absence previous to that should not be counted. But the critics did not wish to be satisfied. One day Dr. Malan sent for Andrews. "Can nothing be done ?" he asked. "I don't see how I can keep things going, in the face of the European opposition, if the Indian community entirely refuses to help me."†

Andrews refused to be discouraged. He knew everything that could be said in criticism of the South African Indian com-

---

* 16th March, 1927.

† Account in a letter from C.F.A. to J. B. Petit, 10th June, 1927.

munity, and he accepted its weaknesses without recrimination as an incentive to still more devoted service.

"I am by no means in despair," he wrote,* "for the history of all subject and depressed peoples is the same. It makes a vicious circle out of which it is impossible to get except by a sacrifice which means the sacrifice of all. We must go on and on until we win and we must not get angry with anyone but love them all the more because they are weak."

On this occasion he knew well that the underlying motive of the opposition was not honest distrust of the Agreement, but class suspicion—trader against labourer, the "ex-indentured" against the "free." He was distressed at the ruinous political exploitation of social wrongs ; but he was even more distressed by the selfish greed of the wealthy "Arabs," and by the contrast between the luxury in which they lived and the squalor of the "locations" of the poor.

In spite of every obstacle, the Bills implementing the Agreement passed their final stage in the Union Parliament by the end of June, without a single hostile amendment. To Andrews, the most important clause of all was that which recognized the Indian right to education. "It is the duty of the Union Government," ran the pledge, "to provide for the development of all races within the Union up to the highest limit of their capacity and opportunity." It was suggested, as a first step, that Indians might share in the provision made for higher education by the Fort Hare Native College. A few of the Indians thereupon declared arrogantly that it was impossible for them to be classed with the natives in this way. Their attitude was the antithesis of everything that Andrews had fought for in their name, but he answered temperately :

The position that Indians should not attend an African college is quite untenable. Nothing but good can come of the warm friendships that have already taken place between those who will be African leaders in the future and our own Indian students. To speak of the African natives in the way Mr. N. does is most insulting, and I hardly like to think what racial trouble he is stirring up by doing so.†

During the months when the Amending Bill was postponed, Andrews visited Southern Rhodesia, where there was work that he could do to help the Indian traders to secure their position in

* To B.D.C., 15th May, 1927.
† *The Modern Review*, November, 1927.

Q

connection with certain proposed "licensing laws." The Indians, who were few in number, were all without exception traders, and the great majority of them were living bachelor-fashion year after year in Africa while their wives and children remained in India. The same custom prevailed largely in the trading community throughout East and South Africa, and was one reason for the unpopularity of the Transvaal Indian trader. Andrews spoke everywhere against it. Such a life, apart from its moral dangers, was, he argued, essentially parasitic ; if the Indian claimed the rights of a citizen in Africa, he must be ready to shoulder the responsibility of citizenship and make Africa more truly his home.

Andrews reached Bombay on August 23rd, 1927, after remaining long enough in South Africa to welcome Srinivasa Sastri as the first Indian Agent and help him to settle in. In his reply to the Civic Address with which the Bombay Municipal Corporation presented him, he enlarged with his usual courteous frankness on the Indian's civic responsibilities in Africa :

"I wish," he stated, "publicly to rebut Sir Sydney Henn's sweeping accusation that the Indian community in East Africa has low commercial and personal morality. He had no right in this way to indict a whole nation. Bombay has given to Africa men of high civic and moral virtues of whom their adopted country may indeed be proud.

"But I would use the same public occasion to counsel the Indian community about three things that badly want saying and perhaps I can best say them. First of all, they need to live in Africa a more settled family life, and not occupy a mere business home in Africa and a family home in Bombay . . . Secondly, I would urge that the money which is being earned by Indians in Africa should be spent in Africa . . . Thirdly, I would urge the Indian community in Africa to foster in themselves and their children a more wholehearted patriotism for their adopted country. Only as they become good South and East Africans will they win their way in the affection both of the European settlers in Africa and of the Africans themselves."*

Gandhi welcomed Charlie back to India with happy congratulations on the "wonders" which he had wrought ; Lord Irwin wrote to him of his regard and gratitude ; but his greatest reward came in later years, when in the ports of East Africa he received the thanks of gentle Indian ladies to whom he had brought a renewal of happy family life.

* Report in *The Indian Social Reformer*, 27th August, 1927.

PART V

THE BRIDGE-BUILDER

CHAPTER XVI

RETROSPECT AND PROSPECT

1927-1928   AGE 56-57

I

WHEN Andrews returned to India in August, 1927, there were factors at work which were to make a great change in the outward aspect of his life. Since he first set foot on Indian soil more than twenty-three years before, he had never been out of India for more than a few months at a time, and his longest absences, in Fiji in 1917-18 and in South Africa in 1926-27, had been spent very largely among the Indian settlers in those lands. Now for nearly ten years he was to live almost entirely in the West, and his visits to India were to be as brief and irregular as his absences had been during the previous period.

During the first few months, however, he took up once more the threads of his old life. Poverty-stricken Orissa, struggling against natural calamities, claimed him for her own. In September, 1927, eighty thousand houses were swept away in another Mahanadi flood. Andrews was on the spot at once, not only to help with the immediate relief work, but to try to find "a way out of the annual calamity." He was one of the first to canvass public opinion for a thorough survey of the whole course of the river, and to point out how much might be learned from the experience of the United States with the Mississippi waterway. A very tender mutual affection grew up between him and the young Congress leaders of the province, to whom he became like a revered elder brother.

The industrial unrest of 1921-22 had been followed by a period of comparative stability. By the end of 1927 however there was a further fall in prices. Employers began to carry out "retrenchments," and this was the cause of many disputes. Andrews attended the All-India Trade Union Congress at Cawnpore in

November and was once more elected its chairman, and much of his time was taken up with negotiations on behalf of the East India Railway workmen at Lillooah and the employees of the Tata Iron and Steel Company at Jamshedpur. The Communist Party was exercising a growing influence in the Trade Unions, and was urging the All-India Trade Union Congress to affiliate itself to the Red International Labour Union sponsored by Moscow. Under Andrews' chairmanship the Cawnpore meeting declined to join either that or the "moderate" Amsterdam International until unity between them had been achieved. A year later, when the Congress met at Jharia, in December, 1928, Andrews was in England. From there he sent a long message urging that Indian labour should retain its independence. The "right wing" of Labour in the west was disappointingly weak and uncertain with regard to imperialism and the "white labour" policy ; the Communists, who made an honest and noble stand against these things, advocated class war and violent revolution. "We should not, if we are wise, join either side," Andrews reiterated. "We have our own work to do and we had better do it alone." This was his last direct contribution to Trade Union affairs. The following year the divergence of opinion within the Congress caused a split that was scarcely healed within his lifetime.

There were signs in other quarters of a spirit of intolerance and coercion, a readiness to stir up religious and communal strife, against which he fought with all his strength. It showed itself in the boycott of the City College, Calcutta, by Hindu students who attempted to force on it religious observances in direct contravention of the Brahmo Samaj principles upon which it was founded. It showed itself in an ugly growth of communalism among Indians overseas—attempts in Durban to incite the "Hindu" poor against the "Muslim" rich, reckless appeals to similar feeling in Kenya and Fiji, trouble-making by rabid sectarians in Malaya. Andrews must have reproached himself more than once that his own idealistic invitations to religious teachers from India, to help to preserve the purity of Hindu ideals among the populations of the "Greater India" overseas,* should

* See, e.g., *Current Thought*, 1925, *passim.*

have given any impetus to a harsh proselytism which was far removed from his own conception of religious service. In India itself one such Hindu controversialist made an ugly and unworthy attack on the personal character of Jesus Christ. Andrews replied in print, in the name of scholarship and objective truth ; but when he saw that his protest only provoked more controversy, he apologized for it with courteous humility, and acknowledged that Christian propagandists themselves had often in the same way wounded the feelings of those who held other names in reverence.*

There were other concerns to be watched over. In Kenya a fresh attempt was being made to get a "white" non-official majority in the Legislative Council, and to bribe the Indians into acquiescence by suggesting that the "trusteeship" over the natives might be shared with the Colonial Office by *both* the immigrant communities, in direct contravention of the principles laid down by the White Paper of 1923.† The position of Indians in British Guiana needed immediate attention. Previous inquiries between 1923 and 1925 had shown that the domiciled Indian community there opposed any renewal of immigration before 1930, and in 1925 Andrews had played his part in getting a premature recruiting scheme turned down. Now 1930 was near, and a fresh inquiry was desirable.

I I

Andrews left Colombo for Europe on June 5th, 1928. The original intention had been that Rabindranath Tagore should go also, and deliver the Hibbert Lectures in Oxford during the autumn ; but he was taken ill and his journey had to be cancelled. Andrews adhered to his own plans. The time had come when an interpreter of India was urgently needed in the West. In the late summer of 1927 Katherine Mayo had published her notorious book *Mother India*, and it was soon clear that its influence on the popular attitude towards India, not only in America but throughout the world, was likely to be both powerful and pernicious. "It was a great shock to me," wrote a South African friend to

* See *The Modern Review*, 1923.

† Andrews' caustic comments may be read in *Young Men of India*, April, 1928.

Andrews, "after the picture of India I had built up from reading Tagore, hearing your lectures, and meeting the Indian delegation."[*] About the same time the Simon Commission on Indian constitutional reform was appointed—without a single Indian member. India's disappointment and indignation were great, and Mahatma Gandhi rapidly recovered the political leadership which he had partially lost in 1922. The two friends talked of the likelihood that Gandhi would need to visit England in person in the fairly near future, and Andrews knew that in case he did so, he himself might do much to prepare the way for him.

A letter was waiting for him when he reached England. It was from Mr. Arthur Hird (of the publishing house of Hodder and Stoughton), and it invited Andrews to come and see him "about writing a book." The letter contained no further details, and some time passed before the meeting took place. Then Hird explained that he wanted a spiritual autobiography—an account of the development of Andrews' religious experience. Andrews was overwhelmed ; he shrank from the greatness and the responsibility of such an undertaking ; but when other people, quite independently, made the same request, he came to feel that he had no right to refuse. Three years were to pass before *What I Owe to Christ* was completed, but from 1928 onwards it was never far from his thoughts.

Andrews set himself therefore to a threefold task. He must set against Miss Mayo's "drain-inspector's report,"[†] a picture of the *True India*,[‡] in which the great religious and cultural traditions should be seen in their full beauty, with Tagore as their living embodiment. He must interpret the political aspirations of an awakened nation, and help the West to understand the life and thought of Gandhi. He must share with devout souls in Europe and America the new vision of Christ and Christian service which had come to him in the East.

Within six months, the foundations of this bridge of understanding had been laid. Andrews had very greatly extended his contacts with the British press, both secular and religious. He

[*] M. E. Rothmann to C.F.A., 10th February, 1928.
[†] Mahatma Gandhi's phrase.
[‡] The title of Andrews' vindication of Indian life, not published till several years later.

had attended a conference of the Fellowship of Reconciliation, come into close touch with peace organisations both in England and at Geneva, and planned a visit to America. He had spent a "red-letter day" with Romain Rolland, another with Eglantine Jebb of the "Save the Children Fund." He had spoken in crowded students' meetings in every one of the principal British universities, and in churches of many denominations. He had established close and friendly relations with political leaders and with Indians in London.

During the same period Andrews edited no less than four books of Tagore's writings (*Letters to a Friend, Fireflies, The Tagore Birthday Book, Thoughts from Tagore*) and saw them through the press. It was a labour of love. After long days of political interviews, or of writing and speaking at high pressure on subjects of clamorous but transitory importance, he would feast his soul on the beauty of the familiar pages, and find new inspiration in the thought that he was helping to spread their message :

> I cannot tell you in any adequate way what a joy it has been for me to do this work for you. I have gone again and again to it when I have been quite tired out in the evening, and found refreshment and peace from your own beautiful words. My debt of gratitude is more than I can ever repay !
> ... It has been a great good fortune that I have had this visit with constant residence in London. Almost every day I have been backwards and forwards about something, and the publishers are so grateful if one takes this personal interest ... What a joy it is thus to be able to work for you and get your ideals known !*

At the same time he was writing to Gandhi about *Mahatma Gandhi's Ideas* :

> I am more anxious than I can tell you that this book which I am writing may really be informing and inspiring, and may also be sufficiently lucid and popular to be read by average people, both in Europe and America ... I really do think, if I might dare in deepest humility to say so, that this year, in which I have been in England and Europe, and the coming visit to America, will both do something to prepare the way for the time when you do actually come.†

In Andrews' public discussions of immediate political issues there occurs more than once the significant phrase "Round Table Conference." He indicted the Labour Party for not withholding

* Letters to Rabindranath Tagore, 22nd November, 1928, 2nd December, 1928.
† To M. K. Gandhi, 10th December, 1928.

its support from the Simon Commission until the "Round Table" principle was recognized : he and Mr. D. Chaman Lall, as representatives of India, withdrew from the Imperial Labour Conference in November, 1928, because their motion demanding that India's constitutional future should be settled by the conference method was ruled out of order. The simple test of sincerity, he wrote, was that the Simon Commission should consent to a Round Table Conference with all parties concerned.

III

A series of articles which Andrews wrote in 1928 for *Young Men of India*, called *A Quest for Truth*, describes the position he had then reached in his religious thought. But the most beautiful reference to his ideals of Christian witness is in a letter to an English religious journal, *The British Weekly*, which was published on 18th August, 1932, as a comment on *What I Owe to Christ* :

> I have longed above all else to make known what Christ Himself has made known to me. But this is rather through sharing with one another the joy of a religious experience than by imposing on anyone a religious dogma . . . Is not the ultimate thing needed for sharing any precious truth with another person just this—to keep the inner light in one's own soul so pure that the truth shines through with its own radiance ? No truth worth knowing can ever be taught ; it can only be lived.

Stories told by two men of widely differing temperament show how the truth by which Andrews lived did shine through his own spirit. The first describes a scene one evening in a Cambridge common-room :

> The old question arose as to the fulness of the knowledge of God held by the greatest non-Christian saint and the humblest old woman in the corner of a Christian "Bethel." Andrews told a story. "Some years ago," he said, "Dame Clara Butt came to seek peace at Santiniketan at a time of great personal sorrow. The last night of her stay we were sitting under the stars, with the students around, talking. 'Would you like me to sing to you ?' she asked, and the poet said we would like it above all things. It happened to be Holy Week, and she sang 'Were you there when they crucified my Lord ?' When the lovely voice had died down, there was perfect silence awhile, and then someone—was it I, or the poet, or no one but the unspoken word of us all ?—answered 'We were all there'."
>
> I have never forgotten that story or the way he told it, and I think I can say that any real understanding I have of the Cross goes back to that hour.*

* The Rev. A. Marcus Ward, letter to the authors.

The second scene is at a weekend conference at Birmingham, where Andrews told the same story :

"Were you there when they crucified my Lord ?" He made the whole of human suffering beat upon my heart in that one poignant phrase, for he made it symbolize all the sufferings of India and the tragic story of Negro slavery. I dare not try to recall his actual words, but the impression of the whole scene and its message remains as something indelible to which I have often returned for its cleansing fire. And I remember one little but symbolic thing, which was that as he spoke Charlie Andrews came (almost imperceptibly) nearer and nearer to us. *Almost* motionless during his address, he was actually moving towards his audience, as though drawn to us by the great desire he had to make these things understood.*

The impression which a casual meeting with him could make is shown by the story of his first visit to his future publishers, Messrs. George Allen & Unwin. "He has no appointment," telephoned the reception clerk to Sir Stanley Unwin, "but I feel it is important you should see him. He is not an ordinary man."

It does not appear that Andrews ever reformulated in intellectual terms those dogmas of the nature of God or the person of Jesus Christ which he had once felt compelled to discard.† When his old friend Stokes had ceased to accept the dogma, he had ceased to call himself a Christian.‡ Andrews was differently made. The centre of his religious experience was an intense personal devotion to a living, human Christ ; his prayers were intimate talks with a Great Companion, vividly, warmly present at his side, the Jesus of the Gospels : his strong visual imagination had been centred from earliest childhood on this beloved Figure. Religion for him was not a system of speculative ideas ; it was the experience of a transforming Friendship ; it was the source and counterpart of the affectionate devotion which he lavished on his friends on earth ; it was *bhakti*, and was content to let intellectual speculation rest.

Christ has become for me in my moral and spiritual experience the living tangible expression of God. With regard to the infinitude of God that lies beyond this I seem able at this present stage of existence to know nothing that can be defined. But the human in Christ, that is also divine,

* Reginald A. Reynolds, letter to the authors.
† See Chapter VII, pp. 102-3.
‡ Letter to C.F.A., November, 1928.

I can really know ; and when I see this divine beauty, truth and love in others also, it is natural for me to relate it to Christ.*

He came to accept and use the historic creeds of his own church as the endeavour to put into human words a divine experience beyond the power of words to express. The Church of England was and remained his spiritual home. But his circle of religious fellowship included everyone, of any creed or none, who served with humility and brotherly love the Living God of all.

* Article, *Why I am a Christian*, written for a Japanese newspaper in 1927, and published in pamphlet form by Friends' Book Centre, London.

CHAPTER XVII

AMERICAN JOURNEYS

1929-1930

I

IT was late in 1928, in London. Sir Gordon Guggisberg, Governor-designate of British Guiana, was waiting for C. F. Andrews at the Army and Navy Club in fashionable Pall Mall. The Rev. A. G. Fraser was with him ; he had known Sir Gordon as a much-beloved Governor of the Gold Coast, and Sir Gordon had asked him to arrange this meeting.

Presently the hall-porter appeared, in all his glory of uniform. "Sir," he said, "there is a man at the door who says he has an appointment with you, but I did not like to let him in till you had seen him." Fraser smiled. "I warned you !" he said. "That's Andrews." They went together to the door. No one who knew the Club's immaculate standards in dress could have blamed the porter for his doubts. From his shabby canvas shoes and shapeless old flannel trousers to the frayed collar of his cricket shirt, Andrews was worse dressed even than usual. But Guggisberg welcomed him gladly and they went in to lunch, while admirals, generals, governors, came up to speak to Sir Gordon and were all introduced to his guest. A quiet talk in an alcove followed, and Andrews' visit to British Guiana was arranged. Then he had to leave, and Sir Gordon saw him down to the street and put him in a taxi. His head bowed, he followed the taxi with his eyes until it was out of sight. There was a silence, and then he turned to his companion. "I feel," he said slowly, "as though I had been honoured to give lunch to my Lord."

Andrews reached the United States in January, 1929, and lost no time in getting into personal touch with Miss Mayo. "I could not feel at all indignant with her," he wrote,* "but could only feel

* To Rabindranath Tagore, 5th February, 1929.

that she was the very extreme opposite of all that we hold dear in the East." After the meeting he felt that she had been sincere, and that he should withdraw the charge of "political motive" which he had made originally against her. "She clearly has political *bias*," he said, "but I had no right to ascribe *motive*."

He met newspaper editors, and discussed with the American Quakers the arrangements for one of their number, Dr. Timbres, to join the staff of Visva-Bharati for anti-malarial work in the villages ; he went to Canada to prepare the way for Tagore's forthcoming visit. What the work cost him, only his most intimate letters reveal. The cold and stormy Atlantic voyage had brought on influenza, and for months he could not completely shake it off. The rush and clamour of life were a continual weariness to his spirit. "It has only been sheer will-power," he confessed, "that has kept me going lately."*

In the latter part of February he went south for an eagerly-anticipated visit to Booker T. Washington's great institute of Negro education at Tuskegee. There he spent ten peaceful days, sharing the life of the school and making friends with great and small. The *Tuskegee Messenger* has preserved an account of his visit :

> Tuskegee has had a messenger from the East. His spirit was a spirit of simplicity, of repose, of reflection and peace. He had a message, a plain unadorned story of the two greatest spirits in the world today, Tagore and Gandhi. Always there was the note of India's aspiration, of the self-denial of its leaders, and of the unity of their cause with the upward striving of all suppressed groups. He desired to establish bonds between Tuskegee in America and Santiniketan in India, which are dedicated in the same spirit to the same cause of emancipation.
>
> He was no recluse. He did not seem of another world ; he was curiously practical. But as he lingered among us his face continuously reflected the joy of his inward spirit. One of the boys said it was just like Jesus himself talking to us.†

In April Andrews went to Vancouver to meet Rabindranath Tagore as he landed in Canada. There he came into personal contact with the little Sikh community, whose struggle for citizenship rights he had followed for many years. Lord Hardinge

* To Rabindranath Tagore, 16th February, 1929.
† Abridged from *The Tuskegee Messenger*, 9th March, 1929.

had intervened on their behalf at the Imperial Conferences of 1917 and 1918, but by that time their number was reduced to about twelve hundred. When Andrews arrived their wives and children had been permitted to join them, and the whole situation was much happier. They gave him a tremendous welcome, drove him to the Gurdwara for prayers, and held a feast of rejoicing. It mattered nothing that he was not himself a Sikh— he was a man of God, and one of themselves. Andrews did all he possibly could to help the community to obtain the full citizenship rights which were still withheld. "You have astonished me," wrote one onlooker.* "by the amount of work it is possible for one man to get through in a quiet way without getting flurried." But in this matter all his efforts were unsuccessful.

II

When Tagore left for San Francisco, Andrews started on the first stage of his long journey to British Guiana, travelling five days and nights to Halifax, Nova Scotia, to embark for George-town. The ship called at the Bermudas, Santa Lucia, and Port of Spain, and everywhere Andrews went ashore and gathered information about the numbers and welfare of Indian settlers. He found, as in British Guiana itself, that their isolation from India was extreme ; no Indian news appeared in the press, and even letters took months to travel.

In Georgetown the East Indian Association welcomed him with ready co-operation. Weeks of travel followed—adventurous journeys through heavy rains and flooded rivers. A very full record of the first three or four weeks has been preserved in Andrews' journal, which, checked by men of long experience in the country, was intended to furnish the material for a book. These notes give by far the fullest picture extant of the method and spirit of his colonial investigations ; they enable us to watch the process of his thought ; and for that reason they are recorded in some detail, though in much abridged form and in the third person.

Andrews reached Georgetown on Saturday, May 18th. On

* Noel Robinson of *The Morning Star*, Vancouver, 16th April, 1929.

Sunday, the 19th, his first act was to attend the early morning service in Georgetown Cathedral. Then he went straight out to some deserted sugar plantations on the East Coast of Demerara, where Indians were still living in the ruinous, unhealthy old indentured labour quarters. Morning and evening he spoke in Hindi at church services to which the Hindu people crowded, hungry for Indian news and the sound of their own language. At a long talk during the afternoon with the Canadian missionary, and another in the evening with leaders of the Indian community, he tested out his own preconceived ideas. There was little or no racial prejudice, he was told, but owing to the extreme isolation of the uprooted community from India, and the weakening of religious sanctions which followed the decline of the mother-tongue, there had been a grave increase in social vices such as rum-drinking and gambling.

The whole of Monday was spent in interviews with Indian visitors, followed by a two hours' meeting of the committee of the East Indian Association which discussed the improvement of communications with India, and then by an overflowing meeting of welcome at the Town Hall. "I want to meet *all* communities," Andrews told them, "and to study the welfare of *all*. I am not here to ask favours for one community only."

Inoculations had been necessary, so Andrews spent the next day "resting"—that is, reading up his subject and writing up his notes at the house of the Bishop, whose guest he was. On Wednesday he discussed with the English Immigration Officer the tentative results of his three days' investigation : the need for one major social reform, the registration of Indian marriages ; and the benefit both to the Indian and to the under-populated colony if an adequate grant of land were offered as a counter-attraction to the free return passage to India.

During the next three days Andrews had many interviews with members of the Negro community. How far, he asked, could there be organised co-operation between Indian and Negro groups for such common objects as the control of drink and gambling ? In mixed gatherings of Indians and Negroes he made the definite proposal that all *de facto* Indian marriages should at once be legalised by recording, and that in future the community should agree to a simple form of registration.

On the second Sunday, May 26th, Andrews paid a promised visit to the West Coast. He was the guest of an Indian landlord, and the colony was prosperous and healthy, but he was at once aware of a sense of constraint on the part of the tenants. He suspected, and later inquiry confirmed his suspicions, that rents could be heavy, and restrictions on the milling and sale of rice irksome. He determined to study the young rice industry, with co-operative credit in his mind as a possible solution of its difficulties.

For the next few days he was surrounded by unemployed Georgetown malingerers whining to return to India. Work could be had on estates close at hand, but they would not take it. He spoke to them very frankly about the tragedies of Matiaburz. Land, he thought again—that was the only solution. If people could be invited to register for it, that would be the right psychological approach.

On Saturday June 1st, Andrews spoke to a great meeting of school teachers, and a new aspect of the situation presented itself. Not a single one of them was an East Indian. Andrews believed more firmly than ever that "without education the foundations of national life would be built on shifting sand," but he found little interest in education among the Indians. He saw too that there might be few openings for Indians, even if they entered the teaching profession, in schools which were almost all Christian denominational schools. Perhaps, he thought, these schools might be required to accept non-Christian teachers of good moral character as a condition of receiving Government aid ?

The next day, Sunday, was spent in a visit to a sugar estate. In Andrews' eyes it compared unfavourably with those of Natal. It seemed to him that the industry needed a large capital outlay and scientific planning.

Monday, June 3rd, was the King's birthday. Andrews watched the parade ; there were no Indians in the police forces. Surely Indian police, who understood the idiosyncrasies of their own people, might be valuable ? That afternoon he took to the

Colonial Secretary his conclusions about the rice industry. With production organised on a co-operative basis, and a market close at hand in Trinidad, it had, he urged, great possibilities.

A Negro public meeting the same evening gave him a glimpse of a racial consciousness far stronger than among the Bantu. Did they, he wondered, fear Indian competition ? The next day he discussed this with a journalist who was in close touch with the Negroes. By nature, said the latter, the West Indian Negro is a pioneer, not a cultivator (like the Chinese in Malaya, thought Andrews), so that his economic interests and the Indian's are in general complementary, not opposed. But he would resent large-scale assisted immigration, or a large influx of Indians into the teaching profession ; and any East Indian colonisation scheme must be paralleled by a similar offer to *bona fide* Negro agriculturalists.

The following day, June 5th, Andrews concentrated on the educational problem, studying reports and talking to teachers. The whole school system, based as it was on the Oxford and Cambridge examinations, was entirely foreign to the life of West Indian children. Should the aim be a West Indian University system, including Barbados and Trinidad ?—or an *ad hoc* educational structure framed for the needs of British Guiana ? He began to plan how a mixed Negro-Indian school might happily be organized, its teaching centred on British Guiana but reaching out to Africa and India also.

Then came a week of travel further afield, visiting schools, and sounding Indian opinion everywhere on the marriage question, on the drink scandal and on education. He visited excellently-managed estates, where Indian families had separate quarters, good conditions, plenty of land for rice and a chance to keep a cow. He visited others, "managed by an absentee company with no sense of smell," but whose water-logged soil, poor for sugar, would be ideal for rice.

One evening he sat and watched the sun set. What a lovely land it was ! Why should the schools be cramped and ugly ? Why should the houses on even the best estates be set up in rows "like beans on a beanstalk ?" Why should there not be lovely tree-shaded river *ghats*, as in India ? Why not the simple attractive school buildings of Java or the Philippines, which were adapted to this climate ? Why should not the Indian choose his own type of house, provided that sanitary requirements were met ? There was land enough and to spare. Given privacy, and water, land and a cow, the Government would hear little of him ! Meantime, alas, rum shops flourished, and evening meetings were interrupted by drunken quarrels.

Back in Georgetown on June 14th, Andrews held a meeting of all the Hindu Pandits in the colony, and put squarely before them the issue of child marriage. There were about a hundred of them, and two were hard to convince, but at last it was agreed unanimously that the marriage age should be raised to fourteen. The meeting lasted for four exhausting hours, but "was well worth it ; never before had the Pandits reached a unanimous decision." He told them frankly that he regarded this decision as only a beginning, but he knew that neither the priests nor the community were ready to go further just then.

III

As Andrews had stayed in South Africa consolidating the achievement of 1927, so he stayed on in British Guiana studying the new colonisation schemes, entering into the plans for a co-operative rice industry, discussing the Canadian rice market—and everywhere visiting the schools. For "education, especially girls' education, is central to the well-being of the colony." He met the Planters' Association, answered their last lingering fears that rice cultivation would be a "rival" to sugar and would bring malaria, and showed that it offered the only sure way of stopping the drift to the towns and building up a happy and contented plantation life. With East Indian leaders he discussed the building up of broken self-respect and the gradual fusion of the racial elements of the West Indies into a new nation wherein the Indian people might play a worthy part. Once more the Journal shows him thinking aloud :

"One or more East Indian holidays should be celebrated and recognized, and they should *not* be financed by the rum shops. Should they be religious holidays (like Id-ul-Fitr), or would that serve to accentuate religious differences ? Why not celebrate, as a national event, the first arrival of East Indians by the 'Lord Hungerford' from Calcutta in February, 1845 ? February is a good time for a festival, and might tend to eliminate the drunken *Holi* which has no real religious meaning. The *Tazia* celebrations in August could be rendered unobjectionable by the closing of the rum shops, and such festivals would make for unity and kindliness."

Thus little by little his conclusions were built up and tested.

Andrews left British Guiana with the hope that his visit "may have done something to bring about in this new world a more real understanding of India among the African people of the colony."* His farewell sermon in Georgetown Cathedral was a plea for the children : "I would ask you in the name of the Master who loved the little children, to cherish the health of the young infants, to care very greatly for the education of the little ones, to keep, for their sakes, the marriage tie inviolate. If you will take this one message from me you will find the difficulties of this country grow less and its prosperity increase."

Returning to Canada in October, Andrews set himself to persuade the Canadian Mission to recognize in its schools the claims of non-Christian religious groups, and to interest the Canadian Government in the possibilities of a direct steamer service *via* Trinidad and British Guiana to Capetown and India. H. N. Brailsford, who met him in New York soon after, was greatly impressed by his tremendous powers of concentration and his absorption in his task. "He *lived* in British Guiana : there must have been a special Providence watching over him, so that he somehow escaped death in the city traffic."

On December 31st, 1929, the marriage reforms which he had initiated received the authority of law ; Ordinance 42 of 1929 amended the Immigration Ordinance "with respect to the minimum age at which female immigrants may marry, and the registration of marriages contracted by immigrants according to their religious and personal law."

Two years later, Sir Edward Denham, who had succeeded Sir Gordon Guggisberg as Governor, wrote Andrews a letter which shows how sound was the general policy which he had advocated:

* Circular letter to friends in India, 13th June, 1929.

... The East Indians have shown themselves admirable workers. A loan to the estates by the Imperial Government, to be spent on housing and improved conditions, has been of very great assistance both to the estates and to the labourers ... The rice industry has been placed on a much more satisfactory basis, and the quality of Demerara rice is now never contested. We are establishing markets in Jamaica and San Domingo as well as in most of the West Indies, and sending paddy and rice to Canada ... I hope to obtain an officer from England with experience in Co-operative Credit Societies. The estates have been encouraged to let out their lands to a much larger extent to their labourers, and are showing an increased interest in sanitation and health problems, and starting Child Welfare committees in several centres.

... I put an East Indian on my Executive Council—the first time that an East Indian has ever sat in this Council. I am trying to assist them with their education but there is very little enthusiasm for it.

You spoke to me about the amount of drinking ... I have been most agreeably surprised. We are suffering in revenue from a big decrease in the consumption of spirits and rum, and undoubtedly a considerable change in customs is taking place. The demand today is for soft drinks and motor-car drives.

It was a great pleasure to meet you. You were most helpful to me, as were your notes of your visit here.*

In one thing he had apparently failed ; the Indian community had remained indifferent to the need of education. But his dream of a West Indian University found other advocates, and recent years have seen the dream come true.

I V

Andrews spent the winter of 1929-30 in Canada and the United States. He threw all his weight into the scales against the "Copeland Bill," which proposed to admit Indians into the States on an equal footing with Europeans on the score of their "Aryan" blood. "I am against it," he explained in a letter to J. B. Petit. "It is racial *in principle*, and it would not help non-Aryan Southern India. I am trying instead for a quota system into which racial distinctions do not enter."

These things were the subject of long discussions with Senator Porter of the Foreign Relations Department, with whom Andrews had much in common, for he had been leader of the

* To C.F.A., 9th June, 1931.

United States delegation to the Opium Conference at Geneva in 1924. The quota system, Andrews argued, might give India a very small immigration figure, but it would be "more righteous and more practical" than the hurriedly passed and obnoxious Asiatic Exclusion Act of 1924, and would make possible its repeal. Andrews missed no opportunity to drive home to the consciousness of the West the dignity and importance of the Asiatic lands. He commented ironically in *The New Republic* on Herbert Hoover's Armistice Day address in November, 1929 :

> The racially insulting Asiatic Prohibition Law of 1924 still remains on the Statute Book of the United States ; the colour bar legislation still keeps its grip upon South Africa ; the Kenya policy still implies racial discrimination in favour of the European race. Nevertheless, we seem wearily to be satisfied with the sedative "All quiet on the Western Front," and assure ourselves that if the Young Plan for naval parity goes through successfully we shall then have almost within our sight "World Peace."

He travelled ceaselessly, speaking everywhere, and wrote much for magazines. The pace of life was tremendous, and his body cried out against it as "a daily crucifixion,"* but he was upheld by one sustaining purpose—rightly to interpret the life of India and thereby to correct the misleading picture given by *Mother India.* He was working in every spare moment at his book on Gandhi,† which was finished and published during the year, and stories of the work of national regeneration carried out by Gandhi or under his inspiration filled all his speeches ; for once even Tagore took a secondary, though still important, place.

> "He has done more than has ever been done before," wrote J. T. Sunderland, the American friend of India, "to give America a true idea of what India's great saint and public leader is and is not, and what he is and is not endeavouring to achieve for the Indian people."‡

Andrews' own personality made its mark on all sorts and conditions of men. After he had spoken at the Starr Commonwealth, letters from many schoolboy correspondents followed "Uncle Charley," filled with boyish discussions of "that way of fighting without guns." A boy at a Quaker school in Philadelphia was unforgettably impressed by the way in which his mere

---

* Letter to Rabindranath Tagore, 20th November, 1929.

† *Mahatma Gandhi's Ideas.*

‡ *The Modern Review,* June, 1930.

presence in a room seemed to change its whole atmosphere. An attorney in New York, after a short meeting with him, was moved to write, "I cannot tell you how much I enjoyed our brief interview the other day. Your visit brought me inspiration." "I have been present at three luncheons where Andrews was the guest of honour," reported another. "At two of them he told the story of the Vykom struggle, and I have not seen in years an audience so moved by a speaker. 'Cynic as I am supposed to be,' said a lawyer present, 'tears came into my eyes as Mr. Andrews talked'."

A group of Indians in the United States, however, publicly attacked his work by means of long "Open Letters" to Mahatma Gandhi. They resented his declaration of belief in Miss Mayo's sincerity, and his retraction of the charge of "political motive" which he had made against her. They objected to his dramatization of the Vykom story, claiming that it distorted the picture, and was calculated to impress America more with the cruelty of the still-existing wrongs than with the widespread and unobstrusive character of the reforms which were taking place. They were annoyed by his frank discussion of rifts in Indian unity, such as the swing over of the Trade Union Congress towards communist ideology, and the claim made by the Aga Khan that the Moslems of India constituted a "nation" in themselves. The real source of their anger, however, was Andrews' opposition to the Copeland Bill which proposed to grant Indians privileges as "Aryans." The group had supported the Bill, and they ridiculed his non-racial principles as "idealistic humbug," and went on to suggest, rather illogically, that his arguments "had been obtained at the office of the British Embassy in Washington."

It cut to the quick to be called a "British spy." He had borne hard words before, and would do so again, and silently ; but he was wounded none the less. An Indian friend, Mr. Hari Govil, who was with him when the taunt reached him, describes how Andrews turned to him with quivering lips : "If I inspire such feelings, after all these years, then I do not deserve to stay in India. Shall I go to China ? I am receiving many pressing calls." "You would do violence to your own inner self," was the reply.

Andrews pressed his friend's hand. "Come with me," he said, "we will go to N's office." With quiet humility he met his cynical critic face to face and told him of his ideals of service. He appealed to him with a warmth of genuine friendliness which was irresistible. "You and I," he said, "have both dedicated our lives to our country—for your country is my country. Let us not advocate methods for the liberation of India which are against the genius of our people. Let us work with *ahimsa* and truth in our hearts."

Cruel and unfair as much of this criticism was, the grain of truth in some of the charges may be recognized by Andrews' closest friends and warmest admirers. His whole temperament predisposed him to worship his ideals incarnate in human heroes, in symbolic situations. The fear that his dramatic and symbolic use of the Vykom incident might have in some quarters the opposite effect from that which he intended, was perhaps not unjustified. It was a friendly reviewer who felt that his book *The True India* is "out of focus," and that the figures of Miss Mayo as "villain" and Mahatma Gandhi as "hero" loom so large that they obstruct the view of the country as a whole. Again, while most of Andrews' prophetic pronouncements on Indian affairs have been amply justified by time, the very intensity of his feeling sometimes warped his judgment of *when* and *where* he could most effectively speak. When deeply moved he found it extremely difficult to exercise self-restraint ; his agony over the "racial churches" in South Africa was poured out sometimes even more strongly to Hindu audiences in India than to the Christians primarily concerned ; and it is difficult not to feel that his championship of the Indian point of view in 1919-21 might have been more effective if more of it had found expression (as later on it did) through British newspapers and magazines as well as Indian ones. Similarly, in America, his fears and hopes about India's political and social welfare and India's relations with Britain were sometimes poured out with insufficient regard for the impression they might make on audiences whose equipment for judging the issues at stake was vastly inferior to his own.

Andrews made no public answer to the attack ; he did not write to the press as he had written in 1923 about the taunts flung at him in Kenya. His only reference to the subject is in two private letters to Benarsidas Chaturvedi :

"It is indeed hard to be a peace-maker, but we were never told that it would be easy. . . . I have not written anything about that attack on me, for it is better entirely forgotten. The harm done unfortunately has been great, but in the end it will turn to good. I am so glad that it did not disturb me as I was disturbed some time ago when I was attacked from East Africa. This time I was much quieter and calmer and understood better the words of the *Gita* about *Nishkama Karma* . . . The very best thing I have found is silence. The praise I have received has been far too great and undeserved. It is a blessing to have something to restore the balance on the other side."*

At Christmas, 1929, among the simple Negro folk of St. Helena's Island, Andrews had revised the opening chapters of *What I Owe to Christ*, which were the fruit of these stormy months. Not long afterwards a group of young Christian leaders, coming to meet him one evening in New York, and looking into his face, had recognized the secret of his life. "Don't tell us about India," said one of them abruptly, "Teach us to pray." The phrase was harsh with urgency ; to Andrews the incident summed up as in a parable the one great need of the strident western world to which he had come.

* To B.D.C., 12th January, 1930 and 12th February, 1930.

CHAPTER XVIII

THE ROUND TABLE CONFERENCES

1930-1932

I

A NEW phase in the political relationships between India and Britain opened in October, 1929, when Lord Irwin returned to Delhi after a visit to England, authorised to invite Indians to a Round Table Conference. Statements made by responsible leaders such as Mr. Ramsay MacDonald led Indians to expect that this Conference would draw up a constitution giving India "dominion status." When this was denied, with certain ill-judged remarks by British politicians, the bitter disappointment in India led to a violent reaction ; in December, 1929, the Lahore Congress passed a resolution in favour of complete independence, and celebrated the 26th January, 1930, as the first "Independence Day." In April, Gandhi challenged the Government by his dramatic three weeks' "salt march", for illicit salt-making. The Government did not choose to accept the challenge, but when this was followed by widespread commercial boycott and sporadic outbreaks of mob violence, Gandhi and many others were arrested and imprisoned, ten special "ordinances" enacted, and certain districts placed under martial law. The Simon Report, which was to form the basis of discussion at the Conference, was

"a document unhappy in form and in the circumstances of its appearance. . . . The emphasis was laid deliberately upon the diversity of the Indian people and their communal dissensions, while the account of recent events wholly disregarded the depth and intensity of nationalist feeling . . . No effective change was suggested in the Central Executive until the States were prepared to come into a Federation and the country was capable of defending itself, provisos . . . which made the future dependent upon two factors, neither of which was under Indian control."*

When Andrews returned to England from the United States in April, 1930, he felt it was his immediate duty to put before the

* Thompson and Garrett, *The Rise and Fulfilment of British Rule in India*, p. 635-6.

English public the Indian point of view on the vital issues which the Conference would discuss. *India and the Simon Report* was written at top speed in the early summer, and finished in the first days of July at Mrs. Ellis' quiet home at Wrea Head, near Scarborough, one of many friendly retreats now open to him. When the news of Gandhi's arrest reached England in May, Tagore was also in the country, and his dignified and moving vindications of India's moral and spiritual claims to freedom made a deep impression, which Andrews reinforced by including them in his book. When the Conference began in the autumn of 1930 the Simon Report was quietly shelved.

Andrews himself was by that time in the United States again, with Tagore. Then came a cable from South Africa ; grave racial issues had raised their heads in the Transvaal. He hurried back to London, and sailed at once for Capetown.* He returned to England again in April, 1931, to find a changed situation. The Gandhi-Irwin pact had been signed in India, and confirmed by the Congress ; the Congress had named Gandhi as its sole representative at the Second Round Table Conference, which was to take place in the autumn of 1931.

Andrews plunged at once into the task of preparing for his friend's coming, and of keeping Gandhi in the closest possible touch with English opinion. He sent him Hansard's Parliamentary Report for May 23rd, asking him to study the part played in the India debate by the Lancashire cotton depression. "When you come," he wrote, "you must meet Lancashire face to face as I myself am just going to do." Sealing his letter he went into the Indian Student Hostel canteen. A group of Indian friends were just sitting down to a midday meal. "I'm just off to Manchester," he told them, "to see the Lancashire unemployed—*Dahl* and half-rice, please," he added to the waiter. This dish then cost three-halfpence. "Let us call you a taxi," said the friends when it had been eaten. "Oh no, I think a bus will do," was the gentle vague reply. The total assets of the traveller, apart from his ticket, were discovered to be threepence.

The distress which he found in Lancashire made him plead with

* For an account of the developments in South Africa, see Chapter XX.

Gandhi to call off the foreign cloth boycott, as he had called off passive resistance in South Africa in 1914. Gandhi's reply shows how well he understood his friend's temperament :

> As is your wont you are distressed over what your eyes see and your ears hear. This time it is the terrible unemployment in Lancashire. What you see and hear acts as an effective barrier against perceiving the truth. I have always found it true that hard cases make bad law ! .. What you say about South Africa is a false analogy. The way you suggest is not the way to help Lancashire.

But he promised that he would visit the Lancashire workers.

Andrews found also that widespread misunderstanding of Gandhi's attitude to Christian missionary work in India was being dexterously fostered by a section of the press. His own two books on Gandhi* were of great assistance in reaching a truer perspective, and immediately on his return from South Africa he plunged into the task of completing the third (*Mahatma Gandhi at Work*) and seeing it through the press. He supplied editors of Christian journals both in Britain and America with material for the Christian reading public, and spoke again and again at public meetings on the same theme.

But it seemed very possible that Gandhi might not come. In India there was acute feeling on both sides that the Gandhi-Irwin Pact had been dishonoured, and Congress workers accused the officials of continuing to obstruct the village industrial programme even after Irwin had pledged his support. In England there was profound distrust of Gandhi's integrity of purpose. Andrews bent all his energies to the removal of this obstacle. Day after day in interviews and letters, in Whitehall and Downing Street, he reiterated what was to him the crucial issue.

> "I can only tell you that after nearly twenty years' experience I have never known a more essentially truthful man. If you are to deal with him at all it will be necessary for you to share that belief with me . . . On no other basis except this confidence in Mr. Gandhi's honesty and sincerity, can the situation in India come to a right settlement."

It was during these months that Andrews first met Agatha Harrison, who became his closest collaborator in this work of conciliation. She has vividly described their first meeting in the house of a mutual friend :

* *Mahatma Gandhi's Ideas* (1929) ; *Mahatma Gandhi : His Own Story* (1930).

He entered the room with his arms laden with papers, and carrying an attaché case brimming over with unanswered letters from all parts of the world, his book *Mahatma Gandhi at Work*, chapters of his half-finished book *What I Owe to Christ*, partially finished articles long overdue. It is a familiar sight. He wasted no time in preliminaries ; he knew that I was deeply concerned . . . We began on the over-full attaché case.

II

Mahatma Gandhi arrived at last. C. F. Andrews met him at Marseilles and was responsible for all the arrangements for his visit outside the Conference itself. Gandhi insisted on living at Muriel Lester's Settlement in the East End of London, among the poor whom he understood ; but this congenial home was several miles from the centre of political activity at Westminster, and Andrews, anxious that all Gandhi's energies should be conserved for his supremely important task, was convinced that he must also have office accommodation near the Conference head-quarters. Gandhi consented only with very great reluctance to the cost of renting No. 88 Knightsbridge—in fact, they came nearer to a quarrel over Charlie's "extravagance" than they had ever done before. But at last the matter was settled ; Charlie's old friends, Dr. and Mrs. S. K. Datta, took over the care of the house, and he himself was established in a "sky-parlour" there, where in the odd moments that could be snatched from hectic days he worked on *What I Owe to Christ*.

Such moments of peace were very few. Visitors poured in at all hours of the day, and Andrews constituted himself door-keeper in chief, guarding Gandhi from the merely importunate, as he had done at Delhi in 1924, and deciding whom it was, and was not, desirable that he should see. It was an onerous responsi-bility ; some of the "undesirables" returned again and again ; but Andrews could and did remain firm.

A much more important contribution to the value of Gandhi's visit to England, however, consisted in the far-sighted strategy with which Andrews planned for him to meet, in an atmosphere of quietness and leisure, with some of the best minds in the country. With the co-operation of Henry Polak and other friends, he arranged a series of week-end visits to the Provinces.

One of these was the promised visit to Lancashire ; the ordinary working people quickly sensed that whatever might be the rights and wrongs of the Indian cotton boycott, Gandhi was a comrade in the fight against poverty, and they readily gave him their affectionate respect. "I am one of the unemployed," said one man, "but if I were in India I would say the same thing as Mr. Gandhi is saying."

With the sophisticated upper middle classes it was more difficult to find common ground, but Andrews did very much. He took Gandhi to Canterbury, to meet his friend Hewlett Johnson, the Dean—the "red" Dean as he was called for his concern for social justice. Another week-end was spent with C. P. Scott of *The Manchester Guardian* ; another in the beloved surroundings of Pembroke College, Cambridge ; another with Quaker friends of India at Birmingham ; another with Dr. Lindsay, Master of Balliol College, at Oxford. Andrews himself summed up the results which he felt had been achieved :

> His unique personality gripped the best English minds, and his originality of thought set those whom he met thinking as they had never done before. They were not always in agreement with him ; but they all immensely respected the greatness of soul which they found in him. England is a very small country, and impressions like these go round very fast indeed. No serious-minded man or woman could any longer take the view, which had been very widely held before, that Mahatma Gandhi was only an impossible fanatic after all.*

With regard to the Round Table Conference itself Andrews could only feel that Gandhi's visit had been "a magnificent failure." It was indeed a period of great disappointment. By the time the second conference met, the Labour Government which had initiated the conference method had been put out of office by a General Election, and though Ramsay MacDonald remained Prime Minister, the attitude of his Cabinet to the nego- tiations had noticeably stiffened. On the Indian side, with the exception of Gandhi himself, almost all the delegates were "moderates," and again and again as the Conference proceeded Gandhi was obliged to record his opposition to proposals which the majority of his colleagues were prepared to accept. It became

* From an article, *Mahatma Gandhi in London*, written in 1932.

clear that two alternatives were open to the Government : they could either ignore Gandhi's point of view, in the hope that the "moderates" would be able to put through their proposals in India ; or they could recognize that as representative of the National Congress he represented India more truly than all the rest put together, and make terms with him accordingly.

Andrews, strongly supported by Datta and Polak, did his utmost to persuade MacDonald and his colleagues to take the second, and as he believed, the only realistic course. Together they arranged with Dr. Lindsay for a second week-end at Oxford, and got down to serious business. Lord Lothian was present, and Mr. Malcolm MacDonald attended as his father's unofficial representative. Professor Coulton, of Cambridge, and Dr. Lindsay himself took a leading part. Andrews and Mrs. Lindsay gently persuaded them to come down from the constitutional clouds to Gandhi's practical concern for the welfare of the starving Indian peasant ; progress was rapid, and it seemed as though real agreement was in sight, and as if, in Dr. Datta's phrase, the week-end might "make history." But there the matter ended ; the Cabinet, for whatever reason, failed to follow up the path that had been opened, and the hope of an understanding withered away.

III

The attempt to reach responsible government for India had failed, but Andrews exerted himself with unabated energy to get the essentials of the situation recognized. Even within the framework of the existing constitution, he pointed out, it was possible for the Government of India to become "a real Indian Government instead of a British Government in India" run, in all vital matters, from Whitehall. The proclamation of 1917, he argued, was a pledge not only to work for responsible government, but also to associate Indians in the administration. The British Government, he suggested, might guarantee the sincerity of its intentions by carrying out the latter part of the pledge, and by issuing *constructive* Orders-in-Council requiring from Government officers active co-operation with the Congress in the promotion of village industries.* This last proposal was made in

* Letter to Ramsay MacDonald, 26th November, 1931.

the full expectation that on Gandhi's return to India constructive village work would be vigorously pressed forward. But events took a tragic turn. Within three weeks of his landing in India in January, 1932, Gandhi was once more in jail and the Congress had been proscribed.

Andrews was in South Africa when the news arrived. He was needed there to prepare the way for the India-South Africa Round Table Conference of 1932. Some of the South African Jews were concerned about the growing Arab-Jewish tension in Palestine, and had offered to pay Andrews' expenses for a visit of conciliation there. He had also been making tentative plans to visit the flood-stricken areas of China in company with the Dean of Canterbury.

But when Gandhi was arrested he cancelled everything else, and went straight from South Africa to India. When he arrived in mid-March over thirty thousand people had been interned in connection with "civil disobedience" offences. Lord Willingdon, who in 1931 had succeded Lord Irwin as Viceroy, believed that the latter's policy had been a mistake and that a "strong hand" was essential, especially in regard to Abdul Ghaffar Khan's "Red Shirt" organisation on the Frontier. The civil disobedience movement, the Government claimed, was deliberately designed to incite the police to actions calculated to alienate public opinion. While the Central and Provincial authorities were making every effort to prevent or punish excesses on the part of their subordinates, the main responsibility for creating the conditions in which excesses were possible lay, they argued, with the Congress, and the alternative to repression was chaos. Three English Quakers, who at Andrews' request were visiting India on an independent mission of conciliation, sadly recorded their impression that the Government officials "were out not for peace but for victory."*

Tagore, at Santiniketan, shared the general gloom ; but after long talks with Andrews and the three Friends he gave them a finely-worded appeal "to all who have the welfare of humanity at heart," in which he pleaded for the abandonment of suspicion and hostility, and for a profounder belief "in the mighty power of creative understanding between individuals and nations." Neither

* Percy W. Bartlett, Journal letter, 1st April, 1932.

Andrews nor anyone else was allowed to deliver this appeal in person to Gandhi in jail, and the Government would say no more than that they would "consider" forwarding it with a covering letter.* Andrews himself was served with a police order restraining him from leaving Delhi, and though his hot protest to the Home Member brought a prompt apology, the incident indicates the atmosphere that prevailed. "It is like 1919 in the Punjab," he wrote to the Home Department, but his warnings made no impression.

It was Holy Week, and the shadows lay heavy on his spirit ; he was physically ill as well as being sick at heart. He had promised to preach an Easter sermon at one of the Delhi churches, and wondered in the darkness of his despair what message he had to give. Then, *ex tenebris lux*. Light and faith and hope came flooding back on Easter morning as he read the story of Mary meeting her risen Master in the Garden, and he set himself with a new courage to his task. In the first week of May he landed once more in England.

All his energies for the next two months were given to personal interviews. He saw Lord Irwin, Lord Sankey, and the Secretary of State, Sir Samuel Hoare. He sought out Ramsay MacDonald in the midst of his golfing holiday at Lossiemouth, and they walked round the golf links together while Andrews put his case. Could not the expiry of the Special Ordinances at the end of June, he pleaded, be made the occasion for a new effort of reconciliation ? He found that once more he had to combat propaganda which cast doubt on Gandhi's personal integrity, and, in addition, to overcome the ordinary man's distaste for any further discussion of the baffling and complex problems of India. "The whole subject of India was tabooed," he writes. "If I had not come back I hardly like to think what would have happened."†

The end of June came and went, and public policy remained unchanged. Andrews was defeated on the surface and with regard to his immediate objective, but he knew that real progress had been made. In July he set to work to reach the Christian conscience of England on the moral aspect of the Indian situation.

* This appeal was afterwards printed and widely circulated in England.
† To G. D. Birla, 9th July, 1932.

S

For this work the doors were now wide open ; *What I Owe to Christ* had been published earlier in the year, and a third reprint had been called for within a fortnight. Invitations to speak in Christian circles began pouring in, giving him the opportunity for a wider "ministry of reconciliation" than he had ever exercised before. He began tentatively to ponder a new book, in which he would share still more fully the secret of his own inner peace.

Suddenly there came a tragic call for help. Tagore's only grandson, Nitu, then a student in Germany, was struck down with tuberculosis. He was dying, and the parents had been summoned. Andrews had known the boy from childhood, and the parents were his friends. During the agonising days that followed, he lifted every possible burden from the stricken father and mother. It was he who read the burial service in the little Black Forest churchyard, and, indescribably weary as he was, strove to comfort those in India by long letters telling of the affection with which they had all been surrounded, and the beauty of the lad's last resting place.

Andrews' letters to friends in England reveal the depth to which this tragedy stirred him. The beauty of the mountains around brought no comfort then ; the poignant contrast between their majestic peace and the agony he was called upon to witness and to share was well-nigh intolerable. Comfort lay elsewhere—in the Cross. Out of suffering which had strained his faith to its foundations, came the new book, *Christ in the Silence*. The outline of it had sprung clear to his brain on a sleepless night journey through Germany as he hurried to Nitu's side, and he knew that it had been kindled to a living power by the searching experiences which had followed.

When all was over he went on from the Black Forest to Switzerland, where he had promised to attend a "House Party" of the Oxford Group. Physically exhausted, he shrank from the new demands which it would make upon him, and he longed for the homely familiarity of English soil instead. "What a comfort it will be to be back in dear England again," he wrote. " 'Here rests his head upon the lap of earth.' In a very true sense I want to lay my head upon the lap of English earth once more."*   But his sense of duty held him to his promise.

He was richly rewarded. The House Party at Ermatingen brought him no further strain, but a healing peace. The sunny hillside above Lac Leman, with its joyous fellowship of young life, was "like a Galilean spring after Gethsemane." He rested, and dreamed of writing another book, which should pass on to the eager young spirits around him some of the heroic inspirations of his own life. As he sat with his eyes on the high snows beyond the Lake, his thoughts went back to the snow-capped ranges beyond Kotgarh and the fastnesses of Tibet towards which, in 1926, Sadhu Sundar Singh had set his face in a journey from which he never returned. He made his plans for *Sadhu Sundar Singh : A Personal Memoir*. But the book was not to be written yet.

* To A.H., undated, August, 1932.

CHAPTER XIX

INDIA AND BRITAIN

1932-1935

DURING Andrews' absence from England in August, 1932, momentous developments were taking place in India. Some groups at the Round Table Conference, including Dr. Ambedkar, the representative of the "untouchables," had demanded that in the new Indian constitution their respective communities should be granted a species of communal franchise, with separate electorates for the legislatures. Gandhi had warned the conference that if need be he would resist this policy "with his life," and he meant exactly what he said. His imprisonment in January, 1932, had prevented him from carrying out his plans for a personal campaign against the proposal, and when Ramsay MacDonald's "Communal Award" was published in August, 1932, he felt that his objections had not been adequately met by its terms. There was however a clause in the Award which made possible the modification of its provisions by agreement between the parties concerned. Gandhi therefore commenced a fast, in order by moral pressure to induce caste Hindus and "untouchable" leaders to make an agreed demand for modification of the Award in the direction he desired. The result was the compromise known as the "Poona Pact."

Both the method and the motive of this fast were not unnaturally widely misunderstood in the west, even by thoughtful and sympathetic Europeans, who wondered whether such moral compulsion was truly "non-violent." Andrews himself shared these doubts and questionings of the *method* of fasting, and poured them out freely in his own letters to Gandhi ; but in his public writings he gave himself entirely to the interpretation of the pure underlying *motive* of his friend's action. It was, as he saw it, a fruit of the compulsion of love :

He saw these poorest of people, whom he loved so deeply, taking a wrong turn, which led to a hidden precipice. With all the reckless daring of devoted love he threw himself across their path . . . Surely in such a deed there is a beauty, rare and wonderful, which brings back to mind the words, "Greater love hath no man than this, that a man lay down his life for his friends."*

Andrews had been in Manchester when the news of the fast reached England. He returned at once to London and got into touch with the Prime Minister, the India Office, and the group of influential friends such as Lords Irwin, Sankey, and Lothian, who understood the situation. He also cabled to Gandhi to ask whether he should start for India to help him there. Gandhi cabled back that he was assured that the fast was in accordance with the will of God, and that Charlie should remain in England. The record of the days that followed can never be fully written ; it is very possible that nothing but the intensity of Andrews' planned, sustained, and concentrated work saved Gandhi's life.

The India Conciliation Group, including Carl Heath, Henry Polak, Agatha Harrison, Horace Alexander, and other British friends of India, took a temporary office in the centre of London, and they and Andrews held daily consultations there. The power of the press to help or hinder was recognised from the first, and with Polak's and Alexander's help Andrews drew up a statement of the issues at stake, which was sent out to every daily newspaper in England and to about two hundred and fifty weekly papers of many kinds. American and Canadian news agencies also cabled to their correspondents to seek Andrews' help in interpreting the facts ; the Editor of the *Christian Century* sent him a warm personal letter of thanks for his assistance.

As day after day went by, the cables from India reflected the terrible anxiety felt there over Gandhi's increasing weakness, Andrews devoted all his time and energy to the task of getting a public statement from the Prime Minister that if an agreement between caste Hindus and "untouchables" should be reached, the British Government would at once accept it. At last on Septem-

* *The Christian Century*, October, 1932.

ber 23rd he was assured that this would be done "if the scheme were practicable." Late next day, Saturday, September 24th, the news of the Poona Pact came through. Most of the ministers concerned were out of town for the week-end ; Ramsay Mac-Donald himself was in his country retreat at Chequers. By seven o'clock on Sunday morning Andrews was on his way there ; all that day he went from interview to interview, while Agatha Harrison sat at the telephone in London and passed on to him the latest items of news as the long cables came in one after another from India. It was the climax of all his months of patient, courteous, friendly contact with British officials. The coldness and hostility of 1923 had long since been dispelled ; at the India Office, in Downing Street, every door was open to him. Time was all-important : the Prime Minister's decision must go out immediately, and it must be rightly worded—an error of judgment there would be fatal. As so often in the crises of Andrews' life the sense of a divine upholding cleared his brain and sharpened his intellectual powers. There was no false step. The message went out and Gandhi broke his fast.

The next day Andrews sent a characteristic letter to *The Manchester Guardian* :

"The news that Mahatma Gandhi has been able to break his fast and that the Legislative Assembly at Simla has received the news of the British Government's decision with prolonged applause may mark a turn in the tide of sentiment in India and Great Britain towards goodwill and peace . . .

May I, as one who knows some at least of the extreme difficulties which had to be faced, pay a heartfelt tribute to the Prime Minister for the high qualities of courage and statesmanship which he has shown ? It is very difficult for the general public to understand the risks that were involved and the way they were boldly overcome.

The first thought is that of deepest gratitude to God who has brought such great things to pass. The second is that men and women of goodwill in either country may use this great opportunity for His service.

"My attention has been drawn," wrote MacDonald, "to that very generous and fine-spirited letter by you which appeared in *The Manchester Guardian* yesterday. It is just the man whom I have respected so much for a good many years now, and I would like to let you know how it impressed me."*

* To C. F. Andrews, 28th September, 1932.

It was Andrews also who publicised in England the protest made by Bishop Azariah of Dornakal, in the name of true religion and true patriotism, against separate electorates for Indian Christians. It was Andrews who brought to the notice of the Government the fresh moves towards Hindu-Muslim agreement which resulted from the fast and the Poona Pact, and who urged, successfully, that Gandhi should be allowed even in prison the fullest freedom of communication for this vital work of re-conciliation.

Andrews himself felt that the purpose of his own life had been clarified.

"For the rest of my life," he wrote to Gandhi on October 14th, "I must dedicate every moment to this supreme issue. That is reality, that is truth for me. It will take me to India, to South Africa and elsewhere, but wherever I go this must be the conscious object—to deal a blow at 'untouchability' within the Christian church . . . You have brought me back, with a shock, to the one purpose for which God gave me life and health and strength. I thank God for that."

He challenged the conscience of England with the thought that Gandhi's dramatic action called for a parallel effort in these other fields. "I long for the day," he declared to nearly a thousand Christian ministers at the Congregational Union Assembly at Wolverhampton, "when untouchability shall be removed, not only in India but in South Africa, the Southern States of America, and everywhere where Christians refuse to worship with their brethren whose complexion is slightly darker than their own."* The fulness and sympathy with which this speech was reported in newspapers of every political colour is a measure of the change which he, more than any other single man, had wrought in the general British attitude towards India, and towards Gandhi, between June and October, 1932.

II

Early in November, 1932, a certain M. Kelappan began a "fast unto death" to secure for the "untouchables" the right of entry into a temple at Guravayur in South India, and Gandhi declared that he would do the same on January 1st, 1933, if the right were

* October 6th, 1932.

not granted. The news of this decision brought him a long letter from Andrews, in which he raises the whole question of the ethics of such a fast, if carried to the point of suicide :

"The whole of my own religious upbringing has been such as to make any thought of suicide on my part impossible.

"I am really troubled still . . . such a practice as this will certainly be used by fanatics to force an issue which may be reactionary instead of progressive. Human madness or even doting affection may become tyrannical in this way. How far my anxieties and fears are mixed with weak human affection I can hardly myself understand. I *do* know that I saw you finally giving your life itself for the depressed classes, in your last fast, and I was glad—I saw in it the "greater love." I can see you now preparing to do the same thing on January 1st, if the temple authorities do not give way.

". . . It seems to me that I would very gladly lay down my life to remove 'untouchability,' between the white race fanatics who call themselves Christians and the other races. But you have evidently come to the point of *forcing the issue*—literally *forcing* it, and I have to think that out in terms of Christ.

"I think He *did* force the issue, when He set His face steadfastly to go to Jerusalem. He saw then, I think, that only His own death could call the Jewish leaders to a halt. There is one strange saying of His, 'The Kingdom of Heaven suffereth violence, and the violent take it by force.' Again I am not sure whether His act in cleansing the temple was not of the same character, i.e., forcing the issue. But the method of fasting, committing suicide, still instinctively repels me."*

When 1933 opened, the burning topic of the day was whether legislation to permit Temple Entry would be allowed. Gandhi had postponed his threatened fast, but the thing that concerned Andrews was that a government of conservative tendency might take refuge behind the principle of "religious neutrality" and refuse to permit even a private Bill on the subject to be brought forward. He set himself to help the India Office and the Cabinet to realise the tremendous importance of the issues involved. Lord Allen of Hurtwood, Ramsay MacDonald's trusted friend and counsellor, promised to give him every help possible in "straightening out the Indian tangle," and at his own suggestion Andrews prepared a short memorandum for his use :

I have had long talks this week with the India Office, and have put before them certain things which I should like you to know.

* To M. K. Gandhi, 10th November, 1932.

(1) I feel quite clear that if the Viceroy blocks legislation both at the Centre and in the Provinces, this will lead to a very dangerous explosion . . . Gandhi would certainly fast if this were done, and he would have the sympathy of every thinking man in India with him . . .

(2) This does not leave the Viceroy without a veto if bad legislation is passed. He still has the power of refusing to sign the Bill, and he can send it back to the Legislature if he feels that it would lead to religious strife . . .

(3) I pressed with all my might that the Viceroy should declare himself openly and frankly in favour of the removal of the curse of Untouchability. He should do this at the opening of the Central Assembly at the end of this month at Delhi. The British Government has always refused to recognise Untouchability under the law, and the time has fully come when the Viceroy, representing the King-Emperor, should declare that this blot on Indian social life must be removed . . . It is possible to regard religious susceptibilities in the process of removing Untouchability, but it is not possible to hold up the whole reform movement indefinitely in order to do so.

(4) On this matter of removal of Untouchability the Government of India is already co-operating with Mr. Gandhi. He is most grateful for the facilities on this subject, which they are allowing him . . . I urged the Government officials at the India Office to do everything possible to continue the co-operation with Mr. Gandhi and also to call into consultation the leading non-co-operator, Mr. C. Rajagopalachariar, who is out of prison. I pressed the India Office to bring Mr. Sastri also into consultation, and to see if an all-India decision could not be found which should unite Congress leaders with Moderates. I think you will see the enormous importance of using to the full this area of co-operation and united action. . . . You have to consider carefully the extreme risks involved in keeping Mr. Gandhi in prison in this way. You are not dealing with an educated community, but one in which legend takes the place of fact. If for any reason, Mahatma Gandhi dies in gaol, he will be a legend for hundreds of years to come, and the power which imprisoned him will undoubtedly be regarded as the cause of his death by popular legendary opinion. Is it worth while running this risk, when he has already declared that he is giving the rest of his life as a hostage to the Untouchables ?*

This letter brought a prompt reply from Lord Allen, saying that he considered its suggestions to be so helpful and important that he had left it to be studied at Downing Street.

The Temple Entry Bill was allowed.

The "White Paper" on Indian constitutional reform which was published in March, 1933, was an unsatisfactory document,

* Letter to Lord Allen, 14th January, 1933.

"written for the British politician with the whole emphasis laid upon safeguards against the dangers implicit in the new experiment."* But Andrews implored the India Conciliation Group in London, with whose work he was now very closely identified, not to dissipate energy over "a matter of political detail and bargaining," but to concentrate on Untouchability.

> "Here is by far the most serious outlook for the whole of the future of India, because if this immense effort to remove Untouchability is squandered away by delays and official deferments, then everything that is vital for building up a real constitution from a solid foundation will be undermined.
>
> "I feel this so strongly and our Christian obligation with regard to it so keenly that every day and night I am wondering if I have any right to remain in the comfort of this country without actually sharing the life of those Untouchables in India. If this great Untouchability Removal Movement goes wrong through our neglect, we shall be far more responsible for that than we should be if we tried to take up some points in the White Paper and failed to get what we wanted there. If only the issue was understood thoroughly, I for one am certain that the heart of England will be with Mahatma Gandhi. They would not allow politician to wreck the greatest social reform movement of our own generation."

India seemed indeed to be on the eve of great reforms. The goodwill between caste Hindus and Harijans† even at strongholds of orthodoxy such as Benares, seemed "not much short of a miracle."‡ The accounts of the breaking down of immemorial social barriers, which were contained in every issue of Gandhi's new weekly *Harijan*, were used by Andrews with careful strategy among the officials and in the religious press.

Amid these high hopes Mahatma Gandhi felt himself constrained by the will of God to undergo a three weeks' fast of purification for service. This time the news was received in England with no cynicism, only bewilderment. Andrews himself cabled to his friend, "Accept your decision and understand. Love, Charlie"—a message which brought Gandhi great happiness. "I treasure the telegram you sent me," he replied, "I was thankful to God that you had understood."

Andrews himself felt a quiet assurance that all would be well,

* Thompson and Garrett, *loc. cit.*, p. 645.
† Harijan (people of God) is Gandhi's name for the "untouchables."
‡ Bishop Chitambar's description in *Mahatma Gandhi: His Life, Work, and Influence.*

very different from the terrible strain of the previous September. The fact that the ordeal was to be for a limited period made all the difference to him. But when the news came he nevertheless spent four days in London urging the importance of Gandhi's immediate and unconditional release from jail. The sentence was in any case due to expire on May 19th, 1933"; Gandhi was set free on the evening of May 8th, the day on which his fast commenced. While the twenty-one days lasted Andrews sent him a "D.L.T." cable message almost every day. "This is not economical, I know," he commented recklessly, "but I cannot help it and he will be delighted."

He set himself serenely, but with a mischievous twinkle in his eye, to his own immediate task—the combating of Winston Churchill's imperialist propaganda in Lancashire by the quiet suggestion that, after all, there could be no trade without goodwill !

III

All through these months Andrews was making his home at the Quaker settlement of Woodbrooke, on the outskirts of Birmingham, where in 1933 he held a Fellowship.

His relationships with the Quakers at Woodbrooke had been growing closer ever since 1928 ; the personal contact with Santiniketan there had been strengthened by the Council's grant of a Fellowship to a Santiniketan scholar, Dr. Amiya Chakravarti, and by Tagore's two visits in 1930. The informal family atmosphere and undogmatic religious inspiration of Woodbrooke reminded Andrews of his beloved Indian home, and increasingly he made it his headquarters when he needed leisure for writing, as he did in the early months of 1933. The material which came in so plentifully with regard to the social reforms in India needed much thinking out in order that it might be used to the greatest advantage, and the work could be far better done away from the hurry of London. His most important letters were written deliberately by hand. "You see," he explained, "letters in a personal handwriting with no enclosures, count far more in these days when everyone is overwhelmed with typed circulars !"

Moreover, Andrews felt that the time had come when *Christ in the Silence* must be finished and published.

> "It is quite literally true," he wrote, "that what I have been able to do in England for India has increased tenfold in value since this new book (i.e., *What I Owe to Christ*) appeared. Before this book I was looked upon as a Gandhi enthusiast and nothing else. Now it is quite different. They take me very seriously. But this is still precarious : it has to be kept in evidence. And the book I am now writing will certainly increase that serious side . . . Every part of it has a glimpse of India in it—a yearning for the quiet which the East has maintained and the West has nearly lost. I know that you will see with me that this must be done, and it can't be done *quite* with the rush that the other more objective book about active life was prepared in 88 Knightsbridge."*

On Christmas morning, 1932, Andrews had come for the first time into the presence of that veteran champion of the African, John White of Mashonaland, now bedridden and slowly dying of cancer in his home not far from Woodbrooke. During the first three months of 1933 he paid daily visits to this kindred spirit, which were spent much in prayer and consultation about the forthcoming book. On Easter Sunday, a day of glorious April sunshine, when the two friends shared the Holy Communion in John White's sickroom, they were able to rejoice together in the completed task, and Andrews could look back with gratitude at the wonderful lifting of the shadows which had clouded the previous dark Easter in Delhi.

The other great new friendship of Woodbrooke days was that of Dr. Rendel Harris, the witty and devout Quaker scholar. "Notwithstanding, rejoice not in this," he commented when *Christ in the Silence* was published, "that the publishers are subject unto you ; but rather rejoice because your books are indited from heaven." Gandhi wrote to Agatha Harrison in similar vein : "Like his economy, Andrews' *purdah* is a fraud ! He pretends that he needs quiet for his writing, and then sits down to write in the midst of bustle and produces quiet from within."

"Indited from Heaven"—"quiet from within." The mystical experience of Heaven—of an inward ecstasy of peace and joy which the world could neither give nor take away—did indeed recur more and more frequently in these later years, especially in

* Letter to A.H. (undated), March, 1933.

such hours of prayerful concentration as Andrews gave to the meditations on St. John's Gospel which make up *Christ in the Silence*. By its very nature this experience was rarely mentioned, but a few sentences in a letter written at this time refer to it :

> The borderline between sense and spirit has almost broken down and I seem to be continually passing beyond the veil of sense—or is it rather that He is ever "coming" in spiritual ways beyond all telling into my own life ? Yet I have no continuous, untroubled faith. "A little while and ye shall see me, and again a little while and ye shall not see me" is very real to me.

It is not surprising that he was completely at home in the quiet, unprogrammed meetings for worship with which each day's work at Woodbrooke began, and would not infrequently break the silence with some simple message of comfort or insight. He speedily became the spiritual adviser of students drawn from many different countries, some of whom had been little touched by any religious influence before.

Quietness for him was not quietism, but the secure foundation of much active service. No man agreed more heartily with Milton in his distrust of "a fugitive and cloistered Virtue, un-exercised and unbreathed." During the precious weeks when no major crisis arose in India, and there was no call to London, he would spend the morning hours, often from 4.30 onwards, in thought and writing. In the afternoons he would disappear into the byways of Birmingham, seeking out the sick, the lonely, the needy. Gandhi's comment to a mutual friend goes to the heart of the matter : "To visit people in power is a task upon his mind. To visit people like you and me is a matter of perennial joy to him. He derives his strength from his association with those whom the world calls weak and helpless, and who often but wrongly feel so themselves."

No one will ever know how many of these "weak and helpless" there were, but chance has preserved the record of a few of them. "You have unconsciously helped me," wrote one of the world's "failures" from a London County Council lodging-house. "I was in the spiritual waste land that we all must cross sooner or later, but the moment I saw you I felt an inrush of new courage." That man spoke for very many, and Andrews gave himself unstintingly to all. A young Japanese, writing from Kyoto after his return home to "C.F.A. wherever he may be," recalled with gratitude "the quiet talks I had with you in Berkeley Square . . . Ah, why is there no such saint in Japan as you ?"* His friends protested in vain that his energies should be saved for "more important work." An old lady kept sending him postal orders, which he suspected that she could ill afford. "Henry (Polak) got quite upset with me for using a whole day to go down and see her, but it was well worth it . . . and anyway (turning the tables) Henry has a wonderful fund of sentiment which he absurdly tries to bottle up and then it goes pop !" His own family claimed his care also. A younger brother suffered from concussion after a motor accident and had to enter a mental hospital for a time. One of the sisters in New Zealand lost her husband and had a breakdown in health. Out of the proceeds of *What I Owe to Christ* Charlie gave generous help to both, and rejoiced that he was able to do so.

In personal matters he remained the same incorrigible Charlie. Bewildered hostesses did not quite know how to manage a guest who might be found seated outside the front door at 5.30 a.m., writing newspaper articles in the early summer sun, and then take his morning walk in his bedroom slippers, become lost to his surroundings in prayer and intercession, and return an hour late for breakfast. The stories about his wardrobe are innumerable. Mrs. McGregor Ross, his former Kenya hostess, once telephoned Agatha Harrison to say that "C.F.A." had left the main part of his pyjamas at their house, and that he was spending that night with Eleanor Rathbone ! Never, it was said, did he leave a restaurant in the same hat as he had worn on entering ; and he remained apparently unconscious of any shortcomings till pyjamas or socks were beyond all repair. He could be, in fact, an incarnation of the "absent-minded professor" of legend.

One of the best stories of all tells of how Andrews sat one evening absorbed in a talk with an Indian friend in his hotel room in Central London. He had kicked off his shoes and was comfortably relaxed in his stockinged feet. Suddenly he looked at

---

* From Gi-ichi Otani, 17th March, 1933.

the clock—the last Underground train to his own Hampstead lodgings was due to leave within five minutes ! He leaped to his feet and dashed for the stairs and the street. His footgear, abandoned and forgotten, caught his host's eye. Snatching them up, he pursued his guest along the city street to the Tube station, where breathless with haste and laughter he thrust them upon their owner as he took his ticket.

The gentle, unworldly saint, the shepherd of needy souls, the counsellor of Cabinet Ministers, was still also the Birmingham schoolboy who had gone, drunk with beauty, through the Sutton woods half a century before. After thirty years of wandering, there surged up in him a great joy of home-coming :

"To be in my own home in England again ! To see once more fields of spring flowers which I had almost forgotten. To watch the sunlight shining through them with all its radiance ! And to take the daffodils on Easter Sunday to the grave where my father and mother were laid to rest—for all this I cannot thank God enough !"*

I V

As soon as *Christ in the Silence* was finished Andrews began to work at the memoir of Sadhu Sundar Singh, but his interlude of peace was coming to an end. He agreed with Gandhi that he must make his contribution to the cause of India at a "deeper level" than political bargaining. That level, for him, was the level of personal friendship begetting trust. He kept himself in close touch with the leaders of the churches and with more unconventional religious movements, such as the "Oxford Groups," which were seeking to break new ground. He himself felt† that his friendship with the Archbishop of Canterbury, Dr. Cosmo Lang, had helped the latter to make his great contribution to the cause of India in the Joint Parliamentary Committee. He sought by the same personal friendliness to win the confidence of another key member of the committee, Dr. Ambedkar, and went over with him each detail of his community's needs and claims. In Whitehall he pleaded for a like friendly approach to India as a whole, and strongly supported the weighty petition from India for a political amnesty and a fresh start.

* *Christ in the Silence*, p. 290.
† Letter to M. K. Gandhi, 26th August, 1933.

This, however, was not to be. In July, Gandhi had recovered from the effects of his May fast, and a conference of Congress leaders resolved to withdraw Civil Disobedience altogether from August 1st, "provided an honourable agreement was reached with the Viceroy by Mahatma Gandhi." The Viceroy, however, regarded this as illegitimate "bargaining," and refused the interview for which Gandhi asked.

On August 1st Gandhi therefore marched from Sabarmati with a few followers to lead a campaign for "individual civil disobedience," was arrested, and was sentenced to one year's simple imprisonment in Yeravada Jail, Poona. He then requested the same facilities to do *Harijan* work which he had been receiving before his release the previous May. This was refused, though certain partial facilities were offered instead. These conditions Gandhi felt he could not accept, and on August 16th he started a voluntary fast, intended solely "for his own consolation."

The next day, August 17th, Andrews landed in Bombay. When the Congress resolution of July 22nd, declaring "individual civil disobedience," reached him in England, he had decided to start at once for India. The conviction that he must do so had come to him in prayer, and the eagerness with which the suggestion was welcomed by Lord Irwin, Lord Sankey, and General Smuts (who was in England at the time), confirmed his assurance that he was divinely guided in his decision. "God bless you," Irwin had said, and added, "Give my affectionate remembrance to that strangely good man." Andrews therefore had adhered to his plans in spite of a cable from Gandhi advising him to stay in England. "I do hope," he wrote to Gandhi in announcing his arrival, "that it will be possible for you to see me before finally taking any drastic step—though in that matter your own judgment is far better than mine."*

On August 1st, before leaving England, and again from the ship, Andrews cabled that he was coming. These cables never reached the prisoner. Had they done so, Andrews was convinced, the fast might never have occurred ; but Gandhi knew nothing of his friend's decision. He sank very rapidly during this tragic

* Letter dated July 26th, 1933.

fast, and on August 20th was removed to the Sassoon hospital in Poona. "The anxiety and strain have been more onerous than I could bear," Andrews wrote that day to London, "but I have been kept up by the feeling that God himself ordained that I should come out at the exact moment when I did."

On the 23rd, Gandhi was unconditionally released. A letter from Andrews reveals something, if only a part, of the share he had in a decision which undoubtedly saved his friend's life :

On Wednesday the danger zone was reached. When I saw him at 11.30 a.m. he could only speak with difficulty . . . he had distributed his little things as last bequests. My own visit rallied him, and I made him promise he would fight for life and (said) that if I felt the last word had been said by Government, I would be the first to tell him and let him die in peace ; but I did not believe it. I got him to promise to continue to struggle for life and take water. Then I hurried to the Home Secretary, but I found that the doctor had already warned him. Just as I began to tell the Home Secretary what I had seen personally, the doctor came back and very soon after that the release order was signed.

Fortunately there was no one about when the doctor and I went together through the passages to tell him he was released. We both pressed him to take his orange juice before the ambulance came, and I said Sanskrit prayers and sang his favourite hymns, "Lead, Kindly Light," and "When I Survey." Dr. Cama came to say goodbye. He raised his head with great difficulty and said : "Thank you, Doctor, for your exquisite kindness !"

Added to other difficulties, the house where I was staying in the city was in a plague-infested quarter ; the inoculation had to take place on the very day of the crisis and there was not a moment to take rest. In consequence, high fever set in that night and I am only just "through" with it after five days. Three days after the release your letter came telling me of the death of my dearest friend, John White, and I spent Sunday in a wonderful peace with a sense of the nearness of his presence.*

Days of recuperation followed, which Andrews employed in writing long letters to Agatha Harrison, Henry Polak, Carl Heath and others who could best interpret what Gandhi stood for to the people of England. "He feels," he wrote, "that the suffering of his fast is needed to purge the atmosphere. When I said to him, 'I can see that you as a Hindu have a different idea of the spiritual effect of suffering from us,' he said at once : 'Yes, that is so. And it came clear to me in reading your new book, *Christ in the Silence*. You are very 'English' in that, but also you are Indian.

* To H.G.A. for the India Conciliation Group, 28th August, 1933.

273

T

I can see two strains in you. I want *you* to interpret the English side. I can see that I am antagonising them, and it is the last thing I want to do—I want to win them.' "

A letter of another kind went to Sir Samuel Hoare :

> We have escaped from a catastrophe almost by a miracle. Mahatma Gandhi's life is far too precious to be hazarded over a mere trifle. He is our greatest asset against the *real* danger facing India at the present moment, namely individual terrorism leading to mass violence.
>
> I have been with him every day, and I can say with truth that every moment his thoughts have been bent upon an honourable peace. But he will not relinquish the one principle of civil resistance which he regards as fundamentally necessary for a healthy political life. He does not wish to put it in practice, if that can be avoided, but he will never relinquish it as a weapon.
>
> He openly declared that *mass* civil resistance in India has led to bad results. Therefore he has substituted individual civil resistance. For he believes with all his heart in pure and religious suffering as the highest means of bringing to an end those man-made laws which are destructive of human liberty. These "Ordinances" he holds to be thus destructive. He could never rest satisfied if they were actively put into operation. He would also be in honour bound to seek for the release of all those non-violent resisters who had suffered with him.
>
> During the critical days of his last fast, Mahatma Gandhi more than once lamented to me the fact that the "human touch" was absent. I have often seen that when he meets someone whom he trusts, all goes well. In any mutual efforts towards peace this question of human touch ought to be carefully borne in mind.*

The danger of terrorism which Andrews mentioned in this letter was a very real one. Some years earlier a youth named Bhagat Singh had murdered an English police officer and had suffered the death penalty. There was a section of Indian opinion which glorified him as a martyr to be revered and a hero to be emulated—the "Michael Collins of India." Other murders and attempted murders followed, committed by girls as well as young men. The use of assassination as a political weapon was alienating the sympathy of many well-disposed Europeans.

Andrews, along with all responsible Indian leaders, condemned the cult of terrorism, but as an Englishman he strove to make his fellow-countrymen in Simla see that merely punitive measures would by themselves only aggravate the disease. True statesman-

* Letter dated 4th September, 1933.

ship, he argued, would deal constructively with its root causes ; it was no accident that the Bengali student, who had suffered so long from repression and espionage, and who was suffering acutely in the 'thirties from the economic crisis, should be most susceptible to terrorist influences. Once more he pleaded for sympathetic understanding of the Indian student's point of view, and for generous and imaginative action calculated to call out in return the warm generosity of the Indian character.

He met with little response. Jawaharlal Nehru's action in signing (together with many responsible and moderate-minded men) a dignified and weighty petition against the use of the Andaman Islands as a penal settlement was interpreted by Government supporters as "encouragement of terrorism" ; and Gandhi himself was charged with conniving at the "Bhagat Singh Cult" which he had publicly and in the plainest terms condemned. It was not easy for Andrews to speak with restraint in the face of so cruel and unjust an accusation, and sometimes undoubtedly he weakened his own arguments by over-statement. The case for penal reform was a very strong one ; it was not strengthened by Andrews' undiscriminating repetition of charges against the Andamans administration to which in 1932 it was no longer open, however well justified they may have been in 1919. He occasionally needed Polak's warning against relying on "insufficiently authenticated evidence" in some cases of alleged "repression." He did his utmost to prevent Bina Das, a Bengali girl student guilty of attempted murder, from being sent to the Andamans ; his cause was wise and merciful, but he did not help it forward by the warm-hearted exaggeration with which he described her to Lord Irwin as "one of the noblest-hearted young girls of Bengal." Such failures of judgment did lay Andrews open to the charge, so frequently made by friendly onlookers, that he was "one-sided," or that "his heart ran away with his head."

V

At the end of November, 1933, Andrews was back in England, urging that the gravity of the political and economic situation should be met with drastic and imaginative action calculated to restore confidence and goodwill—honest, searching, independent inquiries into the situation in Bengal and the state of the prisons ; a drastic scaling down of debts to meet the agricultural crisis. "I am working as a propagandist," he said to an interviewer,* "for the development of our moral sense in relation to India." He planned to concentrate not on London, but upon religious and university centres in the provinces, "where public opinion is formed and the moral sense of this nation is developed."

This programme was never fulfilled in the form in which it was planned. Instead, Andrews became once more "a shuttlecock," impelled hither and thither by his immense desire for reconciliation between India and the West, and 1934 was a year of almost incessant travel.

On January 15th one of the most disastrous earthquakes of modern times devastated the province of Bihar. Tagore sent Andrews a long and detailed cable, describing the extent of the destruction and the widespread need, and Andrews threw himself into the organisation of relief funds. During the next four months he travelled about the British Isles and through the chief cities of Western Europe, speaking, writing and broadcasting his appeal. He put together at top speed a publicity booklet called *The Indian Earthquake.* Pierre Cérésole, the Swiss founder of the *Service Civile Internationale,* led a little team of volunteers to Bihar to share with Indian peasants in the actual manual labour of reconstruction. Andrews was delighted with a gesture of practical goodwill so much in the spirit of Gandhi, and wrote letter after letter to India to prepare their way. Then, in the middle of May, he started once more for South Africa, pouring out last-minute directions, cables, instructions, as the boat-train drew out of Waterloo. "Saw C.F.A. off," reads Agatha Harrison's diary. "On the station platform put shoes, Eno's Fruit Salts, books and apples into his case. . . ."

Andrews did his very utmost to raise funds in South Africa for the earthquake victims in Bihar. He was thinking not only of their need, but even more of the great influence for good which such a friendly gesture would exert on the relationships between the two countries. The appeal failed, but he was not disheartened.

* Leonard Matters in *The Hindu,* Madras.

An effort which took up nights and days and might have gloriously succeeded has ended in failure. But only think what it would have been if it had succeeded ! It would have been the first good contribution outside England, and would have taken away much of the bitterness against South Africa. But one has to take these disappointments lightly if any good is to be done. I do not regret having made the effort.

On this visit to South Africa, Andrews was not primarily concerned with the welfare of the local Indian community, though he was inevitably involved in their affairs. He was thinking now of wider issues. He wanted a consultation with General Smuts, who was to be in England again in the autumn, about the great constitutional changes in India which were now imminent. Smuts' influence carried weight in London, and he was anxious that Smuts and Gandhi should fully understand each other. From Capetown he travelled north through Rhodesia, meeting John White's African friends in Mashonaland and his English fellow-worker, the poet Arthur Shearly Cripps, and gathering material for the memoir which he published in 1935. By August he was in India again, sharing with Gandhi and the national leaders his now unrivalled knowledge of the factors and personalities which influenced England's policy towards India, and learning in his turn the trends of Indian opinion. The economic situation was even graver than in the previous year. Long-continued unemployment and hunger were sowing the seeds of violent revolution ; a younger violent section within the Congress was growing in strength. Jawaharlal Nehru was still in Naini Jail.

For six weeks Andrews went from one trusted friend and beloved home to another, leaving behind him everywhere the warm glow of affection and the echo of good-humoured laughter. "It does Bapu* good to have him," wrote Mahadev Desai ; and Gandhi, in high spirits, delighted to turn aside from politics to tease his old friend about his "wonderful beard." In Allahabad, besides the Naini Jail, there was another place of pilgrimage, for Sudhir Rudra had settled there, and among his little children Charlie at once claimed the proud status of grandfather. Last and dearest of all came Santiniketan. "C.F.A. arrived this morning,"

* The intimate, affectionate title by which Gandhi was known among his younger friends and fellow-workers.

wrote Amiya Chakravarti. "The whole ashram is astir, and the poet is delighted like a child to meet him again." As for Andrews, he no longer felt any conflict between Santiniketan's claims on his love and the demands of his own vocation. "The circumference of Santiniketan," he wrote to Tagore in 1932, "is the larger world, and I have to travel round that circumference in order to be true to the centre."

Back in England in October, he installed himself in Mrs. Alexander Whyte's house on the edge of Hyde Park, where he took his quiet morning walks. At the India Office his was now a familiar figure, and he kept in the closest touch with Sir Samuel Hoare, Lord Irwin, and the Archbishop. The points he made were listened to with a greater friendliness and deeper interest than ever before. He spoke of the economic crisis and of the rising tide of violence. He pleaded for frank and friendly generosity towards Gandhi and those who with him stood for non-violent nationalism, and above all for the release of Nehru.

General Smuts had arrived in Britain, and declared in his famous address at the University of St. Andrews that "the issue of freedom cannot be evaded." He and Andrews discussed ways and means of avoiding the threatened deadlock when the Joint Parliamentary Committee on Indian Constitutional Reform published its report. The Government of India Bill was to be introduced in February, 1935. Andrews accepted an invitation from the British Broadcasting Corporation to take part on the eve of its introduction in a broadcast discussion of the principles at stake ; he therefore returned once more to India, landing there on December 6th, in order that his knowledge of the reactions of representative Indian leaders to the Report might be as full and recent as possible when his turn came to speak on January 22nd.

VI

The records of the winter of 1934-35 show very clearly the double nature of Andrews' conciliation work. To the British public he appealed in his broadcast as man to man, on broad human moral principles. Here is the keynote of his speech :

The first thing to be done is to meet the psychology of India rather than impose upon India what we in England think is good for her. If full freedom, full nationhood, and complete racial equality are accepted by us as basic principles and acted out in our lives, there would be very little quarrel about terms. For it is the psychology of India that matters most of all. We have never yet touched India's heart, and therefore, in spite of all our good intentions, we have blundered.*

In his particular criticism of the Bill he appealed equally to the moral conscience of the nation :

> The omission of any mention of Dominion Status from the Joint Parliamentary Committee report, when the whole Round Table process had been started with the assumption that that was the goal, comes near to a breach of faith and is regarded as 'such by Indian opinion. The contention that the new Constitution is framed to protect the poor is completely inconsistent with the setting up of a Central Legislature where reactionary social and financial interests would be so strongly intrenched.†

The same note runs through the book *India and Britain, A Moral Challenge*, which he began to write very shortly afterwards, and completed during the next three or four months.

On the other hand, among men who had detailed knowledge and direct responsibility, he put forward definite practical proposals designed to meet Indian criticism of the Bill. The central principle for which he argued was that there should be included, as a substantive part of the measure itself, automatic machinery which would make possible the emendation of the Act by Indians themselves without the need of reference to Parliament. This was the principle upon which he had agreed with Smuts ; the chief application of it which he envisaged was the revision of the "Communal Award" by mutual agreement between the communities concerned before the ten-year period prescribed in the Bill had elapsed. If this could not be done he saw the most dangerous potentialities in Bengal, where the enormous weightage given under the Communal Award to European commercial interests and to the Depressed Classes pressed most unfairly upon the Hindu community. On board ship on his journeys to and fro, and in India itself, he carried on long discussions with the leaders of the parties concerned, seeking unweariedly for some practical and just method of conciliating

* Report in *The Listener*, 25th January, 1935.
† *Ibid.*

conflicting interests which might point the way to an agreed solution. His letters show how very nearly these discussions succeeded in their object.

Sir Samuel Hoare however answered, though with the utmost friendliness and sincerity, that the Bill already "went to the utmost limit that was possible in the present Parliament," and that any amendment in the direction Andrews desired might make it impossible to carry it through both Houses. Moreover, the India Office officials did not share his view of the Communal Award. After six years of disturbance, they argued, it was essential that things should be given time to "settle down" without any fresh controversy being introduced, and that the "saving clause" which had made possible the Poona Pact must lapse with the passing of the Act.

Andrews told them plainly that he considered this an illogical position :

> The present settlement is really creating fresh disturbance. It means, I'm afraid, a cat-and-dog fight between Muslim and Hindu for the next ten years with no possible compromise. Extremists on each side would be elected and try to stir up things. If the chance for mutual agreement were left open to be had for the asking, a lasting peace might be secured in two or three years' time ; if it has to run the gamut of a Parliamentary Bill, vexatious minority obstruction will have far more scope. The suspicion is as deep-seated as possible that the British Government wishes this quarrel to continue. People will point to this new act of Government as justifying the suspicion.*

There were two other points which Andrews pressed upon the attention of the India Office. One was the key importance of the treatment accorded to the Christian community in India. Strong sections of Christian opinion disapproved of its inclusion in the Communal Award, and Andrews believed that "a move towards joint electorates there might 'precipitate' a solution of other difficulties in the Punjab and Bengal." The Christian Church was concerned also in the proposed treatment of the Ecclesiastical Department as a reserved Central subject. This association of the church with the alien power of the State was a matter which had troubled Andrews ever since early days in Delhi. He

---

* From notes of a confidential talk and letter to Mr. W. D. Croft (now Sir William Croft), Private Secretary to Sir Samuel Hoare, India Office, April 24th, 1935.

contended now that the provision for Army Chaplains should be part of the *military* budget, the grant for other chaplains being voted by the Assembly. The Christian Church, he urged, must not be stigmatized as part of the "foreign" impedimenta of Government. It must and could place its confidence in the reasonableness and generosity of an Indian Assembly.

The second concession for which he pleaded was that the Royal Jubilee in 1935 should be celebrated in India by the liberation of Jawaharlal Nehru and Abdul Ghaffar Khan. The official refusal to consider this further application of the principle of trust and generosity roused him to some plain speaking, though the friendliness of the conversations remained unbroken :

> Government has become so hopelessly imperialistic that it never appeals to the popular imagination. The Viceroy has said many times that the sternness of the Ordinances was only one side of a dual policy, the other side of which was constitutional reform. He has asked the mass of sensible citizens to accept sternness in order that he might bring the gift of reforms. But the gift has been meagre, and the press is muzzled in a way which would seem outrageous in England.*

These practical suggestions for conciliation were not confined to one side. Andrews argued equally frankly with Mahatma Gandhi, whose request to visit the Frontier for Harijan work was regarded with suspicion by the authorities. Government of India officials told Andrews that they feared Gandhi was all the while "holding a pistol up his sleeve." Andrews passed on the phrase, and gave his opinion that Gandhi's own devastating openness about Congress faults, and the sincerity of his work for reform, would be certain in time to dissipate such suspicions if they were not re-awakened by a too-hasty insistence on the visit to the Frontier.

Andrews had already made up his mind to go back to India in the summer of 1935 and to put the reforms to what, for him, was the crucial test—were *men* of goodwill on the two sides being brought into real and effective personal contact, or were they being imprisoned in a machine ? Soon after he arrived, the disastrous Quetta earthquake occurred. Widespread and quite avoidable bitterness was caused because the official communiqués

* *Ibid.*

to the Press were marred by much blatant racial discrimination. "There were hundreds of military there," Andrews wrote, "who could have taken and despatched the names of the survivors. That would have given comfort. But for four days the papers were full of every English name surviving, died and wounded ; and even Civil Servants who were Indians were not recorded. The atmosphere in Simla was electric." Things got worse when Gandhi was refused entry to the stricken city. Andrews spent hours in the Secretariat, but got little satisfaction. "It is impossible to get one grain of commonsense into their heads," he exploded wrathfully. "They are convinced that every Indian all over India is quite happy about what has happened and that the only one who was disturbed and stirring up racial feeling was C. F. Andrews !"*

Another test case for him was the Italian attack on Abyssinia. In Simla and elsewhere, he took pains to learn the Indian reactions to the Fascist plea that a distinction was drawn by Italy between backward and savage Africa and highly cultured Asia. "Such distinctions do not appeal to me," he declared, and he knew that he spoke for an angry India whose noblest men kept silence only because of a bitter sense of their helplessness (with foreign policy a "reserved" subject) to back their words by deeds. Indians, he pointed out, could see in Britain's half-hearted opposition to Italy in the League only a desire to secure her own sea route to India and Australia, and in its catastrophic ending the failure of Europe as a whole to pass the acid test of sincerity in its relations with coloured peoples.

Lastly, Andrews felt as his own the bitter mortification to India of the Frontier "police bombing" policy. Indian peace lovers reflected that for the sake of a police method in whose efficacy they did not believe and in whose control they had no voice, England had blocked the Air Disarmament Conference at Geneva in 1933. That Lord Londonderry, the Secretary of State for Air, should have chosen May, 1935, to recall with satisfaction his achievement in "preserving the use of the bombing aeroplane" was not likely to sweeten India's reflections on Quetta and Abyssinia. England had failed, once more, to touch India's heart.

* To A.H., 7th June, 1935.

CHAPTER XX

INTERLUDE IN ZANZIBAR

1934

I

ANDREWS' three short visits to South Africa in January, 1931, January, 1932, and June, 1934, mark a change in his approach to the Indian problem there. From this time onwards his judgment was that South-Africa-born Indians (who now included almost the whole community) should cease to look to India for protection but should fight their own battles as South Africans. He continued to help them to do so, no longer as an emissary or representative of the Indian people, but as a Christian and a friend. In the fight against the colour bar his thoughts turned less and less to the "sanctions" which might be applied by the Government of India, and more and more to the moral influence of a Christian Church purged from racial prejudice.

When Andrews was called back from America to South Africa in December 1930, he had spent his last evening in England with some members of the Oxford Group movement. Since his last visit to South Africa in 1927 their "teams" had entered the country, and had won notable victories over race prejudice in some of the churches. Weary, ill and anxious, he asked for their prayers and support in the difficult task ahead of him. The "almost miraculous opening of doors" which he experienced when he reached South Africa was certainly due in part to their influence, and he never ceased to remember it with gratitude.

The main trouble was in the Transvaal. Much of the friction there was caused by a small section of the Indian traders, who had ignored Andrews' pleading for a better home life in Africa and had continued their essentially parasitic habits. An Asiatic Land Tenure Bill was now proposed, which aimed at racial segregation.

The outlook seemed very dark, but Andrews set himself to obtain postponement of the Bill, pointing out that within a year the whole situation created by the Capetown Agreement would be reviewed by a second Round Table Conference. Liberal European newspapers supported him, and beyond all expectation he succeeded. On March 13th, 1931, the Land Tenure Bill was suspended. He himself called it a "wonderful victory" ; a South African correspondent called it "the greatest victory over race-prejudice for over twenty years."*

One factor in his success was undoubtedly that he was whole-heartedly a South African to the South Africans. "We here," he would write naturally and unconsciously, as he expounded the South Africa Indian viewpoint to friends in India. His name was included in the South African *Who's Who*. He would scold the poor Indian labourers of Durban as no "outsider" would have dared to do, for their slovenly housekeeping or their childish party feuds, and they meekly accepted his rebukes. In Capetown, in Durban, in Pietermaritzburg, throughout the Union there were homes—Indian, Cape Malay, English, Afrikaander—where "Uncle Charlie" was hailed with a rush of delight, where his birthday was lovingly celebrated with flowers and gifts, and where the old joke, that he would always turn up for the grape harvest, never grew stale.

In East Africa his methods were of a similar kind. He assisted the Kenya Indians continuously in their long struggle against the communal franchise and segregation policy, and gave evidence with them before the Joint Parliamentary Committee of 1931. There was one campaign however in which Andrews did call for the direct assistance of the Indian public in the homeland. This was in Zanzibar in 1934.

Over and over again Andrews had spent a day among the Zanzibar Indians on his journeys to and from Kenya and South Africa. Zanzibar, he would say laughingly, was a little Paradise. Arab landowners, African labourers, and Indian merchant-financiers had together built up the trade in cloves on which the prosperity of the island depended. Indian enterprise had initiated

* Letter dated 20th March, 1931.

it, and the relationships of Indians with the other communities and with the Sultan and the sprinkling of English officials, were tolerant and kindly.

But when Andrews reached Zanzibar in August, 1934, on his way from South Africa to India he found the island in an uproar. A post-war boom in cloves, in which many of the Arab landowners had speculated recklessly, had been followed by a sudden slump in which the price fell to less than the cost of production. The speculators were bankrupt ; Zanzibar itself was dangerously near to bankruptcy. A group of European officials believed that the remedy was to be found in a Government-subsidised monopoly, the Clove Growers' Association, through which they claimed to be able to maintain a "just price," but which spelt ruin to the Indian merchants who crowded round Andrews on the quay. As he listened to their talk, his mind went back to a scene a few weeks earlier in Rhodesia, where a similar Maize Control Board had come into operation. He had talked there to an Indian storekeeper. "The small African farmer can't understand it," said the latter. "He comes in thirty or forty miles with his four or five bags of maize on a little spring cart, and naturally wants the full price at once. When I say that I can only give him five shillings a bag now, and he must come back for the rest later, he thinks he is being cheated and refuses to sell. It means ruin." He flung open the door of his grain store—it was completely empty.

Here then, thought Andrews, was yet another way in which wealthy vested interests might manipulate Government machinery for their own ends, regardless of the fate of the poor. But in Zanzibar the monopoly policy, which was not in itself racial, had been coupled with another piece of legislation, racial in principle, which was designed to protect the bankrupt Arab landowner against his Indian creditor. This was an Ordinance which forbade the alienation of land to a non-Arab or non-African, the argument being that it would be derogatory to an Arab State like Zanzibar if large areas of it should pass into non-Arab hands. Yet the Indian also was Zanzibar-born ; he was the architect of the fortunes of the island. To make the land inalienable was moreover to destroy the credit without which the clove industry could not survive.

Andrews went to work with his usual thoroughness. He saw the officials concerned ; he studied recent Zanzibar Government reports drawn up by Mr. C. F. Strickland and Sir Alan Pim, which dealt with the economic needs of the island, and he pointed out that the monopoly policy was not in accordance with their recommendations. He suggested that extortionate money-lenders, whether Indian or Arab, could be controlled by less invidious means than racial discrimination. The intensity of the campaign he conducted in India can be measured by the fact that in the first two weeks after reaching Bombay from Zanzibar he spent no less than ten nights in trains, in order to get the situation understood by everyone whose influence would count. He wrote long articles for the Indian press, and a pamphlet, *The Zanzibar Crisis*, which are models of lucid and temperate exposition.

Events justified his fears. Within a year more than two hundred Indian merchants had wound up their businesses, and others were insolvent. In February, 1936, there was an Arab riot directed against the monopoly laws ; a local English solicitor,* commenting on its causes, said of the monopoly that "every phase of native life, every trade and occupation, has been interfered with to its detriment," and of the Land Alienation Ordinance that "no decree has so seriously affected *the Arab and the native* or caused so much distress among them." But still no effective change of policy was made. Finally India, Zanzibar's largest customer, started a boycott of Zanzibar cloves. Andrews threw his whole weight into making the boycott a success, and wrote in support of it even from his sickbed in Simla in 1937. By the end of that year the revenues of Zanzibar had fallen by £30,000, and the Colonial Office had appointed the Binder Commission to investigate the working of the clove decrees. In January, 1938, Lord Dufferin, the Under-Secretary of State, visited Zanzibar, and during the next few months an agreement was reached. The monopoly was abolished in favour of a licence system which was satisfactory to the Indian traders concerned.

* Mr. A. R. Stephens, reported in the Zanzibar press.

Andrews' part in this result is not easy to assess, but the campaign (supported by the Indians Overseas Association) illustrates vividly his quick intellectual grasp of a situation, his persistent thoroughness, and the warm human sympathy which made it impossible for him to refuse to take up any cause when once he had met the sufferers face to face.

CHAPTER XXI

TRAVELS AMONG STUDENTS

1935-1937

I

THROUGHOUT his life Andrews had maintained the closest personal touch with University students whether in Britain or in India. When he first returned to England in 1928 much of his work of interpretation had been directed to the Universities, and he had delayed his departure for the United States until January, 1929, in order that he might be present at the big Quadrennial Conference of the Student Christian Movement at Liverpool in the first days of the new year. To that conference he gave a message which is the keynote of all his student friendships of later years :

> I am nearing the age of sixty and this body of mine has been tried by much illness in the tropics. But if it were only possible to deliver over to the keeping of the young this one supreme longing of our hearts, this longing to remove from the fair name of Christ the racial reproach, and to bring to an end for His sake these racial churches, then we who are old could joyfully make way for others, whose young idealism is untouched by the caution of old age and whose lives are still adventurous with high courage.

Six crowded years of work, not noticeably marred by "the caution of old age," had passed since then ; but early in 1935 two incidents, one at Oxford and the other at Cambridge, marked the opening of a period during which Andrews' influence on students throughout the world, especially on Christian students, was deeper and more far-reaching than it had been since *The Renaissance of India* reached the pre-war generation of 1912-13. In the last week of January, Winston Churchill had made his contribution to the B.B.C. discussion on India ; the hot debate that the speech provoked among Indian and British students at a meeting in

288

Oxford at which Andrews was present, determined the form into which the argument of *India and Britain* is cast. A few days later he was speaking at Cambridge. His mind was still full of the arrogance of Churchill's claim to hold India as a British "possession" in British interests ; he thought of the contrast between this attitude and that of Pierre Cérésole's little team of volunteers, who were working side by side in the earthquake-ravaged fields with the Bihari villagers who called them "brother." Out of his great desire to commend to young England this latter way of service, Andrews spoke as one inspired. He made a deep and lasting impression on many of the students present.

In February and March he redeemed a long-standing promise to visit West Africa. He had known the Rev. A. G. Fraser, the Principal of Achimota College on the Gold Coast, many years before in Ceylon, and Fraser had been instrumental in 1928 in bringing him and Sir Gordon Guggisberg together. His great concern for African welfare made him desire to see both West African education and West African industry. He spent six weeks in the country, lecturing at Achimota on "Christ and Prayer" and studying the culture of the people, the conceptions of life which shaped their social observances, and the impact of the Christian religion which they had accepted on their national life.

He found time also to go inland to the Ashanti territory and see what was going on in the new gold mines. What he saw did not please him. The gold boom which was then at its height seemed to him to be of very doubtful value to the country. It was characteristic that he should lay his finger on two features of the new industry which on a long view threatened disastrous consequences for the health and happiness of the people—the destruction of the forests, and the destruction of family life by the employment of men drawn from distant parts of the country :

"The enormous wood-fuel consumption has led to such extensive deforestation that there is a very real possibility of disaster—of letting in the desert from the north. There is grave *moral* danger ; thousands of men from the Northern Territory are leaving home for the mines, for the Ashantis themselves won't mine—they own the valuable fertile land and grow cocoa."

U

Of the religious life of the country he wrote hopefully. The Christian religion seemed to him to be working as a positive, constructive social force, which found its expression within the indigenous tribal structure of society, and purified and strengthened the native traditions of the people. "He was not shocked—he was delighted," writes an observer, after they had watched together the tremendous dysrhythmics at a display of tribal dancing, "delighted that objectionable features had been annihilated by trust ; and delighted, I must believe, to find himself delighted."*

The impression which Andrews made on Achimota is vividly described by one of its English staff :

"Nothing that happened in the College during my time there compared in any degree, either in kind or intensity, with the excitement which his visit caused to staff and students, young and old alike. Holiness some of them had seen before ; intelligence all of them (I hope) had met ; energy and endurance they were not unfamiliar with ; but holiness combined with intelligence and ripe experience of men and matters, with great pioneering adventures in practical (and often successful) quixotry, and with a more than feminine tenderness and gentleness and courtesy—that was something they (and everybody else too—the man *was* unique) had never met before, and suspected that if they missed they would miss for ever."†

Andrews noted with interest the growth of a political self-consciousness in West Africa which was ready to claim *Swaraj*, and did not fail to make his sympathies known. "We envy India such a champion," runs a "leader" in *The Times of West Africa*, "capable to interpret to his white brethren that the Indian also has a soul that yearns for self-expression. If we in Africa had such a man, our condition might not seem today to be almost without hope. We are sorry he has to go, we would like to see him living among us. Farewell, Charles Freer Andrews ! Know that you have made us happier by your passing this way."‡

During the summer in India, when *India and Britain* was finished, Andrews' next step became clear. Gandhi and many other friends were urging him to retire from active work (he was over sixty-four years old) and concentrate upon some more

* C. Kingsley Williams, letter to the authors.
† *Ibid.*
‡ *The Times of West Africa*, 30th March, 1935.

"solid" piece of writing. The time seemed ripe at last for that work of religious interpretation between East and West of which he had dreamed when he first went to Santiniketan. His imagination had been caught by the parallel between the *bhakti* poets of the Indian Middle Ages and the mediæval Christian hymns of Bernard of Clairvaux, "written in similar times of stress and having a similar influence on the common folk." His mind turned to Cambridge. In Cambridge, with its libraries and scholarly peace, he might write a book which should interpret St. Bernard's mystical thought to India ; and at the same time he might follow up, with conferences and lectures, the book *India and Britain*, which was to be published in October.

Ways and means were found. It proved possible for Pembroke College, in spite of the unusual circumstances, to offer Andrews an Honorary Fellowship for the two winter terms. He was in high spirits. "His Honorary Fellowship is the only thing I can remember Charlie Andrews being proud of," wrote Arthur Porritt in the *Christian World* after his death. It touched him deeply that his College should have recognized his "quixotic" services, and his presence was a benediction to Pembroke, where the senior members of the College were just then facing difficulties which needed a deeply-founded spiritual wisdom for their healing.

The arrangement, which gave him a set of rooms and dinners in College, but made no provision for other meals, brought him up against problems of which for many years he had known nothing. "Fancy, I have to think of ordering tea and marmalade, etc. !" . . . "I was brought up to a dead-end in housekeeping because I hadn't a single match to light the gas-ring to make tea. What a duffer I am !" Laughing friends came to the rescue with gifts. "Tell Ruth the matches are splendid. I had been using those short little things called Swan Vestas and couldn't find out why they always burnt my fingers." Laundry was expensive, so he bought a sixpenny iron, of which he was extraordinarily proud till he discovered that it had burnt a large hole in his only woollen scarf, which he had used as an ironing blanket.

He was asked to give in Cambridge his lectures on "Christ in Prayer." The Regius Professor of Divinity was allowed by statute to appoint someone "of distinction" to give special lectures, and Andrews was delighted that the choice should fall on him, and that he should be thus honoured by his old University. Three lectures were given in the Michaelmas term and five in the Lent term, and the lecture hall was crowded out. The "radiating goodness"* of the lecturer was as strong a magnet to undergraduates in Cambridge as in Achimota, and a crowd of pressing human interests gave "St. Bernard" little chance :

> "The 'Friends' have welcomed me with open arms, and I have become a kind of 'Friend' of the undergraduate Quakers as well as of the Indians in Cambridge. Then there are College duties—Chapel every morning at 7.30 and evening at 7. Hall every evening at 7.30 with a time for talk in the Combination Room afterwards. Then men come up to see me, and alas it is very difficult to get early to bed ; and you know my inveterate habit of early rising.
>
> "There are great joys—such as Sunday afternoon Service at King's College Chapel—the quiet of the College garden to walk in—the young life all around—the new University Library—the intellectual atmosphere once more. But oh ! at times I get so homesick for the leisurely life of India where one hasn't to keep a pocket diary for a hundred and one engagements !"†

It was inevitable that Andrews should be drawn into the preparations for the "Mission to the University" in the Lent term of 1936. The intimate touch which he gained in this way with students in Cambridge and other Universities led to an invitation from the World Student Christian Federation for him to conduct Universities' Missions in New Zealand and Australia. He accepted this invitation, which meant leaving England almost immediately. When he sailed from Southampton via the Panama Canal, on March 20th, 1936, the projected study of St. Bernard had not been begun, but he carried with him the unfinished manuscript of *The Challenge of the North-West Frontier*.

III

The journey to New Zealand made it possible for him to see for himself the new conditions of life in Fiji after sixteen years of freedom from indenture. He therefore took the opportunity,

---

* The phrase was used by Lionel Fielden of the B.B.C., who met Andrews for the first time during this summer.
† To A.H., November, 1935.

before the Universities' Mission opened, to pay a visit to the Islands.

A thrill passed through Fiji when it became known that Andrews was to spend a month in this country. Why was he coming ? Comes he peaceably, or to stir up strife ?

When the *Mariposa* berthed at Suva on May 3rd last, a strict examination of the baggage of this dangerous man was made by the cautious customs officer. No risks should be taken when this disturbing force reappeared. He submitted with calm dignity, with an amused smile. Within a few hours he had had an interview with His Excellency the Governor, and later was the guest of the Chief Justice, and still later was holding a conference with the Anglican Bishop, the Presbyterian Moderator and other Mission officials.*

The Indian community were anxious for Andrews' advice about a threat to their citizenship rights. In the choice of representatives on the Fiji Legislative Council, the Indians demanded the main-tenance of the elective principle, whereas the Europeans, with some Fijian support, favoured the principle of nomination. Andrews put forward, in a memorandum submitted to the Governments of Fiji and India, a practical compromise designed to preserve the best features of both systems :

"Let the elective principle stand with one modification. Let each race elect, on a communal basis, *three* members of the Legislative Council. Let *one* member of each race be nominated by the Governor with a view to represent minority interests which would otherwise be neglected."

He pointed out that the Governor's nomination might then be used to ensure representation to weak groups, such as the Muslims and half-castes, who might not obtain seats by election, and that either Fijians or Europeans might have their other representatives nominated if they so desired, "provided that the *right* of election is not taken away."

Land and educational problems were, nevertheless, in his view, of far greater importance than this political issue. The visit gave him the material for *India and the Pacific*, which was completed at Simla a year later, and his comments and proposals show the influence of his West Indian experience. In Fiji, as in British Guiana, attractive opportunities for land settlement must check the unhealthy drift to the towns, and the exclusive concentration

* Description by C. O. Lelean in *The Missionary Review*, 5th September, 1936.

on sugar must be replaced by mixed cultivation which would enable Fiji to supply her own people with fresh and wholesome rice. The Colonial Government must find a way of giving the Indian farmers more secure land tenure, and so honouring its pledges to them, without infringing the just rights of the Fijians themselves. In Fiji as in British Guiana education, a truly religious education, was a fundamental need. Here too there was need to insist upon a minimum marriage age of fourteen and the education of girls. Here too he felt the danger of isolation, and laid stress on the importance of adequate communications and a worthy news service, which would enable petty local concerns to be seen in their true perspective against the background of world events.

India and the Pacific is a prophetic book. More than twenty years earlier Andrews had found in J. W. Burton's *Fiji of Today* a breadth of outlook on Pacific problems which had kindled his own imagination. In 1936, with world communication by air no longer a distant dream, he emphasized with characteristic statesmanship the significance which Fiji would assume in any world strategy of either peace or war. He strove with all his might to rouse enthusiasm for a Fiji that could and should be a centre of friendship and understanding for the races of the whole Pacific world.

But the final impression made by Andrews himself was not political, in however broad and statesmanlike a sense. It was religious. On his first arrival hundreds of Indian women and girls had lined the wharf at Suva to welcome a *Deenabandhu* whose Christlikeness of character there was no denying. At an Indian welcome meeting, crowded to overflowing, the Chairman, a non-Christian, paid a glowing tribute to the teaching and character of "the Lord Jesus Christ." "One's thoughts ran back," writes a spectator,* "to the bitterness and hostility to everything Christian which the Indians of Fiji had once shown. Here was a change indeed, and the man who had done more than anyone else to bring it about was there on the platform."

All through the long day he was occupied with interviews ;

* C. O. Lelean, *loc. cit.*

officials, merchants, lawyers, company managers, teachers of the various Indian cults. But he had time for the poor man with a burden on his soul, and for three hours each day he could be seen by anyone who wished to meet him in the vestry of Holy Trinity Church. "I went to the church service at which Andrews preached," wrote an English businessman.* "If you asked me to point out a person who acted, spoke and looked exactly as we imagine one of the saints of old would have acted, spoken and looked, I would have said, C. F. Andrews. All the Europeans there thought the same, and they had not always seen eye to eye with him." And another : "Each morning at 6.30 in St. John's Church, Andrews sat and quietly expounded lessons to be learned from St. John's writings. It seemed as though we were actually listening to the Apostle of Love himself."

The strain was tremendous. "To be in public all day long from morning till night in a climate like this !—I cannot tell you how tired I am !" he confessed in a private letter.† An understanding friend, the Rev. A. W. McMillan, took him to a place of quiet retreat, away from the crowds, for a few days' rest. With earliest dawn Andrews would be seated on the lawn, deep in meditation, or watching with a poet's fervour "God's wonderful pageantry" in the gorgeous sunrise skies. Then came the last days in Suva, when for four successive nights the Town Hall was filled to hear him speak of Christ. "Everyone was there, the Anglican Bishop, the Presbyterian Moderator, Methodists, Congregationalists, Quakers, Plymouth Brethren, Roman Catholics. There were Indians, Fijians and Europeans ; there were Hindus, Moslems, Sikhs and Christians. There was no singing, no chairman even. Andrews simply sat there before us and thought aloud. The reverence of those audiences was wonderful, and a deep impression was made."‡

The Universities' Missions in New Zealand and Australia also made a lasting impression, which even seven years later brought letters to him from those who had not heard of his death. The pace was even greater than in Fiji. Sometimes there were as many

* Anonymous : quoted by Rev. A. W. McMillan in a letter to the authors.
† To A.H., May, 1936.
‡ A. W. McMillan, letter to the authors.

as seven addresses to be given in one day, and in addition there were the hundreds of personal interviews to which he strove to give the major part of his time. His heart went out in sympathy to the young people who crowded to his "confessionals." In the tremendous pressure under which they lived in the great "Europeanised" cities it was desperately hard for them to reach that "joy and peace in believing," which he felt they needed above all things, and he devoted himself to them unstintingly. When finally he reached Fremantle his wonderful endurance broke down at last. He was obliged to rest there for two or three weeks before sailing for Colombo, and again to spend a fortnight in Kandy before going on by sea to Bombay.

During these weeks of rest and travel he put into book form the lectures on prayer which he had now delivered at Woodbrooke and Cambridge, in West Africa and in Australia. In one paragraph, quoted from his own *Christ in the Silence*, he sums up the religious testimony which he was now impelled to give in every place :

> "Jesus is to me the living Christ, speaking in my inmost heart, here and now. He is present with me each day in my daily life. He takes up the words which the first disciples placed on record in their Gospel narrative centuries ago, and makes them his very own. He is His own interpreter as He speaks to my heart, saying 'Come unto Me, all ye that labour and are heavy laden, and I will give you rest.' He says to me each day, 'I am the Bread of Life.' He is my Good Shepherd, who calls me today by name."*

The Customs official at Colombo was of a different stamp from the one at Suva. For him the name Andrews spelt not a "disturbing force," but a New Zealand tennis champion. "Are you the Davis Cup player ?" he enquired of the worn, bearded man of sixty-five. "I have played," replied Charlie gravely, "but am hardly up to Davis Cup form." (Now if he had asked, "Are you W. G. Grace ?" one could have understood it, chuckled the delighted Indian press.)

On his return to India, Andrews submitted to the Education Department a detailed memorandum on the encouragement of post-graduate study for Indian students in Australian Universities.

* *Christ and Prayer*, p. 137-8.

He had first mooted this idea in 1918, but at that time it had met with no support, and he had not pressed it. Now, as a result of his visit, the Student Christian Movement of Australia raised funds to support an Indian student at Perth. The University of Sydney offered three open scholarships to Indians for advanced study. Andrews urged that these friendly gestures should be warmly welcomed, that Australian degrees should be fully recognized in India, and that reciprocal arrangements for Australian students in Indian Universities should be considered. He advocated also the appointment of an Indian High Commissioner for the South Pacific, whose sphere would include Fiji as well as Australia and New Zealand, and the dignity of whose status would help to bind Fiji to these two great countries as well as to India. There was difference of opinion in India about these specific proposals ; there can be none about the breadth of outlook and nobility of purpose which inspired them.

I V

One day in November, 1936, Andrews walked unheralded into the Cambridge Brotherhood House at Delhi to claim the hospitality of his old home while he carried on these negotiations. He found that St. James' Church, near the Kashmir Gate, was about to celebrate its Centenary. The church was very dear to him for its old associations with St. Stephen's College. That evening in conversation the Head of the Brotherhood, the Rev. Christopher Robinson, asked him how he stood with regard to the Christian ministry. Andrews explained his old difficulties about the "Thirty-nine articles" and the preface to the "Athanasian Creed." Christopher laughed. "You really ought to move with the times !" he teased. "Don't you realise that when the Church of India, Burma and Ceylon was constituted an autonomous Church in 1930, those two *bêtes noires* of yours ceased to be incumbent upon its clergy ?" Andrews had not realised this, though he had actually been consulted by Government on some points in the Indian Church Act of 1927 under which the legal union with the Church of England had been terminated. His old friend the Metropolitan, who had come to Delhi for the Centenary celebrations, was staying in the house. Andrews sought him out there and then, and the Metropolitan confirmed what Robinson had said—there was now no bar to the resumption of his ministry. So it came about that on November 24th, 1936, during the week of the Centenary, he once more celebrated the Holy Communion in the church he loved. A slip of paper in his handwriting may be seen in the Church Record Book : "Charles Freer Andrews desires to return thanks to Almighty God for being allowed to renew his ministry after many years." The two other doctrines which had troubled him in 1914—the "Virgin Birth," and the "Resurrection of the Body"—were apparently no longer felt to be stumbling-blocks. The *moral* difficulties had been removed, and difficulties of intellectual formulation, which to many men would have formed an insuperable obstacle, were for him now of very secondary importance.* His description of Jesus in *Christ and Prayer*—"a moral revolutionary but no iconoclast"—might well be applied to himself.

Leaving Delhi he visited the Friends' Village Ashram near Itarsi. "Imagine a heavenly clear morning after flooding rain— Charles Andrews descending from the train all in white *khaddar* and long beard, looking for all the world like an ancient Biblical prophet, and pacing in gentle slowness through our wet jungle and through the stream. Imagine him having lost his purse, which he never recovered, and his *topi*, which was salvaged, and clasping Whitehead's *Adventures of Ideas* in his hand lest that also went the way of all flesh. Imagine an apostolic meal on the verandah, while we were all instructed in the true relationship between the acceptance of Christianity and reverence for other faiths ; and then a retreat to Rasulia and a beautiful address to the students who were just at the end of their Village Uplift work with us, very gentle, very quiet and extraordinarily impressive ; a triumphal passage to the station with the whole body of students attending and a procession carrying shoes, pillows, oddments of

---

* In an incomplete draft of the *Life of Christ* on which he was working at the time of his death, Andrews appends to his account of the Birth stories in the Gospels a note explaining that he himself took the view that the birth of Jesus was a natural human birth ; in the body of the book itself however he is scrupulously careful to write in a way which would not grieve those who hold a different view.

all sorts, following merrily behind. That was Charles Andrews' flying visit."*

A few days later, on his way from Santiniketan to Bombay and England, he went to say good-bye to Gandhi at Sevagram. It was not "Whitehead" that was clasped in his hands this time, but the *Collected Poems and Plays* of Tagore. He insisted that Gandhi, in his own presence, should read at least the wonderful *Cycle of Spring*, whose paeans of unconquerable youth had meant so much to him for twenty years. To Gandhi hitherto they had been a closed book.

Andrews returned to England to keep an engagement made the previous spring. He had accepted Dr. Raven's invitation to deliver a course of lectures on Pastoral Theology in Cambridge in the Lent Term of 1937.† Early in January, before the term began, he attended the Student Christian Movement conference at Birmingham, and spoke once more, perhaps most impressively of all, on "Christ and Prayer." But he was worn out by two years of almost continuous travel, and after the Birmingham conference he had to go to bed for several days. At Cambridge, each lecture took toll of his overtaxed strength, and serious insomnia followed. The spring weeks of March and April were spent, far from the clamour of cities, with Mrs. MacGregor Ross at Swarthmore Hall in Cumberland, and with Forrester-Paton and A. G. Fraser in Scotland. The letters which he wrote during these weeks are filled with the affairs of a multitude of friends, especially of the Indian students in England who sought his counsel and help, but they are free from the "anxiety complex" about individuals which was so often for him the penalty of overstrain. He waited quietly, in the sunshine of friendship, for light on the next step of the way.

* Hilda Cashmore, *Journal* No. 10, December, 1936.

† These lectures form the basis of his posthumously-published book, *The Good Shepherd*.

CHAPTER XXII

SIR, WE WOULD SEE JESUS

1937-1940

I

A LETTER lay before Andrews on his table at Swarthmore
Hall. It was from a non-Christian friend in India, and it
had reached him in 1933, in the midst of the most exacting period
of his political work. It had then been laid aside, but his thoughts
had recurred to it continually.

"You know," it ran, "that during the intimate friendship of all these
twenty years I have never asked you anything about Christ, for your own
personality has been more than sufficient for me. But now I feel you
must tell how Christ lived and how He is still living in the lives of millions
of people. I want you to write in simple English the story of the life of
Christ—that is the most important thing you can do. There are many
people in India, from high intellectuals down to the masses, who take their
conception of Christ from you. You are the only man who can write
this book, for you have lived like Him all these thirty years in India."*

Here was a challenge indeed, yet one which all his love for
Christ and for India leaped out to welcome. This, he thought,
should be the "solid work" of his retirement, the golden harvest
of the years.

His first thought was that he should now visit Palestine. Time
after time during the previous five years he had planned to do so,
as the "Jewish question" grew more and more acute, but on each
occasion some more pressing need had prevented him from
carrying out his purpose. Now he proposed to ask one of his
wealthy Indian friends to bear the cost of the journey, and he
consulted Gandhi about whether he should remain in Palestine
to write the book itself. Once more, however, circumstances
decreed otherwise : the disturbed condition of the country would
clearly make quiet concentration there impossible ; and even had

* B.D.C. to C.F.A., 12th January, 1933.

this not been so, Gandhi felt, and Andrews agreed, that while a visit to Palestine would be desirable during the preparation or the revision of the material, the book would be most likely to speak to the heart of India if the actual writing were done in Indian surroundings.

Then came one of those appeals for help which Andrews could never refuse. An Indian student with an incurable cancer was travelling home to die, nursed by his brave young wife. They would need a friend on the voyage, which would be a hard journey through the worst of the monsoon. Andrews travelled with them to Bombay. What he meant to them, as to so many others, has been well expressed in J. S. Hoyland's account of his "prowlings" in Birmingham in 1933 :

> He would enter a sickroom—perhaps a victim of cancer with the prospect of months of bitter suffering ahead. He would leave that sickroom again with the sufferer calmed, encouraged and literally glorified with the knowledge that this dreadful lot . . . was the most glorious fashion in which a soul could ever be called on to serve Christ.*

When Andrews reached Simla in August, 1937, he was tired out, and overstrain brought on a serious choleraic illness. Speedy medical help, and careful loving nursing in Sir Maharaj Singh's peaceful home at Summerhill, saved his life. For two months he remained quietly, though never idly, recovering his strength.

The days of convalescence brought with them a fresh outpouring of that supernatural radiance which had bathed the universe after his first conversion nearly fifty years before, and at rare exalted moments since. The clear sky, the sun in the latticework of leaves, the snow-clad mountains, the green earth, reawakened in him the poetic impulse of earlier years.† He read and rejoiced in Robert Bridges' *Testament of Beauty*, and in long letters shared his musings with Tagore, who was recovering at the same time from an illness as serious as his own. In another letter of friendly counsel to a young beginner in the writer's art, Bharati Sarabhai, he made confession of his faith as an artist :

> Plato is right for all time. Behind the fleeting beauty is the Eternal Beauty ; behind the gleam of truth is the Eternal Verity. I know there is

* C. F. Andrews : Minister of Reconciliation, p. 63.
† One poem written at this time is quoted in the Appendix.

a lot of talk about Art for Art's sake, and I know that the artist must be fearlessly true in his creative mood ; but I know also that Goodness, Truth, Beauty are eternal, and that ugliness, untruth and the rest are *maya*. So let the theme you choose be measured by the eternal standards. That doesn't mean that you are not to capture a sensation like speeding over the sands, simply because there is no "moral" in it. No ! But it *does* mean "keep the aim high."

And again, in a letter written two years later :

With all of us who write there is a tendency to stop and pick flowers by the way. Not that one needs to be an ascetic in the barren sense of the word. The danger lies not in accepting with both hands the cup of the abundant life when it comes unsought to the lips (it is God's gift) but in clinging to the pleasure of it when the supreme call comes later. If you are true to that which is best in you the flower of joy will change to fruit, and the process involves a change within, which comes by living close enough to reality to understand that there is a truth and a beauty in its very tragedy.*

There speaks the disciple, not only of Plato, but also of Tagore.

Along with this renewal of the creative impulse there came a sober sense of consecration. It seemed to Andrews that his life had been given back to him for the writing of his book on Christ. Other people, however, felt sceptical. "If Mahatma Gandhi had advised C.F.A. to retire to a Tibetan monastery, we might hear of progress being made with the *Life of Christ*," wrote its prospective publisher, Sir Stanley Unwin. "I despair of its ever being written in India !"

Such doubts were well founded. Andrews could not be in India in 1937 and refuse to share in the high endeavour of that "year of grace," when responsible ministries, many of them committed to a noble programme of social reform, were taking office in the Provinces. The men who now bore the new burden of executive authority were the comrades with whom for twenty years he had shared the struggle for national freedom. It was inevitable that his pen should be placed at the service of the renewed campaigns for temperance and for prison reform ; and that he should be involved not only in the "clove boycott" of Zanzibar and the fight against fresh racial legislation in Kenya, but also in inquiries into the "kangani" system of seasonal labour

* To Bharati Sarabhai, 23rd November, 1939.

in Burma and the grievances of Tamil coolies in Ceylon. It was no less inevitable that throughout the autumn he should be in the closest consultation with his old friend Lord Lothian about the implementing of the "Central" provisions of the Government of India Act (where Andrews strongly advised delay). He watched anxiously the dangers ahead : dangers of which he had himself forewarned the India Office—the increasing estrangement between Congress and Muslim League, and the tendency of "leftist" groups to advocate a policy of coercion and violence against parasitic landlords. Where he felt he could rightly do so, he intervened with personal letters of friendly advice.

One subject which specially concerned him was nationalist India's attitude towards the Arab-Jewish tangle in Palestine. The tragic situation of the Jews in Central Europe haunted his imagination. In India he found "terrible bitterness" against them, and in his articles for the press he emphasized the greatness of their contribution to human progress, and the inhumanities to which they were being subjected. A letter to Jawaharlal Nehru is typical of his approach to Congress leaders :

> I intended to write about the Italian open bid for an Arab alliance over Palestine. I think in any word that goes out (sc. from the All-India Congress Committee) to the *Arabs*, the warning should be against compromise with *any* imperialistic power. If the Arabs coquette with Italy and the Jews with Britain, it represents something which we in India should if possible keep clear of ; except to say, as Congress has rightly done, "Come together *yourselves* and have nothing to do with imperialism in any shape or form."
>
> As you know, I try to keep absolutely out of giving any advice in Congress matters, for the essence of Swaraj is—*Swaraj*. But that was what was in my mind . . . the dread of Italian intrigue getting any hold of *us*.*

Nor could Andrews ever escape from the problems of the returned emigrants. In one letter he tells a pitiful story about a prosperous Fiji Indian family who had been persuaded to visit relatives in India, and on their arrival had had all their money stolen and had drifted into misery and want at Matiaburz. "This is only one case," he concludes. "I could go on with one story

* Letter dated 9th November, 1937, in the files of the Foreign Relations Department of the Indian National Congress.

after another that simply tear the life out of one. How *can* I go to Palestine and write the life of Christ there when He is here in these poor helpless people ?"* He proposed to Government officials that while large matters of policy and principle should remain under the ægis of the Government of India, powers should be delegated to the authorities of the three major coastal provinces which would enable them to deal speedily and effectively with the many local emigration matters which touched the welfare of individuals so closely. His memoranda, written to officials such as Mr. G. S. Bajpai who had become his close personal friends, have a note of desperate urgency :

> These local matters have led to endless correspondence on my part. The poor people write pathetic letters to me as tke only one who goes into the details of their pitiable cases. I am nearly seventy years of age, and even the stamp expenses have become too much for me ; yet the extra-ordinary benefit that has often come owing to my being able to get them private assistance makes me unwilling to give it up until I can see some way of its being carried out more effectively.

Once more, as with Andrews' earlier suggestion of a High Commissionership in the South Pacific, competent Indian opinion differed about the practical wisdom of his specific proposals. But the principle underlying them is the same upon which Andrews had always insisted as vital to a genuine co-operative democracy —the principle that personal contact should be made natural and easy between the rank and file of poor citizens and those who had power to redress their wrongs.

During the cold season of 1937-38, and during the same months of the following years, Andrews was at Santiniketan, "at home as nowhere else in India." For the first time in all his twenty-five years of work for the ashram, he allowed himself to be placed in a position of official authority. At the end of 1938 Tagore named him *Upacharya* (Vice-President) of Visva-Bharati, and Andrews accepted the honour because of the opportunity it gave him to lighten the aged poet's burden. It meant a still further increase in the enormous volume of his own correspondence, but when friends protested, Andrews would reply that "God will give me

* Letter to A. H., undated, January, 1938.

THE WRITER AT WORK, ABOUT 1935

the strength necessary for the work He puts before me,"* and would go unobtrusively on.

One department of the Visva-Bharati in particular owed much to his enthusiasm. This was the Hindi Bhavana, which was formally opened in 1939. Andrews had always been anxious that Santiniketan should be a truly all-India educational centre, and that the distinctive literary and cultural traditions of every province should find a home there side by side with those of Bengal. The Hindi Bhavana, on whose behalf he made the last and most successful of his attempts at money-raising, was a step towards the fulfilment of his dream, and it was fitting that it should be Andrews who laid the foundation-stone of its modest building.

I I

After his illness in Simla Andrews never recovered full health ; he had to confess to "a continual uphill struggle," and in March, 1938, he went south to the Christu-Kula Ashram at Tirupattur. At the Students' Christian Conference at Poona in 1920 he had met the two young doctors, S. Jesudason and E. Forrester Paton, who were then planning to found the ashram, and had given his blessing and counsel to the enterprise. He now spent the summer with them and other members of their fellowship, partly in Tirupattur and partly in the Nilgiri Hills. It was a time of quiet and almost uninterrupted writing. Andrews worked steadily at his "reply" to Miss Mayo, *The True India*. No sooner was that completed than he plunged with all the enthusiasm of a young man into plans for a series of school "Readers" in English, in collaboration with Dr. E. E. Speight of Hyderabad, whom he had met long before in Japan.

"The passages chosen will be of such a character," he wrote eagerly to Mahadev Desai, "that the highest ideals of their own country and of the great world shall be put before the boys. I want to bring in the *religious* note, without in any way infringing the religious neutrality. It is quite possible to bring in religion and moral idealism through biographical incidents. The matter is so important from the point of view of non-

* Letter to E. Forrester Paton, 18th November, 1939.

V

violence and truth, that I long to get a talk with Bapu before going further."

Another literary and national interest is reflected in a carefully worked-out series of articles on Indian national languages which appeared in *The Hindu* of Madras. They show how quickly he had entered, in this continuous residence, into the point of view of the South. In them he courteously reminded his North Indian friends that "there is no reason why the blending of language and culture, art and music, should be confined merely to Muslim and Hindu assimilation in the North" ; he suggested also to doctrinaire purists that "suitable words for modern inventions, which have found their way into every continent, are not likely to be stopped by a language embargo on the Indian frontier."

Then the claims of friendship broke in once more upon his peace. "One Sunday morning an express delivery letter was handed in. It was from Mrs. N. in Bombay ; she wrote in great distress that her husband was under arrest on a grave but completely false charge : what should she do ? Charlie asked us to join him in prayer for these friends. By the time our prayer was over his mind was clear ; he must himself go and be with them in their distress. This meant a tedious two days' journey over the plains in the hottest part of the year, and being involved in all the difficulties of a police affair, but Charlie never hesitated. Two or three weeks later he rejoined us, tired indeed, but full of inner joy. The truth had been brought to light and his friend saved from disgrace and suffering."*

The supreme value which Andrews had come to place upon all human affection, and upon the "little nameless unremembered acts of kindness and of love," is revealed in every detail which has survived from those final years. "Whose *friendship* is inspiration," a phrase from the dedication of Whitehead's *Adventures of Ideas*, was his text when in March, 1938, he spoke at the Convocation of the Calcutta University of the place in education of those bonds of reverent affection between younger and more mature minds which had meant so much to him in Cambridge. Six months

* Dr. E. Forrester Paton, letter to the authors.

later, in a second Convocation Address to the Mysore University, he made a passionate plea for University Settlements which might bridge the gulf between student and villager, rich and poor, in the spirit in which he himself had worked at Walworth, but by methods in harmony with the genius of India. The Mysore University Settlement owes its origin to that speech. An ever-widening circle of student correspondents from all parts of India looked up to him as *guru* as once he had looked up to Prior, Westcott and Gore. Every letter from them received a careful, individual, affectionate answer.

On his periodical visits to Calcutta the warmth of his presence brought new courage and comfort into the great hospital wards. Entering a hospital to visit one patient, he would remain to bless and inspire countless others, as the grateful letters which followed him bear witness. Friends Christian and non-Christian turned to him naturally to talk of "the greater things of life," and sought for the benediction of his prayers when face to face with suffering and death. The old barriers of suspicion were completely down. "I never thought of him as a Christian" (*sc.* as one of an alien faith), wrote one Hindu friend for whom Charlie had prayed in his sickness. "It was a great soul who prayed, and the prayer gave me strength."* Charlie rejoiced in his turn that this same Hindu friend, Mr. G. A. Natesan, should publish the series of simple Christian meditations which he gave at the time of evening worship at the Christu-Kula Ashram.†

The appeal of poverty and distress was as irresistible as ever. In 1938, at the time of the failure of the Travancore National and Quilon Bank, he was in Bangalore. Scores of humble folk who had invested all their little savings in it, crowded round him anxiously ; he knew that they were typical of thousands of others, and it was not in him to refuse what help he could. There was widespread suspicion that highly-placed officials in Travancore had "engineered" the crash, which led on to "civil disobedience" in the State and very grave unrest. Andrews laid his own work aside ; twice he visited Madras, twice he undertook the weary journey to Delhi. "It was an abominable cruelty to create a panic,"

* Letter to the authors.
† *Sandhya Meditations*, G. A. Natesan & Co., Madras, 1940.

he wrote.* "I cannot believe that there has been fundamental dishonesty, and I am trying to obtain reconstruction."

Pertinent comments from England, on the incompatibility between these entanglements and the writing of the *Life of Christ* called out a not very penitent admission.

> I am afraid you are right, and that I can no more change now from this kind of life than a leopard can change his spots ! It has got into the blood, as this Travancore business shows. Poor Philip Unwin ! I haven't been able to write a single line on the book for a whole month.†

Before another month had passed, Andrews was deeply involved in other distresses. In some of the remote native States of the Orissa hill tracts horrible evidence of oppression and outrage was accumulating, and desperate refugees poured into the adjacent provincial area. The members of the Congress ministry in Orissa were Andrews' personal friends, with whom he had worked side by side in former years in the administration of flood relief. They turned to him now, and he devoted himself to the task of helping them to present the case of the refugees to the Government of India and the officials of the Eastern States Agency.

Finally, no man of the older generation entered with more understanding and friendliness than he into the feelings of the younger political leaders. A great regard and affection for Subhas Bose made him long to be an instrument of peace amid the party cleavages of 1939, though he saw how sharp the divergence on questions of non-violence had become. "The confusion is beyond all words," runs one of his last letters,‡ "and I can only stand by and hold fast all these bonds of friendship which mean so much. I find more and more that personal friendships are the one abiding thing which clears up the tangle when it has been made."

III

In the second half of December, 1938, a world Christian conference was held at Tambaram, near Madras, under the auspices of the International Missionary Council. It was one of

---

* To A. H., 23rd November, 1938. This is not the place to attempt to unravel the tangled threads of policy in which the affairs of the T.N.Q. Bank were involved. Its failure had many aspects. Andrews saw and felt mainly the immediate distress.

† *Ibid*, November, 1938.

‡ To A.H., January, 1940.

the most representative gatherings of Christian leaders from East and West that has ever been held. Somewhat to his own surprise—for he had thought himself "too much of a firebrand," —Andrews was invited to take part. He threw himself into the preparations, and during the weeks that preceded the conference exerted himself to see that its British and American organisers came into touch with as many Indian leaders, Christian and non-Christian, as possible, and that they met and talked with Gandhi.

The Tambaram conference brought into clear focus much that Andrews had been thinking out intermittently during the previous three years. The major question was how the Christian duty of evangelism was to be truly conceived in relation to the non-Christian religious communities. The question of "conversion" had been brought into the glare of publicity by Dr. Ambedkar's politically-motived proposal to lead sixty million "untouchables" out of Hinduism into any community which would offer them satisfactory "terms." Controversy raged through India about whether and in what circumstances a man is justified in changing his outward religious affiliation. A Hindu friend* asked Andrews for an article for his paper which should explain the true religious meaning in Christian teaching, of the much-misused word "conversion."

The question was one on which Andrews and Gandhi did not see eye to eye. Andrews hated all destructive religious controversy, and was sure that true Christian service consisted rather in seeking to strengthen "the things that remain and are ready to die" in the other living faiths of mankind.† He exercised the most scrupulous care lest the influence of his own personality should lead any young man to become a Christian from any other motive than that of genuine religious experience and conviction. On the other hand, where such genuine experience existed, he would not and did not deny him the right to do so, and men who had learnt of Christ from him did from time to time, with his knowledge and support, seek baptism in the Christian church. After a long

* Mr. G. Ramachandran, then editor of *Matrabhumi*, Calicut.
† Letter to E. Forrester Paton, 18th November, 1939.

discussion with Gandhi in 1937 he embodied his own conclusions in a letter to his friend which represents substantially the point of view which he put forward at Tambaram.

Your talk on religion yesterday distressed me, for its formula, *All religions are equal*, did not seem to correspond with history or with my own life experience. Your declaration that a man should always remain in the faith in which he was born appeared to be not in accordance with such a dynamic subject as religion.

Of course, if conversion meant a denial of any living truth in one's own religion, then we must have nothing to do with it. But it is rather the discovery of a new and glorious truth for which one would sacrifice one's whole life. It *does* mean also, very often, passing from one fellowship to another, and this should never be done lightly. But if the new fellowship embodies the glorious new truth in such a way as to make it more living and cogent than the old outworn truth, then I should say to the individual, "Go forward."

This does not imply the denial of any religious truth in what went before. Susil Kumar Rudra used to declare openly that he cherished all that was good in Hinduism, and yet he was a profound Christian. This is surely in accord with the mind of Jesus Christ. He welcomed faith wherever He found it.

. . . Christ is to me the unique way whereby I have come to God, and have found God, and I cannot help telling others about it whenever I can do so without any compulsion or undue influence. I honour Paul the apostle when he says, "Necessity is laid upon me. Woe is me if I preach not the Gospel !" I feel that the message which Christ came into the world to proclaim is the most complete and the most inspiring that was ever given to men. Thet is why I am a Christian. At the same time, I fully expect my friend Abdul Ghaffar Khan to make known the message of the Prophet, which is to him a living truth which he cannot keep to himself.

I don't think it follows that we shall always be fighting as to whose "Gospel" is superior. There are clear-cut distinctions between Christians, Hindus and Muslims which cannot today be overpassed. But there is a precious element of goodness which we can all hold in common. St. Paul says : "Whatsoever things are true, honest, just, pure, lovely, and of good report . . . think on these things, and the God of peace shall be with you." That seems to me to be a fine way towards peace in religion, without any compromise, syncretism or toning down of vital distinctions.

In 1938, in direct preparation for the Tambaram conference, Andrews wrote a paper in which he discusses more directly the missionary motive. He quotes the words of St. Peter, "There is no other name given under heaven whereby we must be saved, but only in the name of our Lord Jesus Christ," and asks what is to be made of that text in the light of the indubitable *experience* of the presence of the Spirit of God among men who are not Christians.

"These very questionings," he says, "drove me back to Christ Himself, and the result was revolutionary. The scales fell from my eyes, and I saw with a thrill of joy how all outer names and titles—all man-made distinctions —were superseded in the light of the one supreme test, love to God and love to man. This was the Gospel, the good tidings—a gospel from God worth bringing down from Heaven. This is the vision of Him which impels His followers to go out to distant lands across the sea. We go out, not merely to quicken those who are dead in trespasses, but also to welcome with joy His radiant presence in those who have seen from afar His glory."

The presentation of this point of view was Andrews' contribution to the Commission of the Conference on "The Church and Evangelism," whose early sessions he attended. He raised there the fundamental questions—how had Jesus Christ Himself understood the duty of proclaiming the Gospel? How had He practised it? But he was obliged to leave Tambaram before the end of the meetings, and the report of the Commission bears no clear impress of his thought. His other contribution, a passionate address to the whole Conference on "Christ and Race," was based upon a text he had used many times before for such a purpose— Pontius Pilate's contemptuous question at the trial of Jesus, "Am I a Jew?"

Andrews left Tambaram early in order to deliver the Presidential Address at the Indian Philosophical Congress at Allahabad on December 26th. His subject was "Ahimsa." Starting from Whitehead's *Adventures of Ideas*, he linked together Plato's "divine persuasion which is the foundation of the order of the world," the Buddhist Law of Compassion, the Tao Te-King, and the Supreme Moral Energy of Zarathustra, with the "Servant Songs" of Isaiah, and the teachings of Jesus the "prince of Satyagrahis," Tagore and Gandhi. When he sat down, he had made an eloquent declaration of faith : he had touched not at all upon the fundamental question of philosophy—whether the faith does in fact

correspond to Reality, to the truth of life. For his own apprehension was in the final resort not that of the philosopher, but
that of the mystic. "When I hear arguments raised," he had
confessed in an essay written the previous year, "there comes back
to me the line in *Abt Vogler* :

> The rest may reason and welcome ; 'tis we musicians *know*."

I V

On March 27th, 1939, Andrews laid the foundation stone of the
new buildings of St. Stephen's College, the first of the Delhi
colleges to move to the new University site to the north of the
City. It was the fulfilment of his own dream ; but when the
tremendous implications of the choice of Delhi as Capital flashed
across his mind at the news of the King's proclamation of 1911,
he had little thought that twenty-eight years would pass before
its accomplishment began. His speech to the brilliant assembly
was a simple tribute of gratitude to Bishop Westcott of Durham
and to Susil Rudra ; but it was not the words, it was the man
himself, that the audience found unforgettable. As he waited
quietly to tap the stone into position, there was in his very
presence a benediction of peace.

When the celebrations were over, Andrews had to go into
hospital, suffering from high blood-pressure. Throughout the
year he struggled with ill-health. After a few weeks with Tagore
at Puri he went south to the Nilgiri Hills once more, but the
height was too great for him, and he was advised, in spite of the
June heat, to return to the plains. He spent a little while with his
Chandpur fellow-workers of 1921, Bishop and Mrs. Pakenham
Walsh, at their *ashram* near Coimbatore, and then went again
to Tirupattur.

His thoughts turned more and more to the *Life of Christ*. "I
should not allow anything else to take priority over that," he
wrote in February. "The book is now getting hold of me in a
way that did not happen before."[*] In June he had "cut down
everything to a minimum in order to pay more close attention

* To A.H., 17th February, 1939.

312

A JOKE ABOUT TEA
with Benarsidas Chaturvedi, January, 1940

to the one book, which I am now engaged in writing" ; and a little later, "It is really getting on, but it needs much rewriting." Towards the end of July, however, he confessed to Horace Alexander a diffidence and doubt which reflect profound anxiety and exhaustion :

"I have been trying my utmost to get this *Life of Christ* written during this year of crises. Partly for health reasons and partly because the subject is far beyond me, I shrink back, and when I have written chapters I find they are not up to the mark. On the other hand, I certainly *can* do work which does not require such complete concentration and devotion as this. My real question is whether, with the world in its present state, there may not be an insistent claim on me to revive the deep interest of the reading public in Mahatma Gandhi's non-violence, which is so closely allied to Christian pacifism ? Would you say that I was running away from the greater duty if I spent time on this rather than continue to struggle with the one supreme task of writing the *Life of Christ* ? I have found it extremely hard to judge what I should really do and I know full well that a double-minded man is unstable in all his ways."*

The subject he raised—that of religious pacifism—had been much in his mind for years past, but the first of his books to devote space to it was *The Challenge of the North-West Frontier*, published in 1937.

"This is one of the most formidable books that have yet been published on the pacifist side," ran a review in *The Church Times*, "because it deals with a concrete practical issue . . . the charge that air-bombing for police purposes on the North-West Frontier is as unnecessary and inexpedient as it is morally undesirable."

Andrews wrote with confidence on the concrete practical issue, but the book poses in addition the "inner doubts and questionings" of his own mind. Can a balance yet be reached, in the sphere of historical events, between the claims of justice and those of forgiveness ? or is it only "between the fell incensed points of mighty opposites" that human progress can be achieved ? Those words from *Hamlet* haunted him, and he quoted them again and again. During the "Munich crisis" in September, 1938, he was torn by doubts, and his sympathies went out to those who declared that a stand against the devilries of the Nazi régime, even if it led to war, ought to be made at once.†

* Letter dated 26th July, 1939.
† Letter to Rabindranath Tagore, September 17th, 1938.

At the time of the crisis Andrews was giving a course of lectures on the life of Christ at the United Theological College in Bangalore, and he devoted considerable time to a discussion, in the light of Christ's teaching, of the duty of the Christian citizen in wartime. He did not condemn all use of physical force in itself; long ago, commenting on the story of Jesus' cleansing of the Temple, he had written to Tagore : "I confess that the whip of small cords in such a connexion has some satisfaction for me, much more than the *tapasya* of fasting for a fortnight to bring someone to repentance."* He still held to that opinion, and he told the story of the conversion of Jack Jobling at Monkwearmouth as an example of how force might be used in the service of love.†

Andrews gave full weight also to the argument used by earnest Christian people who felt that war might sometimes be a terrible necessity for the maintenance of the just foundations of society. He recognized that the great majority of men and women rightly enter into social ties and obligations within the social fabric ; that the marriage bond is the foundation of a God-given order, and that the Kingdom of God has room for those who feel bound by inescapable duty to maintain that order by force, by war if needs must. But his own thinking contained no practical help for those most deeply-troubled souls. It was quite clear where his own mind lay. His words took prophetic fire only when he spoke of the few, the chosen, who "make themselves eunuchs for the Kingdom of God's sake," maintain the *absolute* standard, and witness by utterly uncompromising love and sacrifice to the more excellent way, "so that the Salt does not lose its savour and the Light is not darkened."‡

Nevertheless it would be a misreading of Andrews' thought to accuse him of an "escapist" attitude towards the intractable problems of life in society. Some of his later devotional books undoubtedly tended to give that impression, and it is probably true that many of those who greedily drank in the quietist teach-

* Letter written March, 1921.

† See Chapter III, p. 23.

‡ A transcript of the Bangalore lectures on which this summary is based was made from shorthand notes taken at the time of delivery. Andrews intended to correct and use the material later, probably in the *Life of Christ*, but this was never done.

ings of *The Inner Life* were only too little concerned that industrial and racial questions should be approached in a truly Christian way. But Andrews himself kept the balance. As one of the critics of his books wrote, "Your own life has linked the devotional and the political in their rightful unity."* The last memorandum that Andrews ever wrote was a protest against the impression which he felt had been given by one of the Metropolitan's broadcasts, that from the Christian point of view any resistance, even non-violent resistance, to injustice and oppression was wrong. "Our Lord," he wrote, "was in the direct line of the great Prophets. He made no secret of His own opposition to the Herodians. He challenged the State rulers in Jerusalem on the debased and corrupt form of their own theocratic rule. He fearlessly dealt, from first to last, with public affairs."†

The fact is that Andrews belonged to the great Christian tradition of practical mysticism, as some of his teachers in the Christian Social Union had done before him. One speaks with diffidence on a subject which he himself held sacred, but the indications are that the experience of ecstasy grew more frequent towards the end. Two young volunteers at the Christu-Kula Ashram who helped him as typists,‡ speak of how, after writing for ten to fifteen minutes at the *Life of Christ*, he would go to his cot, lie down, and enter as it seemed a world of complete quiet and bliss. At his request the typist would gently touch him after a few minutes had passed, and at the touch he would rise and continue writing for another short spell. Such cycles of alternating activity and withdrawal might continue for two or three hours. They were symbolic of his whole life. In his experience the Christ who commissioned him for service, and the Christ who called him, weary and heavy-laden, to taste His rest, were indissolubly one.

V

On Sunday, September 3rd, 1939, when the news of war flashed round the world, Andrews was again in Bangalore. That

* R. Gordon Milburn to C.F.A., 27th January, 1940.
† To the Lord Bishop of Calcutta, 21st January, 1940.
‡ Mr. Richard Chinnathambi and Mr. Dorai Savarirayan, letters to the authors.

evening he conducted service in the chapel of the United Theological College.

"It was an unforgettable experience," wrote one who was present. "From beginning to end one was caught up in an act of pure worship. He gave, not a sermon, but a meditation on love, and seemed to me to be the Beloved Disciple himself speaking . . . As he came out, a frail figure, leaning on Mrs. Harrison's arm, his face was radiant with love and peace."*

He went on to Madanapalle, then to Nagpur to aid the National Christian Council in its discussion of the Indian position in South Africa. At Wardha he found Gandhi "doing some revolutionary thinking," and the two old friends talked over his thoughts together and mingled, as they were wont, serious religious discussions with merriment and jokes. A rest and medical treatment followed in the Sarabhais' beautiful home in Ahmedabad, and some unaccustomed "laziness" in the sea-air at Varsova near Bombay, where Andrews actually stayed in bed, on at least one occasion, till 7 a.m.

At Delhi in December he found a letter addressed to him as a "distinguished author well known to the countries of the British Empire and Commonwealth," which informed him that his ideas "relating to wartime publicity in the overseas Empire" would be particularly welcome to the Ministry of Information ! Andrews would be no party to official propaganda for war, but the Director of the Publicity Department at Delhi was an old acquaintance, and he began to plan, with a flash of his old vigour, how he could help him to spread correct information on Indian affairs.

But the worn-out body was at the limit of its endurance. After the happy Christmas festivities at Santiniketan, there were a few weeks of greatly restored vigour when he went as of old for his morning walk down the Red Road to Surul, and returned in the first cool sunlight to some friend's house, to claim his cup of tea and interchange jokes and laughter before the daily round of interviews and correspondence began. Then ill-health returned and gravely increased. When he was examined in the Presidency General Hospital at Calcutta it was feared that a major operation

* Myfanwy Wood in *The Christian World*, April, 1940.

might prove necessary, and a smaller interim operation had to be performed at once. Recovery was very slow ; speech and writing were difficult for weeks, and decision about the major operation was postponed. Friends surrounded him as he lay in hospital ; after a time he could dictate, slowly but quite clearly and co-herently, letters to dear ones, messages of love and requests for prayer.

Mahatma Gandhi came down to Calcutta and paid a long visit to the hospital ; Charlie looked at his friend with deep affection. "Swaraj is coming, Mohan," he whispered. "Both Englishmen and Indians can make it come if they will. Do you know ? I am quite reconciled to my illness. I think it was God's blessing in disguise." Slowly, fumblingly, he began to repeat Francis Thompson's lines :

> "Does the fish soar to find the ocean,
> The eagle plunge to find the air,
> That we ask of the stars in motion
> If they have rumour of Thee there ?
>
> Not where the wheeling systems darken,
> And our benumbed conceiving soars—
> The drift of pinions, would we hearken,
> Beats at our own clay-shuttered doors.

Oh, it is marvellous—that description of the sweep of the angels' wings." A deep peace settled on his face.

Good Friday and Easter Sunday came and went. Sudhir Rudra, who had been like a son to him for so long, came down from Allahabad during the holiday to see him. "Before we parted he made me join him in prayers. His power of speech was affected, but what prayers !"

Later, when the critical operation had been decided upon, Gandhi sent him a brief telegram of love and blessing. Andrews read it, and sat on for a while in silence. "I have no anxiety now," he said at last. "Once when Bapu was fasting I begged him to consult a doctor and he answered, 'Charlie, don't you believe in

God ?' I am thinking of that great Doctor today. Whatever He does will be right for me and good for India and the world."

Yet he desired to live, and had not grown weary of service.

After the second operation he was rarely fully conscious ; but when he opened his eyes and saw one whom he loved by his bedside, the beautiful smile lit up his face. Bishop Westcott gave him the blessing and he murmured, "That's just what I want." On the fourth day he was sinking, and he died in the very early hours of Friday, April 5th.

A codicil to his Will, dictated shortly before the operation, ran as follows :

> I desire, if anything should happen to me, to be buried in the Christian faith as a Christian, near St. Paul's Cathedral, Calcutta, if possible, with the blessing of the Metropolitan whom I have deeply longed to serve as my bishop, as a priest of the Christian Church and a minister of the Christian faith which I hold with all my heart.

His wishes were carried out. The funeral service, conducted by the Metropolitan, was broadcast from the great crowded Cathedral to the sorrowing multitude outside. The beautiful lines of the twenty-third Psalm rang out clear and confident :

> Yea, though I walk through the valley of the shadow of death,
> I will fear no evil.
> For Thou art with me,
> Thy rod and Thy staff, they comfort me.

To a Hindu friend, listening with tear-stained eyes, the words came home with a new meaning. "Yea, verily, the spirit of Charles Freer Andrews need fear no evil."*

The Calcutta Cathedral Close is not a burial ground : the nearest place of Christian interment is the cemetery in Lower Circular Road. It was in the fitness of things that there should be no carriages, that rich and poor alike followed the simple hearse on foot, and that Christian and non-Christian, East and West, were represented in the little group of friends who carried the coffin to the grave.

The *Life of Christ* had never been written ; it had been, most faithfully, lived.

* Amal Home, *Calcutta Municipal Gazette*, 11th April, 1940.

ENVOI

C. F. ANDREWS OF INDIA

Behold a Lazarus of Bethany,
Who breathes (reborn in this world) that world's air,
And moves as one almost too glad to be—
Of the Immortals' blessedness aware.

Bethlehem's foreglow, Calvary's afterglow,
And April's Easter sun (whose tilted rim
Trips to the music of the Seraphim)
Are in the looks and smiles he brings with him.

Behold a freedman, free to come and go
'Twixt earth and Heaven—he loves his brethren so.

His still small voice, with such enchantments rife,
It charms the pride-puffed adder of our strife.
Be sure the Resurrection and the Life
Are his by faith. Peace, as his proof, he'll show—
The peace that world knows, and this does not know.

ARTHUR SHEARLY CRIPPS, 1934

APPENDIX I

WORKING WITH C. F. ANDREWS

by AGATHA HARRISON

IN MAY, 1931, I met C. F. Andrews, the man about whom I had heard so much in India and other parts of the world. Mrs. Alexander Whyte, with whom I was working at the time, met me one morning with : "C. F. Andrews arrived suddenly last night, put down the work you are doing for me and help him, for he is doing important things." And in came C. F. Andrews. He might have been meeting a friend of long standing ; there were no preliminaries. We set to work immediately on his masses of papers, interrupted by a persistent telephone—for the news of his arrival had spread like wildfire.

The Second Round Table Conference was imminent to which Mahatma Gandhi was coming ; C. F. A. began intensive preparation for this visit. His width of contacts amazed me. He beset Whitehall, Fleet Street and Christian leaders, made provisional plans for Mr. Gandhi's visits to Oxford, Cambridge, Lancashire, Birmingham, etc., and fixed talks with strategic people. All the time the Conference was in session C. F. Andrews stood by his old friend and other Indian leaders. When crises arose he acted as an interpreter. The Mahatma's headquarters at 88 Knightsbridge was an exciting centre ; there was a constant stream of visitors from all over the world. In a Babel that would have confused most people, C. F. A. would clear a small space for his papers and say, "Now let us get to work." We rarely got ten minutes without interruption and it was in this setting that much of *What I Owe to Christ* was written.

As soon as the Conference ended he slipped off to Africa. His last minute instructions showed how firmly our collaboration was set. All his letters were to come to me, extracts from the letters he would send back were to be forwarded to certain people here, and always on his mind were the many lame dogs he befriended—all of whom must be cared for. Myriads of threads were left behind to hold while he was away, some rather tangled !

In 1932 he returned via India, having seen that country practically under martial law. By then, the India Conciliation Group had been formed in London with Carl Heath as its wise Chairman, and I became its Secretary. It was clear that while we had this great reconciler in our midst all help must be given to him. Once again the besieging of Whitehall, Fleet Street and the Christian leaders began. C. F. Andrews had the habit of following up important talks with carefully written letters summarising what had transpired during these talks. Those letters are historic and prophetic. When he was staying out of London we kept in touch by telephone and letter. "If you can possibly set me free for my book this week it will be a blessing," he wrote on one occasion. He seldom got the time he craved, for urgent calls would come

THE GRAVE IN CALCUTTA

for interviews, or he himself, reading the Indian news in the daily press, would feel impelled to go to the India Office, etc., and back he would come to London. C. F. A.'s activities during Mr. Gandhi's Poona Fast are quite impossible to describe, the week-end before the Fast was broken in particular. Finding out where the Premier and certain Cabinet Ministers were spending the week-end, C. F. A. borrowed a car and went from one to the other.

There followed years of comings and goings to India, Africa, Australia, New Zealand and Fiji, also frequent visits to the continent. These were interspersed with stretches of time here in which this country at last realised the manner of man he was. He always had a book on hand but no consecutive time to work on it. He moved from place to place like a human shuttle. Telegrams would come—"Where is C. F. A. ?" Can you forecast C. F. A's latitude and longitude at the end of July, we want him for a conference ?" He would announce simply, "I have booked my passage for next week." The Travel Bureau he always used became accustomed to his frequent change of plans. After altering one of these bookings at least six times, I apologised to Mr. H., the manager. He replied : "Don't worry, if Mr. Andrews changes his booking this is my part of the marvellous things he does. Tell him I will see he gets a good cabin." Transport was easier in the prewar days, and C. F. A. nearly always got a cabin to himself. Which perhaps was as well, for he spread his papers about like autumn leaves, sometimes spilling over into the next cabin if it happened to be vacant. For the first few hours at sea he would rest : "Now I am going to relax and think nothing about the things I have left undone," he wrote back to his friend Alexander Wilson. Then from each port of call would come long letters—"I would like this letter to go round in order to keep people informed of some of the vital developments about which we may need to take action during the coming year" : "Could you tell Mr. X what I am thinking ? . . ." "I have been writing, writing, writing to Cabinet Ministers." (He would send copies of these letters so that we could follow his thought.) Then, as a post-script : "I want you specially to look after Mr. and Mrs. S. and their children while they are in London." When he arrived at his destination a steady record would come of all he was doing, with suggestions for action at this end . . . . "There is so much on my mind. At the present moment it is 4 a.m., Mahatma Gandhi's prayer time, and I am keeping watch with him. Gurudev (Tagore) is fast asleep close by, and this lantern by the light of which I am writing, looks as though it will go out at any moment . . . ."

"I am sitting up late to get this important letter finished. I would like you to circulate it, but of course it is all very private—just my own views which I gather from my daily talks with people here . . . ."

As suddenly as he left London, so suddenly he would return, preceded by cables. One read : "Arriving twentieth. Arrange interview Smuts. Inform Unwin book completed." Urgent letters would list the people he must see the day after arrival. Numbers of his friends would write : "Tell C. F. A. when he arrives that his room is ready." I doubt whether any man had more homes. His sisters in Devonshire kept a Prophet's Chamber for him in the hope that one day he would occupy it for more than one night. What amusing tales his hosts and hostesses, the world over, could tell of this Wandering Christian ! He had few belongings ; what he had were carried in two most shabby suitcases, into which he crammed a minimum of clothes, many books, chapters of whatever book was in progress, letters, possibly a box of dates and always a bottle of Eno's Fruit Salts. If, when setting out, the lid would not shut, he would ask his host to "keep this for me." What a museum of his things must be scattered round the world.

On two occasions I had the privilege of working with C. F. Andrews in India ; in 1936 (when we met in Colombo as he returned from his Pacific tour) and again in 1938-39. Both were unforgettable experiences. In 1936 he was staying at Trinity College, Kandy, and in that lovely setting we had long talks. A sermon preached by him in the College Chapel was one of the most moving things I have ever heard. He was already at work on *India and the Pacific*. Read now, in the light of all that has happened since 1936, his keen insight and gift of prophecy are revealed.

In the autumn of 1938, when I arrived in India, C. F. Andrews was already there. He was supposed to be writing his *Life of Christ* that for years his friends Sir Stanley and Mr. Philip Unwin had urged him to undertake. The political situation was tense ; trouble was brewing in some of the Indian States ; daily he got calls to "come and help," and the Tambaram Conference was much on his mind. Sometimes I would suggest that he spared himself. To which he replied : "What is the use of writing about Christ if one is doing what is not Christ-like ?" Going to see him in a Delhi hospital (he had been ordered complete rest), I found a "No Visitors" notice on his door. The room was crowded of course. When his friends left, C. F. A. turned over a pile of letters to me saying "You answer these for me." As I gathered up the material that would take at least two days to handle, he said with his radiant smile : "This is wonderful, I feel so free."

At his request I went to some Indian States to follow up the work he had been doing. I found that being a colleague of C. F. Andrews was all the passport needed to Indian hearts.

During these months of work together in India a premonition that we should never see him again in England struck me forcibly. Yet he was planning another visit to Africa and to come back to this country after his *Life of Christ* was finished. His letters came regularly till the end of 1939 ; these reflected his agony of mind over the war. But early in 1940 he wrote at longer intervals and when he went into hospital, letters came from his friends.

The following extracts from letters written just before and after the outbreak of war, mirror what he was going through :

"We seem hanging between life and death, war and peace, and it is very hard to sleep . . ."

"I feel I want to write daily during the awful crisis. Tomorrow, I fear we shall hear that negotiations have broken down and the end is near . . ."

When censorship of letters came into force, he wrote :

". . . It seems as though this inspection of one's private letters dries up correspondence that ought to be as free as the wind if it is to be any good at all . . . Not that I worry much, as you know, about who sees my letters or anything I possess—for I have never kept anything under lock and key. But somehow it *does* make a difference . . . ."

The following extract is taken from a beautiful letter Mr. Gandhi wrote to me after C. F. Andrews' death :

". . . Let us forget his death and make him live by working in his spirit at the legacy he has left to us . . . I can't realise that C. F. A. has gone. He was an institution. He was love incarnate . . . ."

London, 1948

APPENDIX II

Memory and Emotion

One example of the caution necessary before accepting Andrews' account of events written long after their occurrence, is as follows :

On page 268 of *What I Owe to Christ*, Andrews states that he renounced the exercise of his clerical orders because of his inability conscientiously to recite the Athanasian Creed in the church at Burdwan, Bengal, on Trinity Sunday, 1914.

The true facts are these. Trinity Sunday in that year fell on June 7th. Andrews was then with Tagore at Ramgarh in the United Provinces. Only on June 15th, as an extant letter to Mahatma Munshi Rama proves, did he arrive in Bengal, at Santiniketan. The Church Service Record Book at Burdwan preserves a complete list of the clergy who conducted the services during 1914 ; C. F. Andrews' name appears on only two occasions, July 19th and August 2nd.

Neither of these two Sundays was a festival day, and the question of reciting the Athanasian Creed could not have arisen on them. The crisis occurred on August 2nd, and was caused, not by the Athanasian Creed, but by the doctrines of the Virgin Birth and the Resurrection of the Body contained in the Apostles' Creed which is recited daily at Morning Prayer. This is clear from the letters of explanation to his friends which Andrews wrote during the following week, some of which have survived. Moreover, it was on these two doctrines, more than on any others, that Andrews' doubts had centred during the earlier months of 1914, as letters written to Tagore in March and April show.

CHARLES FREER ANDREWS

The psychological cause of the mistake in *What I Owe to Christ* is quite plain. Intellectual difficulties such as were raised by the Apostles' Creed were with Andrews a passing phase, which had long been left behind at the time when he wrote. But he had moral difficulties of very long standing about the preface to the Athanasian Creed, which had caused a serious emotional crisis, linked in his mind with his relationship to Rabindranath Tagore, at Christmas, 1912. The 1914 crisis was also linked with Tagore ; the Athanasian Creed is specially associated with Trinity Sunday. At seventeen or eighteen years' distance it was easy to make the mistaken identification.

APPENDIX III

Some Poems by Charles Freer Andrews

1. TO LORD HARDINGE, wounded by an assassin on his State Entry into Delhi, December, 1912 :

> "I leave the word of Hope," our Emperor said.
> "This is my parting pledge, the word of Hope."
> And then beyond the seas' dim westering slope
> He passed, and doubting fears were comforted.
> "I add the word of Faith," the Viceroy led
> The King's word further forward. "In his name
> I give the pledge of Faith." . . . The foul blow came,
> And Faith lay torn and bleeding, well-nigh dead.
>
> O wounded sore and stricken in body and soul
> Trust on, by threats and dangers undeterred,
> And through the Power wherewith the ages move
> Moulding mankind into one living whole,
> Hearts numberless shall pledge thee this last word,
> The greatest of them all, the word of Love.

2.   DEATH THE REVEALER

(written during Andrews' first visit to Santiniketan, March, 1913) :

> One night there came to me a dream so rare
>   That by its touch the veil of earth was rifted,
> All luminous and clear beyond compare
>   Heaven's canopy was lifted.
>
> Holy and calm the passion of that hour
>   When love's full tide through every inlet flowing,
> Flooded my life with unimagined power,
>   Infinite peace bestowing.

324

The veil rolled back and earth reclaimed her own,
 And wings too frail to rise were downward driven,
But I have seen His face—have seen and known,
 This sacrament was given.

And I can wait the dawning of the day,
 The day star on my night already gleaming,
The shadow and the veil shall pass away—
 Death shall make true my dreaming.

3.

THE PALMS AT SANTINIKETAN

(written at Santiniketan, July or August, 1914) :

When the last glow of day is dying
 Far in the still and silent West,
The palm-trees cease their plaintive sighing
 And slowly lull themselves to rest.

Through the deep gloom their shapes grow dimmer,
 Rare as the mist-wraiths of the night ;
Only on high the starry shimmer
 Touches their waving tops with light.

But when the low moon's rosy splendour
 Rises along the darkling earth,
They wake to feel her love-light tender
 Stirring their leaves to new-born mirth.

Through the rapt hours they turn to greet her,
 Queen of the purple night above,
Straining their passionate arms to meet her
 With the full ecstasy of love.

Faint, cold and grey the dawn creeps o'er them,
 Bathing with dew their frondage bare ;
A white fog shrouds the land before them,
 Ghost-like they stand in the still air.

Sentinels set to watch the dawning,
 Silent and black against the sky,
Till the full blaze of golden morning
 Circles with fire their foreheads high.

Now all on flame with arms uplifted,
 Surging above the sleeping world,
Proudly they wave, through the night-clouds rifted
 Banners of dazzling light unfurled.

Then, while the morn's enchantment holds them
  Hushed, and the morning breezes cease,
A glory of azure haze enfolds them
  Veiled in a dream of endless peace.

Peace in the deep mid-air surrounding,
  Peace in the sky from pole to pole,
Peace to the far horizon bounding,
  Peace in the universal soul.

And peace at last to the restless longing
  Which swept my life with tumult vain,
And stirred each gust of memory thronging
  Avenues drear of by-gone pain.

Tossed to and fro I had sorely striven,
  Seeking, and finding no release :
Here, by the palm-trees, came God-given
  Utter, ineffable, boundless peace.

4
THE INDENTURED COOLIE
(written at Simla, July, 1915) :

There he crouched,
Back and arms scarred, like a hunted thing,
Terror-stricken.
All within me surged towards him,
While the tears rushed.
Then, a change.
Through his eyes I saw Thy glorious face—
Ah, the wonder !
Calm, unveiled in deathless beauty,
Lord of sorrow.

5
"INASMUCH"
(written at Simla, September, 1937) :

In the cool Church
A stillness reigned, the beautiful light was streaming
Through the stained glass window, where our Lord in judgment,
With a sad sorrowful face, crowned with awful justice,
Seemed to say, "Is it nothing to you, all ye that pass by ?
Behold and see, if there be any sorrow,
Like unto My sorrow."

The sacrament was ended.
The glory of His love had been remembered.
The comfortable words—"Come unto Me,
All ye that labour and are heavy-laden,
And I will give you rest"—
Had brought us peace and joy. For a brief moment,
We had been with Him in Paradise.
"Lift up your hearts"—"Sursum Corda"—
"We lift them up unto the Lord," we had replied.

Then again I saw them,
As I walked back from Church—
That long line, with their bodies straining, toiling,
Weary and heavy-laden.
For them, no Paradise, no heart-uplifting,
No thrill of joy in God's own beautiful creation,
No peace, no rest.
But comfortless toil, day after day—hungry, thirsty,
Ill-clad, ill-housed, ill-fed,
While His sad, sorrowful face, crowned with awful justice,
Looked down on us in solemn judgment, and He said,
"Inasmuch as ye have done this to one of these—
To one of the very least of these My brethren,
Ye did it unto Me."

APPENDIX IV

(a) BOOKS BY C. F. ANDREWS:

1. 1896 THE RELATION OF CHRISTIANITY TO THE CONFLICT BETWEEN
CAPITAL AND LABOUR   *Methuen*
2. 1908 NORTH INDIA   *Mowbray*
3. 1912 THE RENAISSANCE IN INDIA   *U.C.M.E.*
4. 1916 THE MOTHERLAND (Poems)   ·   *Allahabad*
5. 1923 CHRIST AND LABOUR   *S.C.M.*
6. 1926 THE OPIUM EVIL IN INDIA   *S.C.M.*
7. 1929 ZAKA ULLAH OF DELHI   *Heffer*
8. 1930 INDIA AND THE SIMON REPORT   *Allen and Unwin*
9. 1932 WHAT I OWE TO CHRIST   *Hodder and Stoughton*
10. 1933 CHRIST IN THE SILENCE   *Hodder and Stoughton*
11. 1934 SADHU SUNDAR SINGH   *Hodder and Stoughton*
12. 1934 THE INDIAN EARTHQUAKE   *Allen and Unwin*
13. 1935 INDIA AND BRITAIN—A MORAL CHALLENGE   *S.C.M.*

14. 1935 JOHN WHITE OF MASHONALAND   *Hodder and Stoughton*
15. 1937 THE CHALLENGE OF THE NORTH-WEST FRONTIER *Allen and Unwin*
16. 1937 INDIA AND THE PACIFIC   *Allen and Unwin*
17. 1937 CHRIST AND PRAYER   *S.C.M.*
18. 1937 CHRIST AND HUMAN NEED   *Hodder and Stoughton*
19. 1939 THE TRUE INDIA   *Allen and Unwin*
20. 1939 THE INNER LIFE   *Hodder and Stoughton*
21. 1940 SANDHYA MEDITATIONS   *G. A. Natesan*
22. 1940 THE GOOD SHEPHERD   *Hodder and Stoughton*
23. 1942 THE SERMON ON THE MOUNT *Allen and Unwin*
24. 1938 THE RISE AND GROWTH OF THE CONGRESS *Allen and Unwin*
   (with Girija Mukherjee)
25. 1937 RELIGION IN TRANSITION   *Allen and Unwin*
   (C. F. Andrews and others)

(b) BOOKS EDITED BY C. F. ANDREWS:

1. 1904 THE PRESENCE OF GOD   *by C. H. Prior*
2. 1928 LETTERS TO A FRIEND *by Rabindranath Tagore*
3. 1928 THOUGHTS FROM TAGORE *by Rabindranath Tagore*
4. 1929 MAHATMA GANDHI'S IDEAS *by M. K. Gandhi*
5. 1930 MAHATMA GANDHI—HIS OWN STORY *by M. K. Gandhi*
6. 1931 MAHATMA GANDHI AT WORK *by M. K. Gandhi*

(c) PAMPHLETS AND COLLECTIONS OF SPEECHES AND ARTICLES:

(NOTE : Except for Numbers 1, 9 and 10 these compilations were not made by Andrews himself. They are in most cases undated, some of the publishers concerned have gone out of business, but the nature of the subject matter dates them unmistakably to 1921-1923, when they met a popular demand.)

1. 1920 INDIANS IN EAST AFRICA *Privately printed (Nairobi)*
2. NON-CO-OPERATION *Tagore and Co. (Madras)*
3. THE MEANING OF NON-CO-OPERATION *Tagore and Co. (Madras)*
4. TO THE STUDENTS *S. Ganesan (Madras)*
5. INDEPENDENCE, THE IMMEDIATE NEED *S. Ganesan (Madras)*
6. A CASE FOR INDIA'S INDEPENDENCE *S. Ganesan (Madras)*
7. THE OPPRESSION OF THE POOR *S. Ganesan (Madras)*
8. THE INDIAN PROBLEM *G. Natesan (Madras)*
9. 1923 VISVA-BHARATI *G. Natesan (Madras)*
10. 1934 THE ZANZIBAR CRISIS *Kitabistan (Allahabad)*

INDEX